immortal wishes

ELLEN SCHATTSCHNEIDER

Duke University Press   *Durham & London 2003*

immortal wishes

Labor and Transcendence on a Japanese Sacred Mountain

© 2003 Duke University Press

All rights reserved

Printed in the United States of

America on acid-free paper ∞

Designed by Rebecca Giménez

Typeset in Berkeley by

Tseng Information Systems, Inc.

Library of Congress Cataloging-

in-Publication Data appear on the

last printed page of this book.

Portions of chapter 5 appeared

previously in *Ethos*.

to my parents,

Frank and Emily Schattschneider

c o n t e n t s

a c k n o w l e d g m e n t s

My principal fieldwork in Aomori prefecture (April 1991 to November 1992) was funded by grants from the Fulbright Program (Department of Education) and the Wenner-Gren Foundation for Anthropological Research. Follow-up research in Japan during 1997 and 1999 was funded by grants from the North-East Asia Council (Association of Asian Studies) and the Emory University Research Committee.

I trace my interest in the social sciences to my grandfather, the political scientist E. E. Schattschneider, who was always ready for a good political disagreement and who pointed out that it's the crowd—and not simply the protagonists—that determines the outcome of any fight. Sarah Lawrence College teachers Bradd Shore and Michael Davis sparked my interest in anthropology and in problems of cultural interpretation. The Kawashima Textile School in Kyoto, where I studied kimono weaving under the kind supervision of Kinoshita-sensei, first led me to consider the intersection of aesthetics and labor discipline in Japan.

At the University of Chicago, I am especially indebted to my doctoral committee—Jean Comaroff, Norma Field, Nancy Munn, and Marshall Sahlins. At Emory University, I am grateful to colleagues and graduate students in the Graduate Institute of the Liberal Arts, the Department of Anthropology and the Asian Studies Program for their support and constant intellectual stimulation. By a delightful twist of fate, coming to Emory reintroduced me to Bradd Shore and rekindled my earlier interests in the anthropology of mind and object relations theory. Robert Paul and the Program in Psychoanalytic Studies have provided a rigorous environment in which to explore psychoanalytic perspectives on culture and society. Alan Cattier, Carole Meyers, Adam Lipkin, and José Rodriguez have provided excellent, imaginative computer and technical support.

I've been enormously grateful to the editors at Duke University Press, especially Katie Courtland, Shelley Wunder Smith, and Ken Wissoker, for their patience, rigor, and intelligent advice. I'm also very thankful to the two anonymous reviewers for their careful readings and constructive critiques of the manuscript.

My parents, Emily and Frank Schattschneider, have generously provided emotional and material support—and much patience—throughout my undergraduate and graduate studies, my fieldwork, and the book-writing process. This book is dedicated to them.

My husband Mark Auslander resided with me in Hirosaki for most of my fieldwork, participated with me in many of the events described in the following, and shot the video footage that I have relied on in analyzing Tsugaru ritual performance. Mark has tirelessly served as a critical sounding board for my ideas and interpretations. I am deeply grateful to him for innumerable close readings of this book and for his enduring faith in my work and me.

I cannot begin to acknowledge or thank all the people who aided me during my field research in Aomori prefecture. Professor Mitani Eiichi first directed me to the Tsugaru region. The leading authority on *kamisama* spirit mediumship, Professor Ikegami Yoshimasa (formerly of Hirosaki University, now of Tsukuba University) kindly introduced me to his principal informants in the Tsugaru region during my initial visit to Aomori prefecture in June 1988 and again at the beginning of my fieldwork. He generously served as my Japanese academic supervisor and has been a valued friend and interlocutor. Professor Kakeya Makoto (now of Kyoto University) graciously welcomed me to Hirosaki in 1988. Professor Tanno Tadashi, as chairman of the Hirosaki University anthropology department, secured me office space, access to computer, video, and library facilities, and provided constant intellectual and moral support. Professor Sugiyama Yuko provided thoughtful and invaluable guidance throughout my research; I can never hope to repay her tireless hospitality, emotional support, and critical intellectual stimulation. Professors Sakumichi Shinsuke, Koji Kitamura, and Imai Ichiro were also constant sources of support; I sorely miss our collective anthropology department coffee hours. Yokimori Kenji and Abo Junko were valued friends and colleagues. Finally, Hirosaki University ethnomusicologist professor Sasamori Takefusa kindly introduced me to kamisama spirit mediums and many other aspects of Tsugaru popular culture, especially the poetics of shamanic chant.

Many other people in the wider Hirosaki community helped me throughout my stay. Hosoi Yuko helped teach me Tsugaru-ben and provided extensive assistance in transcribing important ritual events and conversations, especially the July 1992 conversation on which so much of this book is based. Yuko has remained a stalwart friend and interlocutor; I hope this book reflects some of her warmth, humor, and insight into Tsugaru culture. I am also indebted to Kudō Tetsuko and her family, to Kudō Katsuko, and to Dr. and Mrs. Onuma. Dr. Shinegawa Shinryo offered many penetrating insights into the politics of medical practice in modern Japan. Tazawa Tadashi and the rest of the Tsugaru Studies Circle at Miyamoto-san's Buruman *kissaten* generously shared their knowledge of Tsugaru literature, history, and culture. Professor Victor Carpenter of Hirosaki University provided much support in person and on-line.

Since the principal subjects of this book are only identified by pseudonyms, I find myself in the curious position of giving a collective thanks to this extraordinarily diverse collection of singular people. The congregation of Akakura Mountain Shrine (Akakura Yama Jinja) treated me with unceasing hospitality and generosity, opening up their homes, their places of worship, and their imaginations without reservation. They kindly allowed me to participate in sensitive ritual events and to undertake ascetic discipline in Akakura Mountain's sacred precincts. Given their deeply held sense that true knowledge about the mountain is beyond "book learning," I am particularly grateful for their support of my writing a book about Akakura.

Pondering these paradoxes, I am reminded of the words of one of my closest friends and teachers at Akakura, whom I identify below as Sakurai Fumiko. As we hiked together along a high, windswept mountain pathway during an ascetic climb, Fumiko instructed me, "The mountain will teach you through your body" ("Yama ga karada de oshiete"). An academic text, this book is inevitably written at a level of abstracted distance from whatever bodily knowledge I managed to gain from Fumiko, her associates, or the mountain. Yet it is my hope that the chapters that follow are faithful to Fumiko's advice, at least in spirit, and that they do some justice to the elegant system of embodied pedagogy to which she and her fellow worshipers have dedicated their lives.

With some reluctance, I have designated my informants by pseudo-nyms. Most have given permission for their names to be used, some are public personages, and some, I realize, were looking forward to seeing their names in print. However, given the sensitive issues that are at times raised in the pages that follow, it seems better to err on the side of caution and not reveal identities. A list of persons is given as an appendix to help readers keep track of the kinship relations and institutional roles. In giving real and fictitious Japanese names, I follow the standard convention of giving the family name first, followed by a personal or given name, with the exception of scholars who have published in English.

I characterize Akakura Yama Jinja (Akakura Mountain Shrine) as a "Shintō" institution, although it incorporates many esoteric "Buddhist," especially Shugendō, images, concepts, and practices. Following my informants, I at times characterize Bodhisattva and other Buddha manifestations or avatars as *kami*. Although some scholars have argued that the terms *kami* and *kamisama* should not be translated, I have found it appropriate at times to gloss these terms as *divinities, god,* or *gods*. The reader should note that in Tsugaru-ben vernacular, the term *kamisama* may also refer to a human spirit medium and healer, who functions as an intermediary with the kami. I use the terms *spirit medium, medium,* and *shaman(ess)* interchangeably. The term *kamisama* is usually translated as "God" or "gods." In the context of Tsugaru, *kamisama* at times refers to a special kind of spirit medium, often believed to have attained spiritual and healing powers through extensive ascetic exercises and revelatory visions. In this book, I use the term *kami* to refer to gods, divinities, or divine beings. At various times, I refer to those persons who worship at Akakura Mountain Shrine and who respect its affiliated spirit mediums and healers as *clients, worshipers, patients,* and *followers.* I reserve the term *ascetic* for those undertaking the formal practice of austerities (*shugyō*) on the mountain.

I give important vernacular Tsugaru-ben terms as well as standard Japanese pronunciations and kanji (ideograms) in the glossary.

I calculate the U.S. dollar value of the Japanese yen as ¥120=$1, the average exchange rate during my 1991–92 fieldwork.

I took all of the photographs. The diagrams were prepared by Lazer Age of Decatur, Georgia. Unless otherwise noted, all translations are my own.

immortal wishes

Votive Painting: Kawai Mariko's Dream of the Dragon

i n t r o d u c t i o n

Labor and Transcendence

These wishes in our unconscious, ever on the alert and, so to say, immortal, remind one of the legendary Titans, weighed down since primeval ages by the massive bulk of the mountains which were once hurled upon them by the victorious gods and which are still shaken, from time to time, by the convulsion of their limbs. — Sigmund Freud, *The Interpretation of Dreams,* 1900

The bad divinities and the good divinities . . . walk together hand in hand. . . . They are together even on this mountain. . . . The divinities only walk in strange shapes, the divinities only walk in strange shapes. — Narita Emiko, senior spirit medium, Akakura Mountain Shrine, 28 July 1992

A Dream and Its Legacy

This book explores the consequences of a dream. In 1921, Kawai Mariko, a thirty-four-year-old peasant woman living in the Tsugaru region of northern Japan, dreamed the same dream every night for a week. She found herself gazing at Mount Iwaki, the freestanding, three-peaked volcanic cone that towers over the southern Tsugaru peninsula. A dragon arose from the mountain's left-hand peak and flew through the sky to her house. A great hole opened on the roof, through which the dragon quietly descended. Standing beside her pillow, the dragon transformed itself into the shape of a beautiful woman who told her, "Although I appear as a human being, I am Akakura Daigongen [lit., the Great Avatar or Manifestation of Akakura]. You shall listen to me and climb to the peak of Akakura [Iwaki's northern peak]."

Inspired by this and subsequent visions, Kawai Mariko spent years pursuing ascetic discipline (*shugyō*) on Akakura Mountain's rugged slopes and in time founded a shrine on the mountain. In the early 1990s, this unorthodox Shintō institution, Akakura Mountain Shrine (Akakura Yama Jinja), served as my base for field research on female asceticism, spirit mediumship, and the popular meanings of landscape in Tsugaru. On these exposed volcanic slopes, the disciples and successors of Kawai Mariko have braved physical and spiritual dangers for seven decades, performing austerities for the mountain divinities and refashioning their bodies and hearts. For these worshipers, as for Kawai Mariko before them, the incessant disciplinary exercises have engendered transformative and often terrifying visions, which they have sought to concretize and pass on in ritual performance, votive paintings, healing sessions, narrative performances, and dedicated labor practices. The mountain gods hold out the promise of healing and wisdom, safeguarding the health and well-being of worshipers' antecedents and descendants. They may even allow a worshiper to be reborn as a powerful *kamisama* spirit medium, a living conduit between this world (この世 *kono yo*) and the other world (あの世 *ano yo*).

As I was often told, the vocation of the mountain exacts a heavy toll. The faithful are forcibly separated from friends and family, subjected to relentless physical trials, and intimately experience the pain of their followers and patients. Required, at various physical and symbolic levels, to reexperience the developmental challenges of infancy and childhood, they are compelled to face profoundly disturbing aspects of their inner selves and of their relations with their loved ones. For those who know it best, the mountain evokes a complex mixture of "lightness" and "weight," pride and shame, joy and fear, autonomy and dependence. In the words of the Akakura Norito (Akakura Prayer), recited every morning and evening in the shrine's Inner

Sanctuary, ~~the sacred mountain must be approached "with fear and reverence, with fear and reverence."~~

The title of this book, *Immortal Wishes,* evokes these deeply ambivalent reactions to Akakura's (赤倉 Red Storehouse/Granary) sacred mountainscape. In one sense, my title alludes to the Japanese word for "immortal person" (*sennin*). The idealized object of popular religious longing in Japan, the word's ideogram is composed of the characters for "person" and "mountain" (仙人). Through her dream and subsequent service to the gods on the mountainscape, Kawai Mariko gradually attained a form of immortality after her death. She became an honored *kami* (divinity) in her own right, enshrined on the mountain slopes where she is still beheld, from time to time, in revelatory visions by her disciples.

For these mortal followers, service to the immortal divinities is a fraught enterprise. As my friends and informants often told me, even an experienced worshiper may easily be led astray, mistaking a "divinity of disaster" for a "divinity of good fortune." Undertaking ascetic discipline on the sacred slopes of Akakura, Kawai Mariko herself was more than once possessed by the wicked demons of the mountain and sought to lead her followers into the temptations of infantile self-indulgence. As Kawai Mariko often noted, and as her disciples so often repeated, "The good divinities and the bad divinities walk together on the mountain." ~~The sacred mountain of the immortal gods may bless the pilgrim with joyous revelatory dreams or curse her with incessant nightmares.~~ *dangerous space*

Freud and the Mountain: Comparative Reflections

These ambiguous features of mountain veneration hint at another referent to my book title, one that recalls a classic analysis of dreams in an interpretive tradition far removed from the visionary ascetics and spirit mediums of Tsugaru. In the above passage from *The Interpretation of Dreams,* Freud characterizes the all-important psychological function of repression through a geological metaphor that I find deeply resonant with mental life at Akakura. A great mountain cast down by the Law of the Father, the mechanism of psychic censorship encases but never fully silences the thundering, libidinous Titans buried below.[1] Like the Titans, who can never be killed but are perpetually trapped within the underworld pit of Tartarus, unconscious desires are beyond destruction—for the unconscious knows neither death nor temporality. In this sense, "immortal wishes" are the most fundamental of human impulses and longings, rooted in the psychic terrain of infancy and early childhood, concealed but never annihilated by the apparatus of civilization.[2]

Freud's mythic allegory of repression deeply resonates with another important feature of Kawai Mariko's founding dream and of Akakura's spiritual landscape. For many of the psychologist's contemporaries, the burial of the Titans by Zeus in the pit of Tartarus was a quasi-historical account, signaling the suppression of local indigenes, who worshipped gods of the earth, at the hands of patriarchal conquerors, who venerated the celestial Olympian pantheon. In this alleged narrative of violent, political suppression, Freud may have seen a rich analogy for the functions of psychological repression.[3]

Although the product of a very different time and place, Freud's retelling of Hesiod's evocative myth casts an interesting light on the case of Kawai Mariko. Freud's image of the long-conquered pre-Olympian Immortals, buried by the conquering Olympians, has striking parallels to the "good" and "bad" gods of Akakura contemplated by Kawai Mariko and her followers.[4] In the Tsugaru popular imagination, Iwaki-Akakura mountain is remembered as a great battleground between the conquering early Japanese Yamato state, worshipping the new synthesis of Buddhist and "Shintō" divinities, and indigenous aboriginal peoples, oriented toward their own autochthonous gods. To this day, a widely recounted local legend recalls that in the ninth century, the Yamato general Sakanoue Tamuramaro conquered the indigenous Ezo or Ainu peoples of Tsugaru by seducing the mountain's resident "demoness" and appropriating her ritual powers. For centuries, the priests of the large mainstream Shintō shrine, Iwaki-san Jinja (Iwaki Mountain Shrine) on Mount Iwaki's gentle western slopes, have venerated this formerly local female deity, whom they consider fully assimilated into the orthodox Shintō pantheon, safely embedded within the long-dormant volcano.

Yet in the unorthodox visions of Kawai Mariko and her followers, the old indigenous powers of the mountainscape are neither tamed nor quiescent. Rather like the Titans buried under Mount Olympus, conquered signs of an older polity and religious imagination, these local forces continue to convulse from time to time: A dragon bursts from within the mountain and manifests itself as a beautiful woman, recalling the long-repressed pre-Japanese indigenous "demoness" Onigamisama; other "demons," associated with the ethnically cleansed Ainu and Ezo, periodically possess worshipers as they undertake ascetic discipline on Akakura's dangerous slopes; amidst the mountain's rocky crevices, winding paths, and waterfalls, the faithful may glimpse the disturbing figure of the deity Akakura Daigongen manifested as a hirsute, undomesticated "wild man" who recalls the "hairy Ainu" exiled long ago to the northern island of Hokkaido.

The six and seventh lines of the Akakura Prayer, the shrine's preeminent ritual text, command: "By all means, the soul must be governed to become quiet, to become quiet / The heart, namely the kami and the "kami" becomes the master." This play on words conflates the divinities (神 kami) with the body's upper zones (上 also pronounced "kami"), which are implicitly contrasted with the body's lower sections and base instincts. In psychoanalytic terms, the mountain divinities, who "govern" the heart, enable the repression of excessively physical mundane desires. Significantly, the prayer does not draw a Cartesian opposition between mind and body, but rather contrasts and links two aspects of corporeal existence. Ascetic discipline constitutes a resolutely embodied physical undertaking that brings about an integrated unity of the upper and lower halves of the body, productively fusing heart and soul, will and desire, work and worship. Spiritual transcendence is achieved only through unrelenting physical labor on the mountain, which gradually causes one's entire body to resemble the graceful, flowing contours of the physical mountain and its resident divinities.

For the northern Japanese women and men with whom I worked, the volcanic mountain functions as a dynamic, integrated model of the human mind and body. On the surface the mountain is manifestly placid and life-giving, yet it contains within it raging, destructive forces obscured until the moment of eruption. It is for this reason, in part, that the mountain so effectively redresses human illness, death, and anger, all of which similarly reside beyond conventional human apprehension and control. As they return to the source of life, the sacred river that bubbles forth out of the mountain's high rock face, worshipers must traverse a primordial, cratered landscape shaped by explosions, lava, and pyroclastic flows, inhabited both by the spirits of those who have climbed before them and by the demonic manifestations of their indigenous forbears. Their daily climbs thus force the faithful to confront the most fundamental sources of human pleasure and pain. In the words of the Akakura Prayer, "There are times when the heart becomes wretched / since all things in the universe, everything, may be compared to water and fire."

This book argues that the perturbations dramatized by this prayer —and by related poetic and ritual practices at Akakura Mountain Shrine—have been largely generated by a complex set of tensions and contradictions. Like the dreams studied by Freud, opposing forces that allowed for no easy resolution or reconciliation catalyzed Kawai Mariko's revelatory visions. In many respects, these tensions may be understood as social and historical phenomena, some dating back to the region's initial incorporation into the early Japanese state, others emerging out of Tsugaru's uneasy status within the modern nation's industrial and post-industrial economies. Yet in other respects, the salient conflicts have been played out at the level of individual psychological processes, as individual women and men have sought to comprehend and manage contradictory obligations and desires. For decades, Akakura Mountain has simultaneously held out promises of regeneration and wholeness to social groups and to individual persons.

Labor and the Transforming Self

Through dedicated work at the shrine—in the form of demanding ascents up the mountain and ritual and profane labor within the shrine's precincts—worshipers over time project aspects of themselves into this complex landscape. In turn, they are believed to be gradually opened to intimate contact with the purifying domains of divinities and ancestors.[5] Over time, each worshiper comes to associate the variegated mountain landscape with her personal biography, the life histories of certain exemplary antecedents and ancestors, and the collective biography of the extended congregation. On the mountain slopes worshipers seek to relive, and ultimately to transcend, troubled chapters in their own lives and the lives of the honored dead.

These struggles often revolve around the fraught articulation of local domestic units with the wider economy and labor market. In many respects, the Akakura shrine system, built on the model of a local farmhouse, functions as a compensatory "home," a symbolic bulwark against the vast social and economic pressures breaking up extended multigenerational agrarian houses. In the great "storehouse/granary" of Akakura, worshipers find a tangible image of agrarian surplus, moral containment, and ancestral propriety, at times integrated into the larger market economy and at times enclaved from that economy.

In the following analysis, I have built on Japanese anthropologist Masao Yamaguchi's important discussion of the widespread tendency in Japan to assign hidden referents to important displayed objects (Yamaguchi 1991). In Japanese ritual contexts, representation and imitation are not simply secondary acts of substitution or replacement. They are, rather, fundamental components of efficacious worship. Through the willed enterprise of mimesis, the production of tangible simulacra of visible and invisible forces, an actor performatively constitutes a productive link between mortal worshipers and immortal divinities. The divinities and ancestors, in this respect, do not enter into the human world without human creative agency and aesthetic apprehension. All labor at the shrine, I argue, is organized around the fundamental work of imitative representation of divine and ancestral capacity. In principle, all subsequent mundane labor undertaken by worshipers in other domains of their lives—in rice fields, kitchens, or factories—can be reorganized to partake of these efficacious mimetic functions. Asceticism, and the related forms of work it infuses, are thus constitutive, performative undertakings through which actors help to produce the landscapes and work sites within which they labor. Through creative performances of disciplined labor, worshipers actively produce an externalized, multilayered model of their own minds and bodies, leading many to reenact important moments or crises in their psychosocial development and work history.

Like other labor activities, the body of developed ritual practice at Akakura does not in itself predetermine actors' experiences. The Akakura complex presents for each worshiper a field of imaginative possibilities through which she may at various levels dramatize or reflect on the nature of her relations with loved ones, ancestors, and divinities. Yet the shrine system does not in most cases provide simple answers to the predicaments faced by its members. In some cases, worship-

[margin note: links between humans & gods require labor]

[margin note: produce external landscapes of internal minds]

ers come to resolve or transcend traumas in their own lives or in the recollected economic careers of their families and ancestors. In other instances, their ritualized processes of recapitulation have led to deepening crises of the self, the accelerated fragmentation of their households, and apprehended possession by demons or ancestral forces.

For many, encounters with Akakura turn out to be profoundly liberatory, or at least help them carve out fulfilling and meaningful zones of partial autonomy in the context of challenging work and family relations. For others, however, time on the mountain has debilitating effects, summoning up unresolved traumas and tensions without providing a clear path to psychosocial integration and spiritual fulfillment.

Shattered Houses: Crises of Domestic Reproduction in Tsugaru

Kawai Mariko's vision of a penetrated house roof poignantly evokes her predicament at the time she was first called to serve Akakura Daigongen, the preeminent divinity of the mountain. Impoverished, once divorced, and fearful for her chronically ill daughter, she had little sense of control over her own household. As my older informants recall, she felt impossibly burdened by conflicting obligations to her natal family, to her new husband and his children, and to her own sick child. In these respects, her predicament exemplified the recurring challenges faced by many of the women with whom I have worked in Tsugaru. Since the late nineteenth century, local men and women have oscillated between farm labor at home and stints of migrant labor in the Japanese industrial heartland and in the fisheries and canneries of Hokkaido. The early decades of the twentieth century are still remembered as a harsh time for families anchored in the rural communities of the Tsugaru plain, characterized by high unemployment rates, persistent hunger, and extensive infant mortality.

Conditions have improved immeasurably since the MacArthur postwar land redistribution, giving thousands of families the possibility of purchasing modest plots for apple orchards and rice or produce farms. Yet few local farming families have been able to achieve in practice the enduring cultural ideal of a multigenerational extended household living together under one roof, redistributing their resources through an expansive kinship network. Nearly every rural or quasi-rural family with which I worked had to devote at least one "permanent" member to labor migration at least four months out of the year, usually in construction, hotel service, or light factory work in the Kansai region. For over a generation, male heads of agrarian households have found it difficult to locate potential brides willing to take on the extraordinary challenges of running a farmhouse and caring for elderly parents-in-law. As more and more of their younger siblings and cousins have moved permanently to urban areas, it has proven increasingly hard to recruit labor during busy planting and harvesting periods. Often families are forced into the humiliating position of requesting loans from urban relatives to pay agriculture cooperative fees and to buy needed fertilizer. Every adult couple I knew was consumed with anxiety over the educational prospects of their children and grandchildren. With little available cash for the cram schools that are considered essential for success on the all-important educational examinations, they fretted that the next generation would have little chance of upward mobility.

The psychological burdens of these predicaments fall especially hard on local women, who remain responsible for the physical and spiritual welfare of the household. When asked what initially drew them to Akakura or similar popular religious establishments, most women responded with stories of great unfulfilled obligation. They spoke of their never-ending burden of obligations toward their parents, affines, spouse, and children, as well as to their larger circle of neighbors and friends. These burdens were compounded by their double responsibility to the souls of their natal ancestors and the ancestors of the husband's lines.

Consider the representative cases of four women, spanning three generations of worshipers. Born in 1905, Fukuda Chie traced her involvement with Akakura to the unhappy early years of her marriage. Against the will of her father, a wealthy Tsugaru landowner, she had attended college in Tokyo in the 1920s and fallen in love. Her father summoned her back to Tsugaru and attempted to break off the romance by stopping mail from her lover. He also contracted an arranged marriage for her with an adopted husband, informing her new husband that he should "control" his willful bride by pursuing numerous extramarital affairs. The husband followed his father-in-law's advice, and for the first ten years, as Mrs. Fukuda later recalled, he never slept at home. In despair, unsure of her relative obligations to her husband

burdens of obligations

and father, she began to consult Kawai Mariko, who directed her to undertake austerities on the mountain. Through Kawai Mariko and the aid of the mountain kami, Fukuda Chie gained much strength and learned to speak "without fear." Indeed, on the occasion of her fiftieth wedding anniversary, she declined all gifts, announcing that the first decade of the marriage "didn't count" since her husband had never been at home during that period. After the MacArthur postwar land reforms she moved to Tokyo, but she returned each year to visit the shrine to pay her respects to the spirit of Kawai Mariko and to the Akakura kami.

Kobayashi Tomiko, a woman in her early sixties, resided in the farming village of Morita, about five miles from Akakura Mountain Shrine. In the early 1990s, she was torn between worry over her husband, exhibiting early signs of dementia, and her son Kenji, who at age forty remained unmarried, unable to find a suitable bride. Kenji worked hard at maintaining the family apple orchard, but he seemed increasingly depressed. He had been contemplating seeking a Thai or Filipino bride, although this option was deeply opposed by his father.[6] Kobayashi Tomiko, who prayed extensively at the family *butsudan* (domestic altar) for her son's marital success, anguished if she should advise her son to ignore his father's wishes and marry a foreign bride. Worried that she was failing her son and her obligations to the husband's ancestors to see the family line continued, she moved back and forth between visits to two local Shintō shrines and a new religious temple in the area. She was greatly relieved in 1991 when her son Kenji became involved with the junior (*bunke*) branch of Akakura Mountain Shrine, where she expected he would begin to receive the kami's blessings.

Okuda Setsuko, another woman in her early sixties, recalled that twenty years earlier she had been overwhelmed with financial debts to the bank, relatives, and friends. Her husband had been chronically ill and was unable to work efficiently on his small farm, which the family risked losing, thus leaving her eldest son without his expected legacy. Each morning at the family butsudan Okuda Setsuko found herself thinking of her unfulfilled duty to her husband's ancestors, which she associated with her sense of having failed as a wife and mother. She was also worried that her brother, a periodic labor migrant in Osaka, had been unable to perform proper memorialization (*kuyō*) for her late parents and their relatives. That same year, she had been diagnosed with severe cardiac problems and had been given six months to live by a local physician.

In the midst of her anxious despair, she experienced a powerful vision of Fudō Myōō, the fierce Buddhist guardian, clothed in fire. This divinity ordered her to begin ascetic climbs on Mount Akakura, a place she knew little of since she lived a two-hour train ride south of Hirosaki. Fudō Myōō, as interpreted by her teacher Mrs. Nakayama, required Okuda Setsuko to perform shugyō on the mountain in order to memorialize her husband's late relations, as well as her mother's mother. Here, Okuda Setsuko explained, she followed the path of Sakanoue Tamuramaro, the ancient conqueror of Tsugaru's indigenous inhabitants, whom she believes to have undertaken *shugyō* on the mountain more than one thousand years ago.

Over the course of the next decade, Okuda Setsuko was granted further visions and powers by the divinities and became an important kamisama spirit medium. By 1991, she was the second-highest-ranking medium associated with Akakura Mountain Shrine, and she was the only one empowered to perform the important monthly rite of Fudō-ken, the Sword of Fudō. She has not experienced heart problems for nearly two decades. She also reports that all her financial burdens have ceased, in part because Fudō has led her into a profitable Amway partnership with Kawai Mariko's granddaughter, the wife of the current priest of Akakura Mountain Shrine.

Women a generation younger feel no less torn over their familial and spiritual obligations. Sakurai Fumiko, age forty, grew up in a farming village near Morita, but at age twenty-eight moved away with her husband to assist him in running his family's small hotel in the Japanese alps several hundred miles to the south. Although filled with worry about the health and welfare of her mother and her mother's sisters, her heavy work responsibilities at the hotel allowed her little opportunity for return visits. A gynecological condition that left her unable to have children, to the bitter disappointment of her husband and mother-in-law, compounded matters. Painfully aware that she had failed to fulfill a fundamental obligation to her husband's house, Sakurai Fumiko experienced a series of undiagnosed illnesses during her early and mid-thirties. She consulted a male kamisama medium, Mr. Abo, who directed her to spend many months each year, for ten years to come, performing austerities at Akakura Mountain Shrine, the same shrine where her mother had undertaken ascetic discipline a generation earlier.

Sakurai Fumiko explained to her husband that this long period of asceticism was necessary to honor the twin *oshirasama* ritual figurines belonging to his family, who might cause untold calamity for the household if not properly venerated. She often noted that the complex interpersonal relations in the shrine were a constant torment to her, as they reminded her of her fraught relationship at the hotel with her mother-in-law, but that on the high mountain slopes her mind finally became "clear, and free of anger." Sakurai Fumiko's demanding shugyō, to be examined in detail in chapter 5, gradually increased her status in the Akakura network. By the mid-1990s, it was widely expected that she would eventually be called as a kamisama spirit medium.

Gender, Social Class, and Political Consciousness

Asceticism and related ritual practices at Akakura offer worshipers, especially women, extraordinary possibilities for fulfillment and status enhancement within local religious networks. In many different ways, participation in *shugyō*, in the aesthetics of prayer and offering, and in collective ceremonies eases the burden of the class and gender structures outlined above. Women who have successfully undertaken *shugyō* are locally respected and may in time become spiritual healers, a potentially lucrative occupation. Nearly all of them report that asceticism brings them a sense of calmness and greatly reduces their troubles at work and in marriage.

Nonetheless, it would be difficult to argue that Akakura constitutes resistance in any organized sense to conventional structures of power and authority in Japan. To be sure, shrine members knew that in the late nineteenth and early twentieth centuries, kamisama spirit mediums associated with the mountain had been harassed and imprisoned by state Shintō authorities, but such events struck nearly everyone as distant memories of a long-lost era. So far as I could tell nearly all of the worshipers consistently voted for the ruling Liberal Democratic Party (LDP), which they understood as safeguarding the interest of agrarian families. Although many women privately told me of their anxieties over the national government's plan in the late 1980s to locate the world's largest plutonium reprocessing plant at Rokkasho, on the western peninsula of the prefecture, nearly all were convinced by LDP officials' pleas that hosting the plant was their patriotic duty. Shamans and spirit mediums from other ritual traditions participated in anti-Rokkasho public protests, but no ritual specialists or worshipers from Akakura did so. The prefecture's LDP governor, the leading supporter of the Rokkasho plant, received a warm welcome when he attended the shrine's great summer festival in 1991.

Many worshipers labor for part of the year in comparatively low-wage temporary positions in light industrial plants, road maintenance crews, and hotels in Japan's core industrial areas. Many return with stories of unsafe working conditions, unsympathetic supervisors, and unpleasant urban accommodations. Yet such frustrations rarely translate into any form of direct political action or mobilization. For the true worshiper, I was often told, work constitutes the most important form of service and must be pursued with a grateful heart, without complaint. The mountain eases pain associated with economic limitations but does not encourage interest in politics of any formal sort. As Fumiko told me, "On the mountain, we can tell one another stories about all our troubles. Up here, the pain will just melt away." Nor, to my knowledge, were conventional gender hierarchies directly challenged at the shrine or in worshipers' households. Although women perform the vast majority of the physical labor required to maintain the shrine and are often granted great latitude in specific ritual and performance domains, I have never observed any woman (other than the wife of the shrine's priest, herself the granddaughter of Kawai Mariko) query a male administrative decision at the shrine.

Since 1987, I have spent a good deal of time working, visiting, and residing in many quasi-agrarian households on the Tsugaru peninsula. My impression is that, as many worshipers insist, there really exists less domestic strife in the households of Akakura Shrine Association members than in many neighboring households. To some extent this seems to due to the serenity, self-confidence, and good humor of women worshipers who are often gifted at defusing potential conflicts with spouses, mothers-in-law, and children before they spiral out of control. Yet in many instances the appearance of domestic harmony is hard-won and not without costs. Women worshipers emphasize that they often apply the great self-discipline they learn on the mountain to relations with kin, enduring harassment and abuse in cheerful silence as a form of service to the divinities and ancestors. Some acknowledge that this stoic attitude only intensifies the rage directed against them but insist that they must, whenever possible, persevere.

Although Akakura women have been known to obtain divorces, there is considerable pressure within the extended shrine network for women to preserve virtually any marriage, regardless of how painful it might be. Having said that, successful ascetics do bring great strength of character to difficult relationships. The often-cited example of Fukuda Chie proves instructive. She actively refused golden wedding anniversary gifts, an extraordinary act of symbolic separation, yet never divorced her philandering husband. In a similar fashion, the pursuit of harsh physical austerities on the mountain, sometimes for weeks at a time, offers women temporary separation from troubled domestic relationships. Their practices allow them, in complex fashions, to dramatize and work on tangible images of their suffering. To be sure, husbands, mothers-in-law, and children may complain bitterly about their women relatives who temporarily leave their homes and domestic duties to undertake shugyō. Yet in the final analysis, life on the mountain does not encourage women to challenge fundamentally those who trouble them or to disentangle themselves from hierarchical relationships.

Plan of the Book

In the chapters that follow, I attempt to do justice to the collective and personal dimensions of ritual practice and spiritual experience at Akakura Mountain Shrine. These undertakings take place within pervasive structures of power and authority, yet they allow for profound fulfillment within restricted, semiautonomous zones. The Akakura faithful continually emphasize their deep bonds of obligation to divinities, ancestors, family members, and fellow mortal worshipers, yet they also insist that while on the mountain, they are "free."

As we shall see, obligation and freedom are intimately linked at Akakura. Like other followers of kamisama spirit mediums in Tsugaru, many Akakura worshipers pursue highly individuated and creative acts of ascetic discipline on the mountain. Yet, unlike many local ascetics, they also participate in a complex collective ritual life, joining their fellow worshipers for pilgrimages and ceremonial performances many times each year. This study explores why Akakura worshipers insist on the equal importance of individual ascetic discipline and collective ceremonials, and how individual women and men move back and forth between coordinated group ritual and highly individuated revelatory experiences.

Chapter 1 locates spirit mediumship and ritual performance at Akakura within a larger historical geography of remembered crisis and trauma in the Tsugaru region. In varied ceremonial and discursive arenas, mediums and their followers reflect on long-term relations between comparatively indigenous and Yamato (core Japanese) spiritual forces embedded in local landscapes and on the changing nature of labor and social value within an increasingly monetized regional economy.

As chapter 2 emphasizes, the enduring predicaments of indigeneity, household integrity, labor, and kinship have helped structure the shrine's emerging architecture and popular apprehensions of Akakura Mountain's sacred topography. Building on Masao Yamaguchi's treatment of *mitate* (imitation) in Japanese ritual symbolism, I explore how worshipers build up tangible models of the "other world" through mimetic practices at the shrine and come to apprehend mysterious, divinely created resemblances on the mountain's slopes. Human-made structures and human-modified landscape features on the mountain make it possible to regulate transactions between the visible and invisible worlds, establishing necessary resemblances and distinctions among persons, ancestors, and divinities.

Chapter 3 examines the integrative functions of ritual performance within this intermediate landscape, bridging dynamic frontiers between the visible and the invisible, the mortal and the immortal, the living and the dead. In many respects, the shrine's annual ceremonial cycle, largely modeled on the seasonal labor cycles of local agrarian households, merges worshipers, divinities, and ancestors into an extended, idealized "family" organized around the circulation of visible and invisible forces on and off the mountainscape. Over the course of a year, this unified family collectively strives for maturation and rebirth in a manner closely coordinated with agrarian cycles of growth and harvest and popular Shintō-Buddhist cycles of memorialization and transcendence. Yet in other important respects the ritual cycle establishes or reproduces critical differentiations—between women and men, the living and ancestors, spiritual leaders and followers, and worshipers and divinities.

Chapter 4 explores how individual worshipers understand their exchange transactions with divinities and ancestors. By means of songs, prayers, and elaborate presentations of material offerings, worshipers often report profound alterations in their bodies and minds. As they internalize the aesthetic principles of purity, symmetry, reversibility, and flexibility exemplified by offered images of their transforming selves, many assert that they gradually take on physical and mental resemblances to invisible spiritual beings and to the transcendent mountain itself.

As chapter 5 demonstrates, these processes of internalization and transposition are most powerfully experienced by those performing demanding physical austerities on the mountain slopes, the residence of the immortal gods, where worshipers present their bodies and physical labor as offerings to be appreciated and transmuted by the divinities. At times, the emotional intensity of these acts of intimate identification with invisible members of the mountain's cosmological family has profound consequences for the worshiper's relations with members of her conventional human family and members of the extended shrine community.

Chapter 6 traces the micropolitical consequences of these experiences of transforming selfhood and interpersonal relations, with particular attention to revelatory visions by individual worshipers. Over time, an experienced ascetic may become a charismatic spirit medium, believed to "mirror" back to an extended group of worshipers images of their better selves and of their relations with others and the benevolent divinities. Creative processes of personal transformation thus at times have profound ramifications for the social organization of the Akakura community. In turn, the social logic of symbolic action on the mountainscape establishes general parameters within which deeply original and creative acts of revelation and self-fashioning may be accomplished, bringing about subtle shifts in the political structure of the shrine association.

In the conclusion, I reconsider the many different kinds of "immortal wishes" promised to worshipers at Akakura. The mountain, as we shall see, embodies many paradoxes. Climbing on its slopes and ven-

erating its divinities, the faithful strive to return to childlike dependence on external forces while developing mature interdependence on
peers and followers. They honor the Great Mothers of the mountain
while fearing the Demon Queen. They gain great respect and status as
women, yet never overtly challenge conventional structures of gender
relations. They celebrate their status as "Japanese," proudly hanging
the Rising Sun flag over the great gorge each year, yet they also enter
into intimate relations with pre-Japanese indigenous forces embedded
in the mysterious mountainscape.

In the final analysis, then, it is impossible to reduce ritual and labor
practices at this unusual mountain shrine to a single moral orientation. Nor would it be possible to disentangle fully the collective and
personal dimensions of work and worship at Akakura. In some respects, Kawai Mariko's founding vision of a dragon emerging from a
mountain was the product of a local religious history embedded in
shared patterns of agrarian labor. Source of water and fertile soil, the
Iwaki-Akakura volcano has long functioned as the symbolic and practical center of local life-giving economies. Fire-breathing dragons, mobile extensions of the ambiguous mountain, have long been understood in northern Japan as mediators between sky and earth, between
the cosmological family of the immortal divinities on the mountain
and conventional mortal families in the plain below. Local women and
men have long pursued ascetic discipline on the dangerous mountain slopes, seeking proximity to gods and ancestors and blessings for
themselves and their kin. Seen in this light, we can understand Akakura Mountain Shrine as an overdetermined product of a specific social and cultural history, exemplifying its deep tensions and contradictions.

Yet in many respects, Kawai Mariko's dream and its legacies were
deeply original and idiosyncratic, creatively synthesizing regional mythology, local labor practices, and her troubled relations with her own
immediate kin. As we shall see, her innovative ritual practices incorporated many of the conventional work activities she had undertaken
as an impoverished farm wife; in the new world of Akakura, cooking, gestation, childbirth, nursing, cleaning, and weaving became the
bases of spiritual regeneration and cosmological kinship. Having suffered through a joyless, childless marriage and a devastating divorce,
her novel ritual cycle was predicated on a periodic marriage between

co-equal female and male forces through which worshipers were re-born as cherished children of the gods.

In turn, each worshiper who has followed Kawai Mariko's example since the 1920s has encountered a standardized set of practices and received wisdom at Akakura, yet, like the founder before them, has always been encouraged to find her or his original "path on the mountain." Each has brought to the mountain a unique pattern of life experience, born of specific family dynamics, medical predicaments, and personal labor histories. Each has concretized aspects of her own personhood and consciousness in material offerings, ritual acts, narrative performances, and ascetic service in a manner partly prescribed and in part freely chosen.

These acts have thus often had unexpected, indeterminate consequences for individual worshipers, ranging from exultation to despair, from serenity to rage, from integration to isolation. Many of these varied practices and outcomes, emerging from the continuous intersection of collective and personal projects, have over time been incorporated into the changing organization of ritual, space, and time at Akakura, which has continued to function as a staging ground for new acts of self-discovery and self-creation. The immortal wishes exemplified by the sacred mountain reside in this ongoing dialectic between collective forms and individual imagination, between historical predicaments and personal struggle, between acceptance and revelation, between labor and transcendence.

1

p r e d i c a m e n t s   o f   h i s t o r y

Ritual Life on a Japanese Periphery

Memories of Conquest

On a warm summer evening in July 1992, a group of a dozen women
were gathered in the Shinden (Inner Sanctuary) of Akakura Mountain Shrine, located on the lower slope of Akakura Mountain, as the
northeastern face of Mount Iwaki is popularly known. The women had
just participated in the first phase of the shrine's annual summer festival, the climax of the ritual year at Akakura. A senior kamisama spirit
medium had led them in an hour-long performance of the shrine's primary chant, "Saigi, Saigi" (Repentance, repentance) as they had collectively besought the aid of the mountain's great divinities. Now, this
group of women remained seated in the sanctuary for an extraordinary
conversation. Led by the shrine's two most important spirit mediums,
Okuda Setsuko and Narita Emiko, they shared stories of firsthand encounters with the divinities on the rugged upper slopes of Akakura.

   As Okuda and Narita repeatedly reminded the lay worshipers, Akakura is the *ura* (rear, or hidden) face of Mount Iwaki, the great three-

peaked volcano that towers over the southern Tsugaru plain. As such, Akakura is contrastively paired with the *omote* (front, or public) face of Iwaki, the mountain's much more placid southern slope. For generations the southern omote front face of Iwaki has been associated with political authority and the state Shintō establishment. In contrast, Akakura, the more remote ura face, has long been popularly conceived as the site of dangerous, unruly cosmological powers linked to the indigenous *onigami* (demon gods) and Onigamisama, the great Demon Queen.

Yet Okuda, Narita, and their fellow ritual specialists at Akakura did not consider themselves simply successors of untamed local demons. Rather, they understood themselves as emerging out of a complex political and cosmological history that stretched back over a millennium, encompassing both the early, conquering Yamato state and the conquered powers of the indigenous landscape. As they perform rigorous physical and spiritual austerities on Akakura's dangerous slopes, these ascetics tangibly encounter and embody a hybrid history, alternately fusing and transcending the categories of foreigner and native, divinity and demon, male and female, past and present.

At one point during the conversation, Okuda recalled that during an early exercise of shugyō on the mountain, the spirit of the great Japanese war leader Sakanoue Tamuramaro, who died more than 1000 years earlier, had possessed her. As she felt Sakanoue's breath coursing though her, her companion, an asthmatic young man, was purified and cured of his affliction. As Okuda recalled, "The kami said, 'This is the place to set down a little of your burden. This is the place.' And it was awe-inspiring. You could feel Sakanoue Tamuramaro's breath and even that young man, his body was frozen in fright, and something stuck into his body, making the sound, *gichya, gichya*" (rattle, rattle).

In describing her possession by the healing mountain spirit of Sakanoue Tamuramaro, Mrs. Okuda, like Kawai Mariko before her, is heir to a popular mythic history stretching back many centuries. Sakanoue Tamuramaro, a historical personage in the ninth-century imperial court at Kyoto, is remembered in local oral histories as the Yamato conqueror of the indigenous Ezo and Ainu peoples of northern Honshu (ethnically cleansed from Tsugaru in the early modern period). Although most historians consider it highly unlikely that Tamuramaro or any figure of the ninth-century Kyoto court actually came as far north as Tsugaru, popular legend has it that Sakanoue Tamuramaro defeated the indigenous aborigines and colonized the region for the expanding Yamato civilization. He is said to have accomplished this feat by seducing Mount Iwaki's resident Demon Queen or Dragon Princess, variously referred to as Anjuhime, Akakurasama, Onigamisama, or Tatsubihime no Mikoto, who provided him with the ritual paraphernalia with which to defeat the indigenous armies (see Kodate 1980, 1986).

In her possession episode, Okuda moves back and forth between the structural positions of conqueror and conquered, foreigner and native. She follows in the footsteps of the ancient Yamato invader, retracing his ascetic pathways, yet is simultaneously followed by his invisible spirit, which moves on the mountain wind. Like the ancient indigenous Dragon Goddess, seduced by the male general, Okuda herself is penetrated by the presence of Sakanoue and begins to speak with his voice. Yet this process of possession also marks her emerging status in the shrine community; a visible representative of the ancient conqueror, she instructs the young male student in the mysteries of the cosmic mountain.

As noted earlier, Okuda had been compelled to undertake this initial period of ascetic discipline out of her overwhelming sense of unfulfilled obligation to her living and dead relatives, burdens that had afflicted her with terrible debts and seemingly terminal heart disease. Yet now, filled with the spirit of the ancient conqueror, she is granted peace. Her once heavy body becomes "light," and she communicates to her ill companion the words of the possessing divinity: "This is the place to set down a little of your burden." A few months before this mountain climb, she had believed herself entirely isolated and defeated, an utter failure in the eyes of her husband, neighbors, and ancestors. Now, atop the sacred mountain, Okuda is triumphant, a gifted healer and teacher within whose body is fused the divine couple, the foreign general and the native Dragon Princess. On the mysterious, hidden side of the mountain, far away from the familiar world of home and the plain, she is no longer a victim of history but is conjoined with history's victors.

As Okuda's possession narrative suggests, one cannot meaningfully separate the familial crises of obligation that impel worshipers to journey to Akakura Mountain from local and national histories. In many senses, these colliding histories have generated the collective and personal difficulties that motivate pilgrims on Akakura's healing slopes. At the same time, the ritual solutions developed by these actors creatively incorporate features of the remembered past, selectively drawing on mytho-historical personages and processes.

A historically isolated region associated with traces of conquered indigenous communities, the Tsugaru peninsula has long been consigned to the cultural and economic periphery of the nation. Existing precariously within a comparatively impoverished labor reserve, the fortunes of Tsugaru agrarian households have been intimately tied to the course of industrialization and urbanization in the core Japanese regions, yet they have rarely been able to reproduce themselves on their own terms. Under these conditions, a complex range of popular ritual practices has emerged and flourished in Tsugaru, surviving both central state repression and cosmopolitan bemusement. Since the 1920s, the ritual specialists of Akakura have imaginatively drawn on the rich local history of remembered conquest, labor, and symbolic action to create an innovative complex of myth and performance on the peripheral, "hidden" face of the sacred mountain.

Tsugaru Histories

Located at the northeastern tip of Honshu, Japan's largest island, the Tsugaru peninsula is surrounded to the west by the Sea of Japan, to the north by the Tsugaru Straits (which divide Honshu from Hokkaido), to the east by the broad circle of Aomori Bay, and to the south by mountains that run from the Sea of Japan to Lake Towada.[1] The northeastern and southwestern sections are especially mountainous; the coastal plains are composed of marshes and swamplands. For millennia most human settlement has concentrated in the Tsugaru plain, the basin of the Iwaki River that flows north from a confluence near Mount Iwaki into the Jūsan Lagoon and the Sea of Japan. The plain, about forty miles long and between four and twelve miles wide, is bordered to the east and south by mountain ranges, and to the west by the massive volcanic Mount Iwaki and a series of sand dunes that stretch along the Sea of Japan. Although inhabitants have practiced irrigated rice cultivation in this central basin since at least the third century (Ravina 1991, 76), rice yields have never been high or reliable.

The Tsugaru region has short summers and long winters, and receives among the heaviest snowfalls in Japan. North of the protective coverage of Mount Iwaki (which for centuries has served as the symbolic center of Tsugaru ritual life), extremely high winds and snowdrifts buffet the central and northern portions of the plain during the long winter season.

Neolithic Jōmon-era archaeological sites are widely spread in Tsugaru and are particularly concentrated in the well-watered, fertile plain beneath the volcanic fissures of Akakura, the northeastern face of Mount Iwaki. The Tsugaru peninsula provided the last habitat of the aboriginal Ainu and Ezo peoples on Honshu, before the Yamato state's conquest and extermination campaigns forced their gradual expulsion to Hokkaido or their reclassification as Japanese from the eleventh century onward. (The last Ainu in Honshu, residing in the village of Utesu at the northern tip of Tsugaru, were officially registered as Japanese in 1756.) As noted above, various local narratives compress this long historical process into the mythic seduction of Mount Iwaki's resident Demon Queen by the Yamato conquering general Sakanoue Tamuramaro.

Partly because of this relatively recent association with the indigenous Ainu and Ezo peoples, Japanese scholarly circles have widely regarded Tsugaru as somewhat of an ethnological curiosity. The nasal twang of its dialects has been ridiculed, its ritual complexes dismissed as not "fully Japanese," and its populations characterized as "hybrid" or "underdeveloped."[2]

In 1189, when central state control was established over all of Tōhoku, the peninsula was officially incorporated into Mutsu province, comprising the area of present-day Aomori, Iwate, Miyagi, and Fukushima prefectures. Even within this historically underdeveloped region, Tsugaru was long considered especially provincial and impoverished. At the northern edge of the Sea of Japan, the peninsula was relatively isolated from the major Pacific sailing routes to the shogunate's capital at Edo. Difficult overland travel from the south over steep mountains limited exports to rice, lumber, and modest quantities of the distinctive local laquerware.

Under the Tokugawa shogunate, Tsugaru was administered as a feudal domain (*han*) by the Tsugaru family, based in the castle city of Hirosaki at the southern edge of the peninsula, to the immediate southeast of Mount Iwaki. From the seventeenth century onward, Hirosaki developed as the cultural and intellectual center of the region. The Tsugaru *daimyō* (feudal lords) historically stood in opposition to the rulers of Nanbu (the eastern region of Northern Tōhoku), from whom the first Tsugaru lord, Tamenobu, had wrested the Tsugaru peninsula in the late sixteenth century. To this day, Tsugaru residents speak scornfully (or at least jokingly) of their traditional Nanbu rivals.

Periodic food crises and unusually extensive samurai involvement in farming and land reclamation projects marked Tsugaru history during the Tokugawa period (Ravina 1999, 115–53). For example, in the novelist Osamu Dazai's birthplace of Kanagi village in central Tsugaru, samurai owned 62 of 105 homes and controlled 79 percent of the land by the late seventeenth century (Ravina 1991, 84). Though well watered, the basin of the central Tsugaru plain has proved an unsteady site of rice production. Under state-enforced policies of rice monoculture, the region experienced several catastrophic famines throughout the Tokugawa period. Between the early seventeenth and the mid-twentieth centuries, the region's rice harvest failed on average once every five years (Dazai 1987, 62–63). The national Tenmei famine of the 1780s and the Tempo famine of the 1840s proved especially calamitous in Tsugaru. Following the eruption of Mount Iwaki in the tenth month of 1783, the region's entire crop was destroyed, and the subsequent famine and epidemic killed over 80,000 people between 1783/9 and 1784/6 (about one-third of the population of 250,000).[3] This demographic disaster and subsequent labor shortages were followed by an extensive policy in the 1790s of forcibly relocating samurai retainers from the castle town of Hirosaki to rural communities. The policy, which rural elites and peasantries actively resisted, was officially abandoned by the end of the eighteenth century (Ravina 1999, 128–41). However, memories of samurai-peasant tensions as well as samurai-peasant intermarriage have continued for generations, and many of my informants recounted them. The chronic late Tokugawa food crises also led the Tsugaru han to place severe restrictions on sericulture in an effort to maximize available land for rice cultivation and increase fiscal revenues.

Soon after the Meiji Restoration (1868), Tsugaru was merged with the impoverished Nanbu-speaking peninsula of Shimokita to its east to constitute the prefecture of Aomori in 1871. Although Aomori City, a port city on Aomori Bay midway between the two peninsulas, was designated the new prefecture's administrative capital, Hirosaki remained its intellectual and cultural center, and its residents insist that the city is the "true heart" of the region.

From the 1860s onward, American missionaries from Illinois and Indiana based in Hirosaki introduced North American apple strains and commercial apple farming in Tsugaru. Since the late nineteenth century, apple monocropping has become the economic mainstay of the southern peninsula; the sandy western shore areas have emphasized melon growing. With the virtual elimination of hunting and gathering, the central and northern zones have depended on timber, charcoal making, scattered rice production, dairy farming, and tourism. Fishing remains important in coastal areas. During the Meiji and Taishō periods, Tsugaru residents, like other Tōhoku peasants, provided the bulk of migrant, low-wage labor for the fisheries and canneries of Hokkaido. According to popular memory, Tsugaru also provided a disproportionately high number of conscript combat soldiers during the Great Pacific War (World War II).

Following the postwar land redistribution, chemical-intensive smallholder apple agriculture spread throughout the southern half of the peninsula, on Iwaki's slopes, and in the surrounding plains. Through an extremely labor-intensive process, these small orchards produce apples that are nationally renowned for their size, roundness, lustrous glow, and smooth skin. Elegantly maintained orchards fill the hills and flatlands of the region. During the summer months the air vibrates with the sound of pesticide sprayers and buzz saws as farming men and women painstakingly prune back dead branches and thin all but the most perfect young apples.[4] Each remaining apple is carefully wrapped in layers of colored tissue paper, peeled back one or two weeks before harvest to ensure a perfectly ripened fruit. Also shortly prior to harvest, reflective foil "blankets" are spread out on the ground below to redden the bottom side of the fruit, guaranteeing the uniform coloration for which Tsugaru apples are prized. Regional farming cooperatives provide loan packages for seeds, chemicals, and other inputs, and they purchase apples from farmers at controlled prices.

Although the process depends on extensive petrochemical inputs, apple growing has been subject to considerable aesthetic and ritual elaboration over the past century. Many farmers refer to their skill at nurturing apple trees as *ringo-dō* (the way of the apple), comparing this craft to martial arts such as *kendō* (the way of the sword). They speak of an intimate relationship between their own bodies and the "bodies" of the apple trees, which they carefully tend throughout the year. Enormous pride is taken in the autumn harvest. Unblemished, round, glowing apples are considered an excellent offering to the kami. Those who work in them usually consider apple orchards beautiful and tranquil places. For all the physical exhaustion (and possible long-term side effects from exposure to chemical toxins) associated with apple cultivation, the practice has romantic connotations for many farmers and is often spoken of wistfully by those who no longer farm.

Few farming families, however, can subsist solely by commercial farming. All of the multigenerational households with whom I worked depended on remittances from relatives working in urban centers, either in long-term employment or short-term contracts. Many families could recall histories of seasonal labor migration going back for at least four or five generations. As elsewhere in northern Tōhoku, the fishing, mountain, and farming villages of Tsugaru have constituted an important labor reserve for the industrializing core areas of central Japan since the late Tokugawa period. Nearly all of the rural families with whom I worked had relatives in the Tokyo or Ōsaka metropolitan areas with whom they were in regular contact. Most households also depended on seasonal labor migration by at least one middle-generation member in construction or light industry in Kantō or Kansai, or at the increasing number of resorts and luxury hotels springing up throughout northern Japan. Many Tsugaru residents worked as labor migrants in the fisheries and canneries of southern Hokkaido during the late nineteenth and early twentieth centuries; extensive links of kinship and friendship continue between Tsugaru and Hokkaido communities.

During the Second World War, the Allies designated Hirosaki a cultural center and thus spared it the extensive aerial bombardment that leveled the military port of Aomori City thirty-five miles away. Now a city of approximately 180,000, Hirosaki is still celebrated for its scenic Tokugawa-era Castle and Cherry Tree Festival, its excellent National University, its old twisting streets, and its elaborate wards of Buddhist temples, Shintō shrines, and samurai houses.

In the 1990s, Aomori still rivaled Okinawa for the dubious distinction of most impoverished prefecture in the nation, reckoned both in terms of per capita income and locally generated revenues. (During my 1991–92 fieldwork, direct or indirect grants from the national government made up about 70 percent of the prefecture's budget.) Since the 1960s, the state has heavily invested in local infrastructure and development projects, including regional agricultural cooperatives, the northward extension of the Tōhoku expressway to Aomori City, and the Tappi rail tunnel from the northern tip of the Tsugaru peninsula to Hokkaido. However, in spite of frequent campaigns by regional politicians, the high-speed Shinkansen (Bullet Train) line—the preeminent sign of inclusion in national economic space—still has not been extended from Morioka in Iwate prefecture northwards to Aomori City.

In the absence of the Shinkansen, Aomori prefecture is continuously exhorted by national authorities to expand facilities for domestic tourism. On winter nights, a ski lift's powerful lights now illuminate the silhouette of Mount Iwaki. Bus tours from Tokyo bring tourists to experience the rustic villages and extraordinary snowdrifts of central Tsugaru. Several *furusato-machi* (old home-town cultural villages) are under construction in the hope of attracting tourists. A "Santa's Village" has been built in the mountains dividing Tsugaru and Akita prefecture. The Shirakami forest reserve has been developed for metropolitan ecotourism. Extensive efforts have been to made to market the prefecture's "traditional" commodities as souvenirs; the Prefecture's Museum in Aomori City, for example, centers around a giant, walkthrough map of the prefecture that features the "distinctive local products" (available for purchase in the gift shop) of each community in Aomori.

As one of the least politically powerful prefectures in the nation, Aomori has also become the site of controversial nuclear projects successfully resisted by other prefectures. Mutsu on the Shimokita peninsula served as the base of an abortive nuclear-powered ship project in the 1950s. As noted in the introduction, in the early 1990s, the national government overruled extensive local protests to construct the world's largest plutonium reprocessing plant at Rokkasho, an extremely poor community on the southern Shimokita peninsula.[5]

In spite of over a century of intensive effort by the national Education Ministry to eliminate local dialects and accents, Tsugaru-ben remains widely spoken throughout rural and urban areas of the peninsula. All my informants stressed pride in these dialects' virtual unintelligibility to standard Japanese speakers, and they supported recent efforts by local intellectuals and activists to revive schooling, fiction, song, and poetry in Tsugaru-ben.

Besides their apples, harsh winters, and esoteric dialects, Tsugaru and Aomori have several other national claims to fame. The region has been known for generations to produce some of the nation's finest sumō wrestlers. (My informants insist this results from the excellent quality of Tsugaru rice.) The town of Kanagi in central Tsugaru claims renown as the birthplace of novelist Dazai Osamu, who immortalized the community's decaying aristocracy in *The Setting Sun* (1947) and other works. His family's home has become a significant national tourist and "literary pilgrimage" site.

Haunted Landscapes: Memorialization and Cultural Geography

A remembered history of privation, death, and loss informs Tsugaru's contemporary ritual or "moral" geography. To this day in Tsugaru communities, the ninth-century victory of Sakanoue Tamuramaro over the aboriginals is celebrated each August in the Nebuta and Neputa festivals (as the ceremonies are known in Aomori and Hirosaki City respectively). Great lantern floats, painted with the lurid images of demons believed to have been in league with the indigenous Ezo and Ainu, are pulled through the region's cities and villages. Until the early twentieth century, carnivalesque violence between the "upper" and "lower" halves of the city marked the Neputa festival in Hirosaki, as the ancient battle between relative foreigners and relative indigenes was refought each year. Nowadays, the largely sanitized festival offers an exquisite procession of magnificent fan-shaped floats, illuminated from within, constructed over the course of the year by neighborhood associations. Held on the eve of the national Obon festival of the dead, the rites at an inchoate level propitiate the dead souls of the ancient aboriginal population, widely associated with archeological sites throughout the region.[6]

Memories of more recent deaths are also scattered across the local landscape. During planting season in the Iwaki River plain, as I worked with friends and informants in orchards and fields, I would often hear, "You know, there is a body buried in those dikes." During the great eighteenth-century flooding of the river plain, a priest is said to have lain down on the dike at the river's bank and ordered peasants to pound on his stomach with a long pole until he expired. He was buried in the dike, and from that time on the river kept within its banks. The popular Tsugaru Kagura ritual dance, performed by local Shintō priests, especially at Sekihachi Jinja in Kujisama-machi, routinely re-enacts this mythic event and is believed to keep floods away.

The mythic act of pounding the priest's body recalls the common-place act of pounding rice to produce *mochi,* the glutinous rice cakes presented as offerings to the divinities. The myth and rite emphasize the symbolism of enclosure: the priest's blood is kept inside his body and the priest's body is kept within the dike, just as the dike should enclose the river waters. His homogenized innards become the mortar that holds together the river barriers. Through the offered operator of the priest's body, the peasant labor of pounding and enclosure is permanently embedded as a prophylactic feature within the local landscape.

The symbolism of productive sacrifice conjoined with signs of daily labor also characterizes the thousands of oshirasama (オシラ様) ritual figurines found in many Tsugaru households. As elsewhere in Tōhoku, the paired male and female oshirasama are associated with an ancient Chinese myth of a murdered young woman and her horse-lover, killed for their unnatural love for one another. Here and throughout north-eastern Japan, *itako* female shamanesses use the figurines as they enter trance, mime the divinities' sexual union, and reenact the murdered beings' journey to heaven (Blacker 1975; Schattschneider 1996a). In Tsugaru, the silk-wrapped oshirasama have become closely associated with the complex history of sericulture in the region. During the Tokugawa period, the local aristocracy sought to eliminate silk production as it attempted to maximize rice production in order to bolster its position in the national state. Given the relatively poor local conditions for rice cultivation, these moves were often resisted by the peasantry and mercantile class, which sought the security of regular cash income. Amidst the eighteenth-century famines brought on by periodic crises in rice monoculture, oshirasama emerged as powerful household divinities, protecting landowning families from hunger and safeguarding their attempts to navigate the cash economy.

Oshirasama, I was often told, impose many demands on their human owners: they must be given daily offerings, housed with honor within the family butsudan (ancestral altar), clothed in silk brocade and jewelry, routinely taken to appropriate festivals at local shrines and temples, and receive new outer silk layers each year. If denied these tributes, it is said, the figurines will "fly away" during the night, leaving the household vulnerable to the vicissitudes of the market economy.

The ubiquitous stone statues of the Bodhisattva Jizō found throughout the region, especially in zones considered to be *Sainokawara* (lit., banks of the subterranean river Sai), river banks bordering on the underworld, also recall histories of flood, famine, and labor.[7] Many of these popular carvings commemorate children who died of hunger or who fell victim to famine-induced infanticide.[8] The simple wooden *kokeshi* dolls (now a popular curio in the Tsugaru tourist trade) are also widely believed to memorialize the victims of early modern infanticide; like Jizō statues, the dolls help appease the unquiet spirits of the dead and prevent the dangerous circulation of *muenbotoke* (restless spirits) through the land of the living.

In the 1930s and 1940s Jizō-oriented memorialization was popularly adapted in Tsugaru to the calamities of war. Unmarried soldiers killed in battle were married to consecrated "bride dolls" (*hanayomeningyō*) animated by the spirit of Jizō and stored in special temple complexes. Since the war, the practice has been extended to civilian children and young people who die before marriage. In the esoteric Buddhist institutions of Kōbōji (in Kizukuri) and Kawakura Sainokawara (in Nakasato-Kanagi), thousands of dolls are consecrated as spirit spouses, enshrined with photographs of youths who died before their time (Schattschneider 2001).

Oshirasama and hanayomeningyō are closely associated with itako (イタコ), the celebrated "blind shamanesses," who constitute northern Tōhoku's most pronounced claim on the "national cultural imaginary" (Ivy 1995). The annual gathering by itako at Osorezan ("Mount Dread") in Shimokita has been featured in national television broadcasts since 1960 (Blacker 1975, 339). My metropolitan Tokyo friends, on learning that I wished to study Tsugaru shamanism, assumed that I would study itako.[9] The closely related institution of kamisama spirit mediumship—a principal object of my research—is not widely known nationally.

Most northern Tōhoku mediums insist that itako and kamisama are entirely distinct traditions. Itako, people usually say, are born blind, and are initiated in late adolescence or early adulthood into mediumship through intensive austerities supervised by senior itako. All itako in Aomori belong to an overarching regional association (the president of which is usually the husband of one of the area's most prominent itako). Itako have close formal affiliations with Buddhist temples, and like these temples they are principally concerned with memorialization (kuyō) of the dead. Itako are especially renowned for the process of *kuchiyose,* calling down the spirits of the dead to communicate with the living. Throughout Tōhoku, itako are intimately associated with the male and female oshirasama figurines, made of cloth or silk bundled around sculpted mulberry wood cores. Itako at times enter trance by ritually manipulating these figurines, and by reciting *oshira-saimon* chants that recount the mythic death and rebirth of the oshirasama divinities.

Many itako attend prominent Buddhist festivals in Aomori prefecture, most notably the summer festivals at Osorezan in Shimokita and at Kawakura Sainokawara (Kanagi-Nakasato) in Tsugaru. During these memorialization festivals, between ten to thirty mediums sit in lines of special tents outside of the temple itself, within the temple grounds. They hold brief séances for hundreds of clients who may wait hours for a ten-minute consultation. Although repressed and harassed by state and Shintō authorities for generations, in recent years itako have become a prominent tourist attraction; regional tourist maps even picture a cartoon figure of an elderly kneeling itako in kimono superimposed over an image of Mount Osore. In the early 1990s, the prefectural administration unsuccessfully pressured the *itako-kō* (itako association) to keep at least one itako on permanent duty at Osorezan, in deference to metropolitan tourists who expect to see an authentic shamaness at this sacred site throughout the year.

In contrast, kamisama (神さま) spirit mediums (sometimes derisively termed *gomiso,* mystic healer) are said to be sighted, and they are usually called to sacred service later in life through revelatory visions or profound illness.[10] They may be possessed by ancestral forces or divinities and usually perform healing rites. They are usually affiliated with small, independent Shintō shrines, belong to no overarching association, never gather collectively, and do not have the relatively high public profile of itako. They are usually prone to idiosyncratic prophetic revelations, and their followers may often divide or schism. Many kamisama found their own shrines and maintain only tenuous links to more mainstream Shintō establishments. Most kamisama I worked with voiced great distrust of itako and the Inari deity that they associate with itako practice.[11] As many kamisama mediums told me, Inari's foxlike familiars are seductive tricksters that falsely promise enormous wealth and worldly success.

For all this rhetorical insistence on the absolute distinctiveness of these two traditions, my research suggests rather fluid boundaries between kamisama and itako affiliation. Not all itako are blind, and in some cases kamisama may temporarily or permanently reclassify themselves as itako. Many kamisama possess oshirasama ritual figurines, which they deploy therapeutically. In my experience, some itako are possessed by kami (gods) as well as ancestral beings. Both itako and kamisama often regard the fierce divinity Fudō Myōō as their tutelary deity with whom they have been joined in a spiritual marriage. Although they are ostensibly "Shintō," some kamisama have intimate ties with Buddhist temples.[12]

The Two Sides of the Mountain: Iwaki and Akakura

It would be difficult to overstate the significance in Tsugaru's social and cultural history of Mount Iwaki (岩木山 lit., Mountain of Stones and Trees), the great three-peaked dormant volcanic cone (1625 meters) that towers over the Tsugaru plain. Source of the rich volcanic soils of the southern Tsugaru plain, the mountain shelters Hirosaki and its environs from the heavy snows and winds of the northern plain. For many centuries, the mountain has been celebrated in Tsugaru myth, poetry, visual arts, and ritual performance. To this day, simply seeing the mountain is said by many to bring blessings of health and serenity. Many patients in Hirosaki University Hospital would endure considerable discomfort to catch a glimpse of the mountain each morning; many returning labor migrants told that the first thing they did on coming home was "look at the mountain," or climb to its summit.

As noted above, the mountain for centuries has been divided in popular imagination into two halves, the omote (front or public) southern face associated with establishment political and ritual authority, and the ura (rear or hidden) northeastern face associated with the mysterious local onigami (demon gods) and indigenous powers. This inauspicious northeastern quadrant of the mountain is known as Akakura-zawa (lit., Gorge of the Red Storehouse). To this day, the volcanic landscape of Akakura, under Iwaki's northeast peak of Ganki (巌鬼山 lit., Rock Demon Mountain), is marked by "demonic" sites, including Oni no Miharashidai (鬼の見晴らし台 Demons' Lookout), Oni no Niwa (鬼の庭 Demons' Garden), and Oni no Dohyō (鬼の土俵 Demons' Sumō Ring). The Ganki peak, which continued to smoke until the mid-nineteenth century, towers over the Akakura gorge, the most pronounced volcanic formation on the whole of Mount Iwaki.

Various cults and religious movements have been oriented toward the desolate Akakura slope at least since the medieval period, many of them emphasizing an ancient marriage between a foreign male conqueror and an indigenous female divinity on the northern mountain. According to an Edo-era text, the *Iwaki-san Engi*, Iwaki and Tsugaru were presided over by the Dragon Princess, Tatsubihime no Mikoto. A male figure, Utsushikunitama no Mikoto, then arrived and seduced her. As a sign of her subordination to the male divinity, the Dragon Princess emerged from a pool and presented him with a *tama* (a jewel). The same text links this mythic sequence to the region's conquest by the Yamato official Sakanoue Tamuramaro who allegedly mated with the Dragon Princess and secured from her the ritual objects that allowed him to conquer the indigenous Ainu and Ezo. In some versions, the goddess is identified as Onigamisama (鬼神様 Demon Goddess) or Akakurasama (赤倉様) and is said to have told her seducer Sakanoue to use a special staff and place a fylfot (a Buddhist swastika) on his flags to defeat the indigenous peoples and their gods. In gratitude for his victory over the barbarians, Sakanoue is said in the *Iwaki-san Engi* to have enshrined the goddess at Orii no Miya Shrine, at the base of Akakura Mountain.

As we shall see in chapter 3, the mythic marriage between these two figures is reenacted at Akakura Mountain Shrine over the course of the annual ritual cycle, which begins with a ceremonial filling of the Dragon Princess's pool. Sakanoue Tamuramaro is represented by a statue in the shrine's precincts, immediately next to images of Kannon and Kōbō Daishi, the founder of esoteric Japanese Buddhism. Votive paintings at the shrine depict Akakura Daigongen, the great divinity of the mountain, bearing the staff and fylfot given by the Dragon Princess to Sakanoue.

Throughout the region the figure of Sakanoue Tamuramaro — conqueror of the north, subduer of demons, and "founder of Nebuta" — has long been assimilated to the Buddhist deity Bishamon (Sanskrit: Vaisravana, also known in Japan as Tamonten or Bishamonten), one of the four heavenly kings (Shi-Tennō) of the fourth level of Mount Sumeru, the world mountain. Bishamon, the guardian of the northern quarter of the universe, is typically represented as a fierce warrior in full armor, holding a spear in his right hand and a treasure tower, pagoda, or stupa in his left (Inagaki 1988, 13; Bocking 1997, 10). At times revered as the god of war, in Japan he is also renowned as one of the seven gods of good fortune (Reader and Tanabe 1998, 158–59). Since north represented an unlucky, demon-haunted quarter in classical Chinese geomancy, this guardian of the north was widely celebrated as a crusher of demons, and many temples in Japan's "northeast" region (東北 Tōhoku) are dedicated to him. Within Aomori prefecture itself, thirteen or so shrines are dedicated to Sakanoue Tamuramaro as an avatar of Bishamon.

Another Edo-period text, the *Tsugaru ittoshi*, reiterates the mythic pattern of alliance between foreign conqueror and mountain demoness to account for the defeat of the Nanbu house at the hands of Tamenobu, the founder of the Tsugaru dynastic line, in the late sixteenth century. The demon gods of Akakura are said to have granted Tamenobu a dream vision, assuring him victory.[13] In turn, the birth of the fourth Tsugaru daimyō, Nobumasa, is said to have been heralded by a miraculous light emanating from Akakura's sacred slopes.

Religious historian Ikegami Yoshimasa (1984, 1987, 1992, 1999) argues that over the course of centuries, regional and state political elites have gradually sought to appropriate and relocate ritual powers associated with the mountain's disturbing northeastern side — oriented toward the alien, "demon-haunted" quarter — to the mountain's southern slopes, facing the traditional Japanese heartland.[14] Initially, the resident goddess appears to have been enshrined as the Buddhist Bodhisattva Juichimen Kannon Bosatsu (Eleven-headed Kannon) high on the mountain's northern side, but was eventually replaced with an image of Shōkannon. Eventually, this image was transferred to Iwaki-san Jinja, in the village of Hyaku-zawa (百沢 One Hundred Gorges) at the southwestern base of Mount Iwaki.[15] During the Tokugawa era, this village housed a unified Shintō and Buddhist complex, Hyakuta-kuji, in which were enshrined the various male and female divinities of Iwaki, presented as intimate kin of the Tsugaru dynastic house. The mythical figure of Anjuhime, a manifestation of the Dragon Goddess, was included among the five hundred *rakan* (Buddhist guardians) in the Iwakisan Jinja gate. Following the Meiji Restoration and the formal establishment of state Shintō, most of the Buddhist images at Hyaku-zawa were removed to Buddhist temples in Hirosaki. However, the an-cient image of Kannonsama, long linked to the ancient Dragon Prin-cess, was lost during this period.

Although the mountain's female divinity's official Shintō designa-tion is *Iwaki-sama,* or *Tatsubihime no kami,* she is still referred to as *Onigamisama* in local rural communities. Recalling the mythic liai-son between the local demoness and the foreign conqueror, the female deity remains the object of ritualized sexual attraction by the male worshipers who have followed in Sakanoue Tamuramaro's footsteps.[16] Each September, local men climb the mountain at midnight in the *Ōyamasankei* (great mountain ritual) from Iwaki-san Jinja at the base, bearing enormous phallic poles. Until the 1930s, climbing the moun-tain in this (male-only) rite for three consecutive years constituted ini-tiation into male adulthood (Ikegami 1987).[17]

Although the officially sanctioned shrine to the Dragon Princess was formally transferred to the southern side of Iwaki in the eleventh century and assimilated into the establishment Shintō Iwakisan Jinja (Liscutin 2000, 193), many local informants insist that the venera-tion of Akakurasama is most properly associated with shrines that still remain on the northern side of the mountain. These include Ōishi (大石 Great Stone) Shrine at Akakura Mountain's base, dedicated to Batō (Horse Crowned) Kannon, long visited by local women seeking aid in conception and childbirth. Ōishi Shrine has ritual links to the Ubaishi (乳母石 Wet Nurse Rock) Boulder located high on Akakura's "left" ridge, an important site (as we shall see in chapter 5) for Aka-kura Mountain Shrine ascetics. Akakura has also long been venerated at nearby Oni Jinja (鬼神社 Demon Shrine), which both honors the mountain's resident demons and protects nearby villages from their wrath.

For centuries, Akakura has remained the region's favored locale for ascetic discipline among diverse groups and for initiation into varied forms of spirit mediumship and charismatic healing. Growing up near the mountain's base in the late nineteenth century, Kawai Mariko often heard stories of Shugendō and Yamabushi specialists practicing austerities on its treacherous slopes. But she seems to have had no intention of following in their footsteps until a pivotal series of events in the 1910s, to which I now turn.

The History of Akakura Mountain Shrine

Like many important kamisama mediums, Kawai Mariko grew up in an extremely poor rural family.[18] Born into the Kawai family in 1888 (Meiji 20) in a southern Tsugaru village, she was sent out to work as a *komori* (nurse-maid) when she was nine by her impoverished parents. She never attended school and never learned to read or write. She married into a nearby village, but after ten childless years of marriage, her husband divorced her. Ordinarily, a "barren" divorced woman was consigned to the status of a widow, but Mariko soon married the widower Takeda Seiji of the village Hanawa (the present Iwaki-chō, in the eastern foothills of Mount Iwaki). Mariko brought up Takeda Seiji's two children by his first, deceased wife. Years later, Mariko and these two children had a falling out over inheritance issues; Mariko thus elected to retain her natal family name Kawai. It is by this name that her followers still remember her.

In 1915 (Taishō 3) when she was twenty-seven (or twenty-eight by traditional Japanese reckoning), Mariko gave birth to her first child, her daughter Kimiko, who would later succeed her mother as a spirit medium. Kimiko had a sickly childhood; she suffered of dermatitis at the age of two and lost all her hair. Filled with worry, Mariko swore to pay daily visits to the God of March of the Third Year, enshrined in a nearby village. For three years, she visited the shrine every day, praying for her daughter's complete recovery. Many of my informants stressed that Mariko braved rain, cold, and snow to pray in the freezing, dark sanctuary of the shrine until her prayers were answered in 1920, when Kimiko's skin condition and hair loss were cured.

During this period of intense prayer, Mariko underwent a gradual transformation, as people's fates came to be "told to her heart." As Mariko's gifts became known, the women of the village started to visit her for advice. She began to experience a recurrent dream of the three-peaked Mount Iwaki, the mountain she saw every day as she labored in the family fields. A dragon arose from the left-hand peak and flew through the sky to her house. A great hole opened on the roof, through which the dragon descended. Standing beside her pillow, the dragon transformed itself into the shape of a woman who told her, "Although I appear as a human being, I am Akakura Daigongen[19] [赤倉大権現]. You shall listen to me and climb to the peak of Akakura."

Up until the dream, Mariko apparently had only vague familiarity with Akakura as a place where people undertook ascetic practices. After the dream repeated itself each night for seven nights, Mariko finally told the deity that "I cannot go out to the mountains leaving my children behind. I will pray to you here, in the village, however hard it may be." Akakura Daigongen disappeared without a reply.

With the coming of the spring thaw, Mariko became anxious once more about the dream. She consulted a male ascetic who had climbed Akakura Mountain to practice shugyō. The ascetic was moved by Mariko's eagerness and agreed to lead her twice up Akakura. The second time Mariko climbed Akakura, she cut her black hair at the holy ground called Eighty-Eight Places, just below the summit of the mountain. After this, the words of the deity started to "echo in her heart." The god told her, "Even if one is good, not all wishes come true. Instead, I shall protect you and your daughter's generation for life." Mariko was pregnant during these initial stints of shugyō, and later that same year she gave birth to a second child, a son.

The following year, in 1922 (Taishō 10), Mariko went to Akakura three times each month, from March through October, sleeping each night at Ōishi Shrine near the mountain base and climbing the mountain during the day. In December, she received a divine revelation from Akakura Daigongen: "Be confined in the mountain of Akakura and practice a week of silent austerities." The second day of January of the lunar calendar, Mariko accepted her dream's oracle "without hesitation" and left her house taking only meager supplies and a blanket. She borrowed five yen from her husband's mother ("the grandmother of the house"), telling her, "In case I happen to die in the mountain, please imagine you have simply given this money to a Buddhist altar. If I return home alive, I will surely return it to you." Staying at the uninhabited shrine of Ōishi, Mariko endured a three-day raging snowstorm without sleeping or speaking. When the storm subsided on the fourth day, she spread out her red blanket, collected branches of the evergreen cryptomeria tree, and made a fire. Once her body warmed up, she started to feel tired from her sleepless three days and nights, and involuntarily took a nap. When she woke up with the voices of people, three male hunters were looking down on Mariko with guns in their hands. In a panic, Mariko opened her mouth to explain who she was. In so doing, she broke her "silent austerities." Mariko apologized deeply to Akakura Daigongen and fell asleep again. The deity then appeared in her dream in the form of a white-haired elderly man and talked to her gently: "Raise your head. I shall give this to you. Follow the kami's heart. For three years, you should not show or talk about this to anyone, otherwise your life will be endangered." The god then presented her with three scrolls, inscribed with mysterious writing. To her great surprise, she awoke to find three actual scrolls on her red blanket. The moment she saw the scrolls, a violent chill ran through her body. She returned home but within a few weeks came back to the mountain to undertake a successful week of silent shugyō.

In the subsequent months, as her fame spread across the region, Mariko took her growing circle of worshipers on ascetic climbs of Akakura. Among these early disciples was Mrs. Narita, who later became an important kamisama and the official "voice" of Kawai Mariko after her death.

In 1923 (Taishō 11), Akakura Daigongen once again appeared in Mariko's dream and announced, "I will present you with this land." Since one of her followers was employed in the Forestry Office, she was able to obtain permission to build a small shrine about a mile uphill from Ōishi Shrine. Kawai Mariko or one of her disciple's revelatory visions had determined the precise site of this shrine, named Hanawa for Kawai Mariko's second husband's hamlet. Mrs. Narita claimed that she herself also experienced the founding vision as she was undertaking shugyō while based at Ōishi Shrine. Narita said she beheld a vision of a "streak of gold across the deep blue sky." Taking the light to be the sun goddess Amaterasu, the women planned a shrine where the light fell to earth.

Akakura Mountain Shrine was constructed on the site of the old Hanawa Shrine soon after the Asia-Pacific War (World War II), when the MacArthur Constitution legally guaranteed freedom of religious expression. The family and followers of Kawai Mariko's most important disciple, Sugiyama Junko, began construction on a subsidiary (bunke) shrine soon afterward, located about thirty meters downhill of the main (honke) shrine buildings.

Soon after the war, Kawai Mariko began to take an annual pilgrimage to Mount Taihei in Akita prefecture, about 150 miles south of Akakura. During one of these pilgrimages, her disciple Narita Emiko heard a mysterious voice, which addressed her as "the beautiful voice of Tsugaru."

When Kawai Mariko's first-born daughter, Takeda Kimiko, reached adulthood, she, too, received a vision from the kami Akakura Daigongen—in the likeness of a tall man with long black hair. He instructed her to undertake three weeks of shugyō: one week of fasting, one week of sleeping exposed on the mountain, one week of silence. Kimiko went on to become a prominent kamisama medium herself. She married an "adopted husband" (mukoyōshi) who entered into her parents' house and took on the Takeda family name.

The Akakura Mountain Shrine Congregation in the 1990s

In the early 1990s, the Akakura Mountain Shrine association was held together by a core group of about ten people, nearly all of whom had performed shugyō. The priest Mr. Takeda Seiji, the adopted husband of Mrs. Takeda Yuko, Takeda Kimiko's daughter, officially led the shrine. Many years ago, following the death of her older brother in his twenties, Takeda Yuko (b. 1945) decided to assume the family butsudan and to adopt a husband into her family line (just as her own mother had adopted a husband) from a local fishing family.[20] Seiji (b. 1946) spent most of his time in residence at the shrine; he also had affiliate priestly responsibilities at Tsugaru Akakura Shrine in the middle Tsugaru peninsula and at Miyoshi Shrine in Akita City.

Takeda Yuko's own relationship with Akakura Mountain Shrine was ambiguous. A trained nurse, she taught health in a local middle school. Along with the kamisama medium Mrs. Okuda, she was an active Amway distributor. In contrast to most members of the congregation, her presentation of self was distinctly middle-class: she usually wore

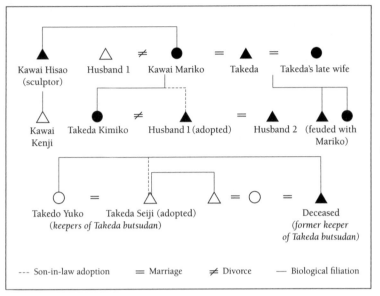

1. The family of Kawai Mariko

stylish clothes, spoke metropolitan Japanese, as opposed to Tsugaru-ben dialect, and studied the tea ceremony, French cooking, and English. She often traveled to visit her only son who studied in Tokyo.

Takeda Yuko often participates in collective ceremonies at the shrine, and helps officiate at important Cooking Pot Ceremonies. However, she has not, as of this writing, undertaken shugyō, and other congregation members do not yet consider her "called to the service of the kami." To my knowledge, she never actually sleeps at the shrine. Even during major ceremonies, she drives home to Hirosaki each night and returns to the shrine early each morning. Although she is usually treated with outward respect, and referred to as "the mother" in shrine conversations, she has a tense relationship with some leading members of the shrine community. Older lay members often noted that Yuko had not performed shugyō and did not understand the true mysteries of the mountain. Nonetheless Takeda Yuko remains a strong candidate to succeed her mother and grandmother as leading kamisama of the shrine.

Mrs. Takeda's closest friend in the Akakura Shrine community is Mrs. Okuda Setsuko, a kamisama of extraordinary vitality and charisma. Okuda, who lives in Akita prefecture, was diagnosed with a serious heart condition in the 1970s and told by doctors that she had only a few more months to live. In great physical pain and faced by crushing financial debts, she had lost hope. But, like Kawai Mariko, she was granted extraordinary visions by Akakura Daigongen and Fudō Myōō. As a kamisama spirit medium at Akakura, Okuda specializes in an athletic form of healing and has become especially oriented toward the divinities Ryūjinsama (竜神様 Dragon deity) and Fudō Myōō. She has a substantial following of her own, and has brought many new worshipers into Akakura Shrine communities. By the early 1990s, Okuda had emerged as the most vigorous and popular kamisama affiliated with the senior branch of Akakura. Nonetheless, she was usually mindful of the prerogatives of the shrine's senior kamisama, Narita Emiko, the official "voice" of the late Kawai Mariko. Although Narita does not have a healing practice (a ritual condition of her position vis-à-vis the founder), she has a loyal following of women from coastal western Tsugaru communities.

In the early 1990s, four other kamisama mediums maintained formal affiliations with the shrine and would from time to time assist in major rites, including the Great Summer Festival in July and the Ancestral Memorialization Ceremony in October. Each of these had their own following of patients and worshipers who would at times participate in collective or healing rites or join in the summer pilgrimages.

As in most Japanese shrines, the entire board of the Akakura Yama Jinja-kō (赤倉神社講 Akakura Mountain Shrine Association) is composed of men. Kawai Kenji (b. 1928), the son of Kawai Mariko's brother, stands as one of the congregation's most active members. He has undertaken extensive ascetic discipline on the mountain and has had a number of important revelatory visions. He helps officiate at major ceremonies and serves as the shrine association's secretary, keeping careful track of donations and financial matters. As we shall see, his relations with Mrs. Takeda are often prickly.

Mr. Kawai is often assisted by Mr. Kinoshita (b. 1938), who also comes from a local apple-growing family. His mother had been one of Kawai Mariko's early clients, and he continues to feel great loyalty to her memory and to the shrine. He had performed stints of shugyō in the 1960s and spent most of his free time living at the shrine, taking primary responsibility for odd jobs and minor ritual activities.

During the time of my fieldwork, the most widely beloved member of the congregation was Mrs. Koike, a woman in her mid-eighties from a local farming family. She was an early disciple of Kawai Mariko and undertook shugyō for many years in the early postwar period. Charismatic and energetic, she often took primary responsibility for the shrine kitchen and related chores. She routinely stood at the kitchen's *genkan* (entranceway), cheerfully welcoming back ascetics when they returned from long mountain climbs.

LAY MEMBERS

In the early 1990s, approximately 1,500 persons were listed in Akakura Mountain Shrine's official records as occasional or regular financial donors. Of these, around 400 attended at least one major shrine function and gave at least one financial donation per year. For the purposes of the discussion that follows, I classify these persons as comprising the Akakura Mountain Shrine congregation. Of the active members, about 320 persons (80 percent) were women. Ten percent were under the age of thirty-five; 30 percent were between the ages of thirty-five and fifty-five. Sixty percent were older than fifty-five. About thirty-five persons had performed stints of shugyō in residence at Akakura. Around fifty occasionally attended kamisama healing ceremonies at the shrine, such as the Sword of Fudō (Fudō-ken). The year's nine collective ceremonies constitute the principal forums in which most worshipers encounter one another. During my fieldwork, the most broadly attended collective rite was the Great Summer Festival, which averaged around 350 participants. The smallest rite was the February Dragon Princess Rite, which only about fifteen worshipers attended, nearly all of them having undertaken extensive austerities on the mountain.

The congregation divided into two basic groups. Kawai Mariko had founded the larger honke or senior branch, and it occupied the major cluster of shrines and residential buildings usually referred to as Akakura Yama Jinja per se. The smaller, bunke or junior branch had been founded by Sugiyama Junko in the late 1940s, and it numbered around 150 worshipers by the early 1990s. As I will discuss in chapter 6, the death of Sugiyama Junko in July 1991 brought into greater evidence long-simmering tensions between the honke and bunke branches. Leadership of the bunke branch passed to Sugiyama Junko's daughter, Yukiko, and adopted son-in-law, Hideo, who began to perform independent ceremonies at their subshrine and in their village home.

Nonetheless, in the early and mid-1990s some of the bunke members continued to attend collective rites held by the main shrine, especially the summer festival and the annual pilgrimage to Mount Hakkōda.

Like Mr. Kinoshita, some worshipers had in effect "inherited" membership in the shrine congregation from their parents, and they continued to attend shrine events partly out of a sense of filial piety. Not all worshipers could easily articulate what drew them to the shrine. Mrs. Sato, a psychiatrist in her thirties from Hokkaido, began to visit the shrine out of "curiosity," hoping that she might learn techniques to aid her patients. She began to practice shugyō on the mountain in 1991 and continued for several years, on and off. Mr. Yamamoto, a young man in his early twenties, was born into a local agrarian household and from time to time worked in an automobile factory in the Tokyo metropolitan area. When he began shugyō in early 1992, he simply remarked that he felt it was the "right" thing to do. At times, he speculated that shugyō would make him "stronger" and increase his endurance working at a car manufacturing plant. My sense is that for Sato and Yamamoto, as for many ascetics, shugyō in time became its own reward.

At the other end of the spectrum, some participants in collective rituals only found their way up to Akakura for specific, time-limited reasons. For example, in May 1991 I talked to a young sailor who had climbed with the congregation to the Fudō Waterfall during the Mountain Opening Ceremony. He expressed skepticism in the whole enterprise. Why, then, I asked, had he participated? He explained that he was first mate on a fishing boat that had been caught in a terrible storm in the nearby Sea of Japan that winter. Just as the boat was about to capsize, the crew had prayed in desperation to the divinity of Akakura. The winds and swells had immediately abated, and the crew and ship were saved. Thus, the man explained, he felt obligated to participate in this year's Mountain Opening to thank Akakura Daigongen, but he had no expectation of returning to the shrine.

Many lay congregants, brought into the shrine community through long-term emotional difficulties, found deep resonance in the Akakura Prayer's eighth line, "There are times when the heart becomes wretched." Like Fukuda Chie and Sakurai Fumiko, many women cited difficult marital obligations as their initial reason for coming to the mountain. Marriage difficulties also brought some men into the shrine.

Consider, for example, the *chōnan* (first son) of Kobayashi Tomiko. Mr. Kobayashi (b.1952), a local apple farmer, was still unmarried at age forty. Worries over his aged, ailing parents, with whom he still lived, consumed him. In late 1991, half a year after the death of the great kamisama Sugiyama Junko, he had a minor traffic accident in front of the Sugiyamas' house. Entering the house to use the telephone, he was amazed by the household's great *saidan* (altar) and entered into conversation with Junko's daughter, Yukiko, and (adopted) son-in-law, Hideo, who prayed for him and his parents. Over the course of 1992, Yukiko and Hideo gradually adopted Mr. Kobayashi as a client, and he began to attend major rites in the Sugiyama house and at Akakura.

Nearly all members of Akakura Mountain Shrine's congregation considered themselves natives of southern Tsugaru peninsula or northern Akita prefecture. A few had married into Tsugaru families from the Shimokita peninsula or southern Hokkaido. Four-fifths of the members identified themselves as coming from "farming families," although many had not farmed for decades. Fifty per cent stated that they had worked in apple orchards at some time in their lives. Many older women were severely stooped from a lifetime of work in rice fields; many of these explained that they had done extensive piecework and did not own family plots. About 10 percent stated that they came from "fishing families," especially from Ajigasawa on the Sea of Japan coast. Around 60 percent had experience working outside of Aomori prefecture, in factories, canneries, or in hotel service jobs. Only 25 percent had education beyond secondary school. There were a number of artisans, construction workers, and mechanics, but only a few "professionals" who worked as schoolteachers, bank clerks, nurses, or engineers. A half-dozen owned or managed *kissaten* (small cafés).

Nearly all congregation members were of modest means. For example, only about twenty members of the congregation had regular access to an automobile; most had to take taxis, hire small busses, or impose on friends or relatives in order to reach the shrine. Few could afford to send their children or grandchildren to *juku* (cram schools), one of the key signs of secure "middle-class" status in Japan. None to my knowledge were homeless or malnourished, but most worshipers acknowledged that they occupied the lower rungs of the Japanese economy.

It is impossible to understand ritual life at Akakura without taking into account these pervasive economic predicaments, especially as experienced by women on the quasi-agrarian periphery of postwar Japan. The ritual practices and discourses of the shrine's leaders are deeply appealing to women oriented toward dense and intricate kinship and community networks that are organized around the exchange of the products of one's own labor. Although these women do not overtly resist or protest dominant social and economic institutions, they do maintain a somewhat skeptical stance toward the highly commodified and abstracted forms of social relations that they associate with mainstream Japanese society.

The lives of the leading women of Akakura exemplify the long-term predicaments of female labor in the Tsugaru region, as well as the promise of spiritual transcendence embedded in these labor processes. For their followers, each woman dramatizes and makes accessible the positive "immortal wishes" manifestly associated with Akakura Mountain and its resident divinities. At the same time, each woman's story hints at the troubled counterpoint of these spiritual quests, evoking the unresolved traumas, tragedies, and crises lodged in Tsugaru's beautiful and poignant landscapes.

Chapter 2 explores how these multiple layers of remembered economic and cultural history have been embedded in the physical architecture of Akakura Shrine and the symbolic topography of the mountainscape, thought by worshipers to bridge the visible and invisible worlds. The ritual process of collective healing at Akakura revolves around the incorporation of diverse worshipers into a united "family" within which mortals, ancestors, and divinities are miraculously conjoined. This cosmological family reproduces itself through the union of opposites, productively joining foreign conquerors with conquered indigenes, male with female, right with left. In the face of systemic historical crises in agrarian households, the shrine itself is structured as an idealized rural farmhouse in which residence, work, and worship proceed in balanced coordination with one another. Performing service (*otsutome*) in these sacred spaces, worshipers repeatedly encounter personages from the community's mythic past and gradually develop lasting relations of spiritual kinship with them and the extended cosmological family of Akakura.

2

b e t w e e n   w o r l d s

Akakura's Architecture of Potential Transformation

Virtually all features of the Akakura mountainscape and the human-made structures on it potentially open the worshiper to transformative encounters with the divinities and ancestors. This transformative potential is, in many respects, a function of Akakura's ambiguous status as a dynamic frontier between "this world," the world of mortals, and "the other world," the world of the kami and of the dead. For the faithful who traverse it, the mountain is in a continuous state of flux, at times offering a relatively familiar face, at other times affording glimpses of the gods' miraculous capacities. As Fumiko told me, "The mountain is not like any other place. Each time you climb, it can be different." Like other pilgrims, she often reported being blessed by transient visions. The clearing beneath the Fudō Waterfall might turn into a great green, coiled dragon. Between rocky crags, one might glimpse the beautiful, mythic garden believed to lie at the heart of the mountain.

Each such encounter may move the devotee into a purer and more transcendent state, closer to the divinities, but each step on the mountain also poses the potential for failure and the diminution of self. Demons may distract or posses the worshiper, reducing her to an infantile state. Incorrect teachings or practices may "confuse" the novice and undercut her emerging intimate relations with the kami, weighing her down with bonds to conventional earthly desire. To be on the mountain is thus to be between worlds, perpetually suspended between the glorious possibilities of transcendence and ever present temptations of the mundane.

As worshipers often assert, the mountain offers no guarantees. Ultimately, health and blessings are gifts of the divinities, bestowed or withheld at their whim. Yet as she negotiates the ambiguous, intermediate landscape and architecture of Akakura, the dedicated worshiper is believed capable of increasing the likelihood of being "seen" and "called" by the gods. As I was often told, a good worshiper strives to become "like" the kami by imitating them in all ways, in her manner of dress, her diet, her mode of bodily comportment, and her exchange transactions. Successfully navigating between worlds depends on the careful labor of imitation within architectural spaces themselves fashioned to resemble both the invisible precincts of gods and the visible dwellings of mortals. The dedicated labor of shugyō on the mountainscape thus in principle enables each worshiper to bridge two different planes of existence, bringing the divinities' blessings to her own human family and gradually integrating her into the cosmological family of the mountain.

Overview: Shugyō at Akakura Mountain Shrine

Although ascetics often shared their experiences on the mountain with one another, the overall function of shugyō was not, in my experience, subject to extensive discussion or speculation. People often recalled the specific problem that had first motivated them to undertake austerities, such as illness, weighty obligations, or family misfortune. Beyond that, one performed shugyō simply because one was obligated to do so—by one's teachers, the ancestors, and the kami.[1] A few mediums occasionally explained, making reference to the shrine song, "Saigi, Saigi," that shugyō cleansed the worshipers of sins (*zaishō*), which they left behind in the high, pure reaches of the mountain. It is for this reason, in part, that novices were warned not to remove anything from the mountainscape, a mysterious and dangerous place at the best of times. Mrs. Okuda, for example, once remonstrated with the ascetic Mrs. Nakamura, who had contemplated carrying two bamboo stalks from a mountain grove: "The mountain belongs to the divinities, and if you bring anything back, you will carry back your own sins."

Over the course of a year, about forty-five women and men undertake shugyō at Akakura. Most of these only perform a three-day austerity and thus only ascend the main shugyō route, up the stream to the Fudō-taki (Fudō Waterfall). On average, about twenty worshipers during the year stay for seven days or more, and they may alternate their climbs to the waterfall with ascents along the Thirty-Three Kannonsama route to the Ubaishi Boulder. Only a very few, who stay for three weeks or longer, are allowed to ascend the physically and spiritually dangerous upper reaches of the mountain, to the summit and the Shōkannonsama statue.

These shugyō visits are generally spaced out through the summer and fall months when the mountain snow has sufficiently melted to allow access along the paths. During the winter months, when the paths above the shrine are impassable and the mountain is ritually "closed," worshipers perform morning shugyō within the shrine precincts, chanting long prayers, engaging in cold water ablutions, and circumambulating the Thirty-Three Kannon statues. Usually no more than four people undergo shugyō at any given time.

One's teacher strictly regulates the length of each interval of shugyō: a worshiper is usually directed to conduct a period of ascetic discipline for a period of either three days, one week, or three weeks. Occasionally, a worshiper will be told to undergo shugyō for three months, or even longer. As we have seen, Kawai Mariko's daughter and successor, the kamisama Takeda Kimiko, received a vision from the kami Akakura Daigongen instructing her to undertake three weeks of shugyō: one week of fasting, one week of sleeping exposed on the mountain, and one week of silence.

I could not obtain any explanation for the standardized length of these periods beyond the usual, "That is how it is done here." However, we may note that the shrine founder Kawai Mariko performed an initial shugyō for seven days and that she endured a heavy snowstorm for the length of three days in the midst of it, which led to her revelatory vision and the divine gift of the three sacred scrolls. Significantly, these two shorter intervals, three and seven days, are the prime (and hence unique) divisors of twenty-one, the longer interval.

Regardless of its length, each period of shugyō up on the mountain divides into a tripartite rite de passage structure. The worshiper separates herself from ordinary life before entering the liminal phase of shugyō itself. She must therefore arrive the afternoon before and attend evening services. In turn, at the conclusion of shugyō, the worshiper must undergo a reintegration period, staying at the shrine a final night, attending morning services, and (if a woman) performing a final cleaning of the shrine before departing. Hence, a so-called three-day shugyō in actuality lasts for five days, a seven-day one nine days, and so forth.

A Day of Shugyō

The experience of shugyō differs dramatically for male and female worshipers. Although both men and women climb the mountain in the morning and engage in kuyō (ancestral memorialization) in the afternoon, women are also responsible for food preparation, cleaning, and the presentation of food offerings in the various shrines of the complex. Thus, in a strictly physical sense, the occasional man performing shugyō had a much easier time of it than women worshipers. He was only expected to climb the mountain, perform ancestral memorialization, attend the morning and evening prayer services, and occasionally help out with equipment repairs, wood chopping, and building the fire that heats the evening's bath water. The rest of the time, he was free to eat and relax. As we shall see, the moral center of the shrine in many respects lies in the kitchen, nearly always off-limits to men. In this sense, men are denied some of the social and emotional rewards of female shugyō.

Regardless of gender, each day's shugyō has a common pattern for all participants. Each person rises at around 4:00 A.M., dresses, and quickly puts away her or his futon. Immediately afterwards, women worshipers in the shrine kitchen prepare special water and food offerings for the mountain kami and place them in the five shrine structures. Simultaneously, the breakfast table is set and preparations are made for the worshipers' morning meal.

By 6:00 A.M. all worshipers have assembled in the Shinden for morning services. Like the preparation and presentation of the offering trays, the sequence of movement during the morning and evening prayer services (from the front Shinden and Reidō shrines to the rear Ryūjinsama, Godaimyōō, and Kawai Mariko subshrines) proceeds from left to right, from inside to outside, and from front to back. It also anticipates the larger movements of the mountain circuits, during which worshipers move from inside to outside, and from the "front" to the "back" of the mountain.

The specific Akakura Shrine prayers (revealed to the founder Kawai Mariko by the kami) are only recited at services in the Shinden, the principal shrine room, where the Buddhist Heart Sutra is also performed. The Heart Sutra is again performed moments later in the smaller Reidō Shrine room, immediately to the right of the Shinden sanctuary. In the Godaimyōō Shrine (Five Lords Shrine), the worshipers recite the *Fudō-son-ken-Kudōku-no-mon*, the special prayers for Fudōsama (which are also recited at Fudō Waterfall). At the small Ryūjinsama and Kawai Mariko Shrines in the back, the worshipers simply bow and clap to greet the kami.

After quickly eating and cleaning up breakfast (usually miso soup, rice, raw squid, spinach, and herbal tea) the worshipers hurriedly dress in white clothes to prepare for the most demanding event of the day, the morning climb up the mountain.

These climbs, which generally take between four and nine hours round trip, proceed along three long-established routes, known to have been followed by the founder Kawai Mariko and the other great kamisama spirit mediums associated with the shrine. The three routes are ranked according to difficulty. Most frequently, ascetics proceed up along the banks of the Akakura gorge stream to the sacred Fudō-taki, about one third up the mountain (approximately two hours one way). Somewhat less frequently, and only during longer periods of shugyō, they may climb up along a high ridge overlooking the Akakura stream following the line of Thirty-Three Kannonsama statues to the sacral boulder of Ubaishi, about halfway up the mountain (five or six hours). Much less frequently, an experienced ascetic may continue along the entire Thirty-Three Kannonsama path to the mountain summit, where there stands a special statue, Shōkannonsama, sculpted by the brother of the shrine's founder. In rare cases, a veteran ascetic may climb up through the mountain's central gorge above the Fudō Waterfall in a winding path to the summit, but this route is considered very dangerous physically and spiritually.

The middle section of the Akakura Prayer, repeated twice each day and evoking upward movement toward transformative sites given by the compassionate mountain, anticipates the process of actual ascent:

The great kami, the local great kami,
The Dragon Princess . . . we respectfully pray and offer [to you]
    above all.
Also, the honorable mountain of Akakura, the deep rock wall
    door, the place where water comes out, [you] have given us,
The first rock passage,
We climb and pray at the second rock passage,
And at the third divine storage place we bow down and make
    offerings.
(lines 25–31)

After descending the mountain, the worshipers (who have usually climbed alone) gather together for lunch. After a brief nap, each worshiper spends about an hour in the two principal shrine rooms, performing ancestral memorialization for several specified deceased relatives. During the rest of the afternoon, women worshipers clean the shrine buildings and prepare dinner. There is usually a pleasant late afternoon break for tea around the wood-burning stove, as worshipers share stories of their adventures on the mountain.

Following dinner, evening services (6:00–7:00 P.M.) repeat the sequence of the morning prayer services, with only two exceptions. The kami receive only hot green tea instead of meals, and the worshipers perform the important chant "Saigi, Saigi." In singing this beloved song at evening services and during pilgrimages, worshipers collectively anticipate and recapitulate the basic process of shugyō, ascending the mountain to a state of progressive purity, cleanliness, and openness. The song's performance thus encapsulates and frames each twenty-four-hour cycle of shugyō, consolidating the just completed day's efforts and anticipating the worshipers' coming efforts the next morning.

After evening services, all worshipers retire to the living room. During my stints of shugyō, I always found this evening period of collec-

ation and relaxation the most enjoyable time of day. All
the shrine gathered around the wood-burning stove to
nt coffee, munch on fruit, and (perhaps most impor-
d listen to stories of the mountain. Exhausted wor-
unted up the remaining days until their shugyō was
, and they talked longingly of all they would do once they
had returned to their families and to normal life. The television was
usually turned on at some point; low-budget samurai dramas were the
general favorite. Worshipers gave each other foot and back massages,
darned socks, mended clothes, and occasionally napped by the warm
wood-burning stove. This was also the time when the priest Mr. Takeda
would address piles of postcards to the congregation, announcing upcoming ceremonies and shrine events. From time to time, he would
use one of the woodstove's pokers to catch one of the stink bugs that
proliferated through summer and late fall and, to general amusement,
would drop it in the stove. In contrast to the intense and quiet direct-
ness of the morning, there was always a good deal of joking around,
with plenty of good-natured, ribald teasing back and forth between
men and women.

By 8:30 P.M., quiet usually fell over the room. One by one, each person would wish the others good night and retrieve a futon from the
wall closets in the main room or in the various sleeping rooms scattered throughout the shrine.

The Power of Sleep and Dreams

The period of sleep, generally between 9:00 P.M. and 4:00 A.M., continues quietly to forge social and spiritual bonds among and between
worshipers and the kami. Sleep appears to function both as a frame
and as a connecting thread. As noted above, the worshiper must sleep
at the shrine the night before her shugyō starts, every night of shugyō,
and during the night after her final day of shugyō.[2]

As I was to learn forcefully from the spirit medium Mrs. Okuda during the 1992 summer festival, it is wrong for one who has undergone
shugyō at the main shrine to sleep anywhere else on the mountain
(for example, at the Sugiyamas' "subordinate" shrine, as I had done).
Such an act is said to "confuse" the kami and could lead to serious
illness for the worshiper or members of her family. In my case, said

Mrs. Okuda, my decision to sleep in the wrong shrine was making my husband Mark ill with a temporary inner-ear infection.

Evidently, sleep realizes or solidifies the worshiper's emerging relationship with the gods. Through sleep may come the vitally important revelatory dreams that command one to go to a certain place on the mountain, or that warn one of lurking demons lying in wait, or that alert one to a coming miracle by the kami. Mr. Kawai, for example, dreamed one night in the shrine of large hands in the Shinden water jug. This dream, he later explained, presaged his important vision three days later of forty-one pieces of *mannengusa* (thousand-year) plant in the jug.

In this regard, it is interesting that Takeda Yuko, who often expressed intense ambivalence over her relations to the Akakura Mountain kami and to the shrine founded by her maternal grandmother, resolutely refused to sleep in the shrine. Even during the annual Great Summer Festival, she would leave the ceremony late at night, drive down to sleep at her house in Hirosaki City, and drive back to the shrine around dawn. Mrs. Takeda was in fact often referred to with the rather dismissive phrase, "She doesn't sleep here." Significantly, this observation was always joined with the observation that she had never undergone shugyō.

The Work of Resemblance

As even this cursory overview of shugyō suggests, those who live and worship at Akakura become increasingly socialized into a world of intense resemblances. From the moment an ascetic awakes in the morning, she must be highly attentive to the nature of likenesses all around her. She must assemble and present offerings that resemble the mysterious configuration and perfect beauty of the divinities. She must comport her own body in a manner that recalls the flowing movement of the kami. She must care for and venerate statues, paintings, and other votive images that are manifestly patterned on other images, elsewhere. Climbing the mountain paths, she must carefully observe a vast range of landscape features that are said to be "like" specified beings or entities. Two intertwined pine trees are "like" the male and female instantiations of Akakura Daigongen. Certain snowmelt patterns are "like" a dragon, hare, or crane. A great stone is "like" a fertile woman, and the vast gorge beside it is "like" a woman's vagina. In the presence of these sites of resemblance, she must perform activities that are "like" other kinds of practices: through her own bodily actions, she must mime the process of birth, tangibly represent childhood encounters with her mother's body, retrace the mythic journey and life course of the shrine's founding mother, and tangibly reenact cosmological cycles of death and regeneration. Dreams encountered during sleep each night must be carefully pondered for hints explicating this ever deepening web of resemblances.

Through dedicated acts of producing, apprehending, and reflecting on these likenesses, the successful worshiper gradually becomes bound to the greatest similarity of all: she comes to perceive herself as intimate kin to the divinities, as being more and more "like" the kami whom she serves. Like other mimetic relations at Akakura, these apprehended resemblances are ultimately perceived as fundamentally "true things." Over time, the worshiper comes to speak of the shrine association both as being "like" a family and as being her "real family." In the process, worshipers insist, the health and well-being of their conventional human families "at home" enhance dramatically.

Akakura worshipers recognize two kinds of resemblances. Many human practices are overtly marked as being imitative, patterned after forms and things created by the kami. As we shall see in the next chapter, the ritual cooking pot, heated by worshipers three times each year, manifestly models the sacred volcano. The mirror in the shrine is a tangible model of the mythic mirror through which Amaterasu was drawn out of her cave to restore light and life in the universe. The great rice straw rope hung each year across the gorge serves as a tangible representation of the mythic rope that prevented Amaterasu from returning into her cave. By carefully creating these imitative forms, worshipers labor to open and expand productive conduits between themselves and the other world.

In turn, the mountain landscape, the most important venue through which that other world may be encountered, is the domain of mysterious resemblances markedly not created by humans. The divinities leave opaque traces of themselves and their capacities, which human worshipers try to interpret and comprehend through ascetic discipline, prayer, sacred visions, and conversation. Morning climbs in the upper reaches of the mountain thus often become journeys of discovery, through which each worshiper may become aware of new signs and correspondences that had eluded her peers and predecessors.

Broadly speaking, human-made resemblances and imitative practices characterize the shrine precincts, while the upper reaches of the mountain, across the bridge that ascetics cross each morning, are characterized by divinely generated mysterious resemblances. Yet the line between mortal and divine-created resemblance is a fluid one. As worshipers emphasize, the gods at any moment may manifest themselves in the most unexpected of places, causing a melting piece of candle wax to momentarily resemble a flying dragon or allowing scattered rice grains to look "like" written characters. Conversely, even when they are in the most sacred and mysterious upper reaches of the mountain gods' domain, human worshipers should strive to engage in imitative practices. They should make offerings that resemble divinely created shapes, install statues that look "like" statues at a other sacral sites in Japan, and undertake actions that mime those of their human predecessors, their ancestors, and the kami. Mortal and divine resemblances stand in a complementary relationship to one another, allowing productive traffic between this world and the other world, binding together the living, the dead, and the divinities within the unified Akakura "family."

The Concept of Mitate

My understanding of imitation and resemblance at Akakura builds on the Japanese anthropologist Masao Yamaguchi's discussion of the concepts of *mitate* and *tsukuri* in Japanese culture (1991). *Mitate,* defined by Yamaguchi as "the art of citation," characterizes the widespread tendency in Japan to assign hidden referents to important displayed objects. Composed of two words, *mi* (to see) and *tate* (to stand, to arrange), mitate depends on intentional human creative agency. Like classical artists, lay worshipers carefully arrange presented objects to signal key connections to absent or distant forms and forces. In turn, the term *tsukuri*, usually glossed as "to make," refers to a particular kind of mitate, the "fabrication of something modeled after a primordial object" (Yamaguchi 1991, 64). Thus raw fish piled elegantly on a plate may be termed *o-tsukuri*, evoking the mythic image of Mount Meru at the world's center. A conical pile of sand presented at a shrine will similarly be termed *tsukuri-yama* (made mountain), a simulated mountain that refers to and makes tangible the cosmic mountain (Herbert 1967, 330–31; Nitzschke 1995).

Comparing the cultural practices of mitate and tsukuri to Baudrillard's concept of the simulacrum, Yamaguchi argues that these processes turn the "invisible into the visible" and allow productive interpenetrations of the divine and human worlds: "It is understood that Japanese gods do not appreciate true things; they do not accept things that are not fabricated by means of a device (*shukō*)" (1991, 64).

Representation and imitation, then, are not simply secondary acts of substitution or replacement in Japanese ritual contexts. They constitute, rather, fundamental components of efficacious worship. The willed enterprise of representation, of producing a "simulacrum," is the performative act that constitutes a productive link between mortal worshiper and immortal divinity. The kami, in this respect, do not enter into the human world without human creative agency and aesthetic apprehension.

At Akakura, the sacred mountain itself makes for the most common simulation fabricated in offerings. As we will see in chapter 4, offerings may share some of the mountain's spatial, physical, or sensory qualities, such as a triangular or vertical shape, symmetry, reversibility, verticality, "redness," or hardness. Circular cakes of mochi are carefully piled in the shapes of miniature mountains. Mounds of raw rice are shaped into perfect cones. Offered metal bells are sculpted into vertical, mountainlike towers. The mountain may be visually represented in votive paintings or aurally represented in prayers and songs celebrating ascent up its slopes.

In addition to such direct representations of the mountain's dimensional form, exchanged media may concretize or objectify the usually ephemeral, intangible spiritual and meteorological traffic believed to circulate up and down the mountainscape. Offerings of incense and water evoke the movement of water and mist on the mountain. Every day, "pure" offerings of flowers, fruit, vegetables, fish (especially red fish), and rice wine are presented to the gods in the mountain shrine and along high pathways; the products of the divinities' life-giving flows are thus partly returned to the elevated precincts of the kami.

Imitative Action: Healing, Pedagogy, and Architecture

The Sword of Fudō (Fudō-ken) healing ritual, performed four times each year by worshipers in the small Godaimyōō building in the rear of the complex, illustrates the critical importance of imitative practices at Akakura. A kamisama medium possessed by Fudō Myōō, the Buddhist fire deity, treats each patient with Fudō's great ritual sword. Chanting esoteric Buddhist prayers, she slashes the sword through the air immediately in front of, behind, and above each kneeling patient. In so doing, she is believed to cut the invisible, evil attributes that bind the afflicted to misfortune and suffering. Many patients report that as they are healed, they feel the flaming sword of Fudō cutting through internal regions of their body, destroying impurities and restoring tired muscles, joints, and organs.

In many respects, the Fudō-ken rite dramatizes and encapsulates the diverse therapeutic and representational processes of the Akakura system. The sword, understood as an animate manifestation of Fudō, also represents a microcosmic image of the great healing mountain itself. Through the sword, as through the mountain, the invisible therapeutic powers of the kami are called down into the body of each worshiper, heating and sculpting her so that she will more closely resemble the immortal gods themselves. As we shall see, those undertaking ascetic discipline within the shrine precincts and on the high mountain paths tell of experiences that closely resemble those reported during the Fudō-ken. At varied, ritually charged sites, worshipers recall penetration by invisible forces, being filled with great heat, having extraneous attachments slashed away, and learning to make their limbs conform to the graceful contours of the flowing kami. Healing within the Akakura system, I was often told, is a gradual process of coming to "learn" about the kami. As novice worshipers gather from direct instruction and subtle hints, this pedagogic process depends primarily on active encounters with multiple physical sites on the mountain and within the shrine.

The net effect of these encounters tends to be a kind of "interpretive drift," predisposing worshipers toward a powerful set of shared understandings about the divinities, the ancestors, and themselves. Over time, worshipers come to internalize the mountain's extensive healing geography through acts of vision, ritual performance, offering, consumption, and physical exertions on the mountain's upper slopes. As they do so, they are gradually recruited into the larger family of Akakura, developing intimate bonds of cosmological kinship with the kami and fellow worshipers.

Over the course of my fieldwork, I came to understand that virtually every corner of the shrine complex and its surroundings was imbued with symbolic import and emotional weight. In some cases, novice worshipers are told detailed stories about specific sites. In other cases, worshipers only receive tantalizing hints about the mountain's powers and are expected to discover the salient resemblances embedded in given locales. All worshipers spend a good deal of time contemplating and interacting with diverse statues, images, architectural spaces, and landscape sites at Akakura—in group ritual performance and in silent private meditation. Taken as a whole, the spatial organization of the shrine and its mountain environs constitutes the most significant pedagogic medium at Akakura. These sites collectively function as the primary mechanism through which authoritative, secret knowledge about the divinities is transmitted from generation to generation of worshipers and through which the kami and their human disciples are constituted as a unified family.

With this background in mind, let us now consider in more detail the major landscape and architectural sites at Akakura. As we shall see, each of these spaces, in effect, predisposes worshipers toward certain stereotypical imitative acts and certain apprehensions of deep resemblance between different domains of existence. As she becomes progressively immersed in these dense, deeply meaningful sites of resemblance, the worshiper achieves an increasing awareness of new kinds of correspondences between the visible and invisible worlds and gradually moves from being a student to being a teacher, taking on some of the pedagogic qualities of the kami and of their sacred landscape.

Healing Visions: Learning to See Resemblances on the Mountain

One of the first things a novice worshiper at Akakura learns to do is to experience the mountain in the correct visual fashion, apprehending an esoteric set of resemblances not accessible to the uninitiated. For many people in the region, Akakura is simply the northeast face of Mount Iwaki, but Akakura worshipers are quickly taught to view it as a separate mountain with its own peculiar features. Just as Mount Iwaki is universally acknowledged to have three peaks, new worshipers are told, Akakura Mountain itself has a high summit flanked by two lower peaks. (This image is represented in the great candelabra on the main altar of the Inner Sanctuary.) Although Akakura's three summits are not as easily discernible as Iwaki's, worshipers soon come to perceive them as natural features of the landscape; some go so far as to paint these three peaks in votive paintings given as consecrated offerings (奉納 *hōnō*) to the mountain divinities.

Snow covers the upper reaches of Iwaki and Akakura well into June. Because of its northeast orientation toward the flat central Tsugaru plain, sandwiched between the Sea of Japan and Aomori Bay, the Akakura face receives especially high winds and precipitation. At any point of the year, clouds, fog, or mist are more likely to shroud the Akakura face than any other portion of Iwaki.

It is widely said in Tsugaru that the relatively smooth Mount Iwaki resembles the smooth face of a beautiful woman. Hence this side's traditional prohibition to women. (As on many Japanese sacral mountains, the resident goddess or demoness was held to be jealous of female competitors for her veneration by men.) The Iwaki side has for centuries featured as the favored side for male pilgrimages up the mountain, culminating in the annual Great Mountain Rite each September, when hundreds of men climb the mountain at midnight from Iwaki-san Jinja (Mount Iwaki Shrine) to greet the rising sun from the summit.

In contrast, the craggy, volcanic, and weather-beaten Akakura is often said to resemble the rough, unshaven face of a man; hence its greater attractiveness to women. Akakura is especially associated with individual pilgrimage and austerities motivated by severe illness and revelatory dreams.[3] This northeastern face of the mountain is often referred to as the *ura no kao* (reverse-side face) or the *fushigi na basho* (mysterious or strange place). For generations popular tales have circulated of *oni* (demons) that live on the mountain, and of the ghostly forces of the place that have irresistibly pulled people up its steep, windswept slopes.

Whatever its formal designation, Akakura presents a forbidding sight from its base. In contrast to the gentle slopes that house Mount

Iwaki Shrine, the establishment Shintō institution at the southwestern base of the mountain, twisting volcanic features dominate the Akakura slopes. A fast-moving stream, the Akakura-gawa, runs down the mountain to the plain below. About halfway down the mountain, the river courses down the thirty-foot waterfall of Fudō, an important destination point in mountain ascetic discipline, where pilgrims sometimes perform cold-water discipline. A long ridge rises gradually from the far right, culminating in a huge half-dome prominently visible from the waterfall. On the left side of the mountain runs another ridge, along which shrine worshipers have placed thirty-three statues of the compassionate Bodhisattva Kannonsama. Midway along this ridge stands the huge isolated boulder, Ubaishi, another important site for ascetic practice.

The two great ridges converge in the great Akakura-zawa (赤倉沢 Akakura Gorge), a vast, triangular, treeless gash in the higher reaches of the mountain that is visible from the plain below and toward which worshipers learn to direct their visual attention. Enormous, deep red-, charcoal-, and light gray-colored layers of exposed geological strata ripple inward in chevron-patterned, undulating lines on either side of the gorge, converging in a dark horizontal line. The gorge has strong maternal and feminine associations. Many of my informants referred to this unusual formation as *onna no koto* (女のこと the womanly/feminine aspect) or believed it resembled the female genitalia. Above the craggy Akakura gorge, the worshipers learn to see the three peaks of Akakura Mountain.

Beholding Akakura Daigongen

Appropriately, a wrinkled face distinguishes the two human incarnations of Akakura Daigongen, the resident deity of this rough face of the mountain. Akakura Daigongen appears alternately as a wild-looking, black-haired young man whose entire body is covered with thick hair, and as an equally unkempt elderly white-haired man. The former shape, the black-haired younger man, is said to be the god's *shōtai* (true form). In both forms, the god appears in attire recalling an itinerant yamabushi mountain priest who carries a *shakuhachi* (bamboo flute) and a staff with metal Buddhist rings (see Blacker 1975, 36). Votive paintings of the black-haired and the white-haired man both

2. Akakura Mountain seen from the northeast

3. Akakura Mountain gorge

appear in the main Shinden room of the Akakura Mountain Shrine. Although my informants never put it in these terms, I surmise that the double image of black-haired young man and white-haired old man evokes the alternating "faces" of the mountain over the course of the year, as it moves from the vigorous foliage of mid-summer to the desolate, snow-covered appearance of deep winter. As we shall see in chapter 3, the Mountain Opening Ceremony of 1 May, which climaxes half-way up the mountain at the base of the gorge, may be understood as the annual "birth" from this vagina-like opening of the young and vigorous incarnation of Akakura Daigongen. This young incarnation will, in effect, reign for a half-year until the mountain is ritually "closed" at the Great Autumn Festival in November, at which time the elderly white-haired incarnation takes over.

As in Kawai Mariko's initial vision, Akakura Daigongen may also manifest himself as a great dragon (竜神様 Ryūjinsama), whose terrifying and craggy face, which also recalls the sharp contours of this volcanic mountain, is celebrated in many votive paintings and sculptures at Akakura Mountain Shrine. At times, Akakura Daigongen also manifests itself as a pair of male and female dragons, or as a pair of male and female birds.[4]

I understand Akakura Daigongen, the being envisioned by Kawai Mariko in the 1920s, to be a synthetic figure, conflating the alien male conquering figures of Sakanoue Tamuramaro and Bishamonten (Vaisravana) with the older, indigenous demoness figure of Onigamisama or Akakurasama. Indeed, the formal name of the Akakura summit, Ganki (巌鬼山 lit., Rock Demon Mountain), contains the kanji for oni (鬼). At times, the female and male figures are explicitly joined, as in the thirty-fourth line of the Akakura Prayer, "We praise Akakura Daigongen and the Dragon Princess and worship them." In such statements, Onigamisama is not directly named, but she appears in transmuted form as "Amaterasu," "The Dragon Princess," and "The Mountain Princess Deity" (Yama Hime no Kami).[5]

The divinity's bigendered quality becomes evident in Mariko's initial dream: Akakura Daigongen first appears as a violent, phallic dragon, piercing the dreamer's roof, and then turns into a "beautiful woman" on her pillow. In revelatory visions, the diarchic god has continued to manifest itself in male and female forms, often appearing as a male and female pair of dragons, birds, or pine trees, or, as we have seen, in alternating male incarnations. Linked to the cyclical alternation between winter and summer, these two figures also evoke the mythic alternation between older autochthons and new, alien conquerors.

Recall that in performing shugyō at Akakura, the spirit medium Okuda emphasized the accompanying presence of Sakanoue Tamura-

4. Votive painting: Fudō Waterfall, Akakura
Daigongen, Kawai Mariko, and Disciple

5. Votive painting depicting Akakura Daigongen as a young man

6. Akakura Daigongen as an old man

7. Votive painting of two birds

maro's conquering spirit; he himself had once performed ascetic discipline on precisely the same mountainous ground. Like Tamuramaro before her, Okuda roams through a partially alien landscape, seeking to incorporate the powers of its "strange" beings without fully succumbing to them. Yet she, a local woman, is herself at times cast in the structural position of the indigenous demoness, possessed by the alien conqueror Tamuramaro or by the violent Buddhist fire god Fudō Myōō, with whom Tamuramaro is closely associated.

In this sense, ritual practice at Akakura, an interstitial space "between worlds," may be conceived as a kind of unsteady compromise formation, a long-term attempt to contain the dimly remembered powers of an indigenous landscape within an overarching "Japanese" or "Yamato" frame. As we shall see, this project is only partially successful, for traces of indigenous capacity, in the form of "demons" or other "strange beings," continually threaten to possess ascetics who traverse the sacred mountain. The unresolved burdens of regional history, in effect, still weigh on the bodies and minds of present-day worshipers.

The Gendered Landscape of Akakura

While widely acknowledged as a frightening and disturbing place, the concealed or "reverse" face of Akakura is believed to have extensive healing powers. For generations, Tsugaru women have popularly conceived Akakura's topography as a therapeutic and revelatory site, and as a source of medicinal plants and mosses.[6] For over a century, women seeking assistance in conception and childbirth have visited Ōishi Shrine at the mountain's base to pray to Batō Kannon, the horse-headed incarnation of the compassionate Bodhisattva. From the mountain heights flows the medicinal water *kami no mizu* (water of the gods) that cleanses the body of impurities. Climbing the mountain's windswept and exposed rocky slopes, ascetics cleanse themselves of impurities and transcend biophysical and spiritual afflictions. As they stand and pray within the freezing water that spills down the mountain out of the great waterfall of Fudō, they activate their inner "heat" and triumph over mortal ills.

Although my informants did not explicitly speak of Akakura Mountain as a "womb," the imagery of gender, sexual difference, and gestation stands pronounced in all the major rituals at Akakura Mountain Shrine, as it is in many important Japanese mountains. As noted above, many Tsugaru residents conceptually divide Iwaki Mountain along gendered lines, with the north side supposedly exuding greater attraction to women, the south side to men. (Although female religious figures and shamanic healers had apparently been drawn to the mountain for centuries, their presence was actively discouraged from the late nineteenth century onward, as state Shintō and regular medical authorities sought to prohibit their practices.)

From the standpoint of Akakura Shrine worshipers, Akakura mountain embodies varied and overlapping gendered qualities. Its "right" side is more associated with the fierce male deity Fudō Myōō and the wild male form of the deity Akakura Daigongen, while its "left" side stands in closer association with Fudō's female counterpart, the merciful Kannonsama. Images of sexual difference in the standard right-left configuration adorn the Shinden shrine room. In one painting, two trees, one on each side of Akakura gorge, reach out toward one another. The trees themselves rather resemble the two dragon heads above them in the gorge, which smile at one another.

This gendered symbolism is neither static nor absolute. The male-coded Fudō Waterfall is located at the base of the Akakura gorge, which is often explicitly compared to female genitalia. While doing cold-water ablutions at the Fudō Waterfall, the female medium Okuda was possessed by the male spirit of the ancient war leader Sakanoue Tamuramaro. As we have seen, in Kawai Mariko's revelatory dream, the deity Akakura Daigongen transformed from a "male" to a female manifestation. In subsequent revelatory dreams and visions, Kawai Mariko, her daughter, and their disciples also beheld Akakura Daigongen as a hairy black-haired young man or as a hairy white-haired old man. Taken as a whole, the ritual cycle seeks to bring about various productive unions and exchanges between these contrasting potentialities of the mountain kami.

Ultimately, however, worshipers seem to experience Akakura as a deeply maternal entity. The line of carved stupas leading up to the summit all represent female divinities. The spirit of Kawai Mariko, referred to as the "Mother of the Mountain," serves as the worshipers' principal link to the mountain kami. As we shall see in the next chapter, the overall annual cycle at the shrine is structured through gestational sequences and miraculous births. This maternal imagery, in turn, informs the architectural layout of Akakura Mountain Shrine itself.

Human-Made Resemblances: Living with Family

The worshipers' sense that the Akakura Shrine community is "like" a family builds on a series of marked resemblances to the divine world and to the domestic domain. As they labor and worship in each part of the shrine, they are saturated with images and features that remind them of their conventional home and which also point to the invisible mysteries of the mountain. More so than orthodox Shintō shrines in the region, the L-shaped Akakura Mountain Shrine resembles a conventional northern Japanese agrarian household. Like a regular house, the shrine is very much oriented toward the mundane, quotidian labor activities of its human residents. Like local farmhouses, the shrine's unpretentious architecture commemorates the history of its residents and their sustained labor over time. As in regular households, women and the exigencies of their labor largely set the rhythms of life in the shrine. Since its erection in the late 1940s, the shrine has been developed to house and feed a large number of visitors in an efficient, albeit not luxurious, fashion.[7] If the shrine lacks the brand-new furnishings of more prosperous institutions, it more than compensates for this with its warm, hospitable, and homey qualities. As Mrs. Koike put it, "Here, we're really a family. We work together, cook together, drink together."

The architectural layout of the complex contributes to an interpretive drift that leads most worshipers to experience the shrine as a profoundly interior, homelike place. Daily activities of work, worship, and relaxation within these spaces over time promote a pervasive sense of co-residence with the extended family of the Akakura divinities and their human worshipers, living and dead.

The shrine's general informality immediately becomes evident to visitors. Although steps lead directly up from the courtyard to the front of the Shinden sanctuary, virtually all visitors enter Akakura Mountain Shrine from the front parking lot and courtyard through the doorway

8. Shrine residential buildings (on left) and kitchen (on right)

of the main residential building. In the main tatami room, the principal eating, socializing, and sleeping area of the shrine, they greet the priest or other residents of the shrine, who might be drinking herbal tea, heated on a wood-burning stove recessed into the floor in traditional rural fashion. At the stove, one of the social centers of the shrine, old-timers and novices gather to warm their feet, sip tea, recount the day's events, and watch an old black-and-white television set. Futon are stored in large closets behind sliding doors in the far wall of the shrine.

Some worshipers told me that the main tatami room was their favorite place in the shrine. "Here," one woman stated, "I really feel at home. Somehow, all my worries seem lighter when we're together in here." In the evening, ascetics and experienced worshipers gathered in this relaxing space to trade stories of shugyō, revelatory visions on the mountain slopes, and goings-on within the congregation. As in other Japanese domestic, interior (uchi) spaces, this site helps produce pervasive sentiments of belonging and group solidarity. Yet even here the faithful at all times remain attentive to the living presence of the divinities and ancestors, who may manifest their influence through inspired stories or unexpected signs.

Imitative Labor in the Kitchen

The shrine's general function as a "switchpoint" between the invisible realm of the divinities and the visible domestic domain becomes especially evident in the kitchen, in which women labor to produce a range of imitative offerings and strive to transform themselves into tangible images of the gods they serve.

Newcomers usually enter the kitchen through the sliding doors off of the main tatami room, but women on familiar terms with the shrine tend to enter through the kitchen genkan, which leads out to the main courtyard. From this vantage point, the women working in the kitchen usually keep track of the various comings and goings. As in conventional Japanese houses, the easy spatial access to the kitchen marks these women as the most "inside" members of the community.

All sizable Shintō shrines have kitchens, but in male-dominated religious establishments, the kitchen does not carry the enormous social and cosmological significance it does at Akakura. For women, who constitute the vast majority of ascetics and lay worshipers there, the kitchen remains the most intensely social space in the shrine complex. Here women prepare complex trays of offerings for the kami every dawn, clean, process, and redistribute the vast amount of food offerings presented by other worshipers, prepare meals, and exchange news and stories. They manage the sacred kami no mizu (神の水) that flows into the shrine through a faucet in the kitchen. Arguably, a female ascetic's most important socialization takes place during her many hours of labor each day over the kitchen's sinks, counters, and gas cooking rings.

At the kitchen's center stands a large (twelve feet by five feet) stainless steel sink with four spigots. Viewed from the living room entrance, the front right spigot is the source of the all-important "water of the gods" that alone may be used for preparing offerings to the gods and ancestors. In contrast, for example, to the nearly obsessive emphasis on turning off electric lights, this particular water faucet would be left slightly dripping for long periods of time, in tangible testimony to the water's animate and life-giving qualities. A large tiled sink in the back of the kitchen was used for cleaning incoming offerings, such as fish. Over the course of the day, the kitchen constantly received offerings from members of the congregation. Fish, seaweed, fruits, and vegetables would be delivered through the back door that opened out into the central courtyard and parking lot. Every significant food offering to the shrine thus passed through the kitchen, where women cleaned and prepared it for presentation to the kami in the Inner Sanctuary. (The shrine entirely subsisted on offered food.)

The kitchen is an emphatically female space. Although men might occasionally pop in for a moment to chat or check the dinner menu, I never saw a man doing any work in the kitchen.[8] Women especially liked to congregate in the rear "outdoor kitchen" extension near the back door, where they could chat for long stretches in relative privacy.

As I learned when I began shugyō, the shrine kitchen really comprises two kitchens within it, one for the kami and one for humans. The large room stores one set of tableware, trays, and eating tools for the kami, and another set for their human worshipers. The two sets are never mixed.

In the kitchen, women worshipers continually encounter in a highly intensified form the basic shugyō motifs of order and conformity to pattern. Every profane and sacred object in the kitchen must be strictly accounted for and kept in its proper place. Even dish drying could turn into an anxious, nerve-wracking process. The kami's dishes and utensils had their own special drying cloth, which hung on a special peg; this cloth could not be used for any purposes other than drying the divinities' dishes. All dishes had to be put away in precisely the right location. Beginners were often admonished if they inadvertently misplaced a bowl or cup in the wrong shelf or cupboard. I recall that I once, after having cleaned the tatami floor, left a rag in a kitchen bucket. When Fumiko discovered the rag, she angrily demanded of all the women present who had placed it there, and she emphatically scolded me when I sheepishly confessed.

This principle of orderliness was even more drastically enforced for the kami's objects. Women not undergoing shugyō were not allowed to touch the divinities' dishes. Beginning ascetics did not even have permission to wash or dry these sacred things; they could only carry the prepared food trays out to the shrine altars. Eventually an ascetic might be allowed to fill the water and rice bowls, but the important job of preparing full meals for the kami was reserved for the most experienced woman ascetic present. In the absence of any such women, Mrs. Koike, the elderly woman who had undergone numerous stints of shugyō many years earlier and who served as the shrine's informal caretaker during the "open" season from May through October, would take on the task.

Beyond being the site of these important ritual preparations, the kitchen constituted the key nexus of women's social networks in the extended shrine community. Since most of the time only three or four women lived in the shrine, there was usually plenty of room to move around in the capacious kitchen. But on the eve of a major festival—such as the Great Summer Festival on 28–29 July—the kitchen would overflow with enormous piles of food offerings and would bustle with a dozen or more women working hard at the various sinks and counters, chopping, washing vegetables, cooking, cleaning, preparing offerings, washing dishes, and drying, as well as chatting and joking around. For all the hard work and the embarrassment of my frequent mistakes, I considered the kitchen my favorite place in the entire shrine complex. Nearly all experienced female worshipers in the shrine stated that they felt much the same.

The preparation of divine and human food requires a great deal of coordination, and it usually falls into the responsibility of the most experienced woman resident at the shrine. During the time of my fieldwork, this was usually my friend and teacher Fumiko, who was about halfway through her ten-year stint of ascetic discipline.[9] Fumiko and other experienced shrine members exercised strict supervision over less experienced members. This practice followed the model of a standard multigenerational Japanese household, in which the okāsan (the mother of the household) continuously asserts her authority over the oyomesan (the subordinate, incoming bride or daughter-in-law)—especially within the all-important kitchen space. In the shrine, however, one's degree of spiritual experience takes precedence over age. Fumiko, who was in her early forties, would routinely order about much older women in the kitchen, who would meekly submit to her often harsh and peremptory instructions and criticism.

The senior woman present did not only regulate space and time within the kitchen; she also regulated many spatial and temporal processes through the entire shrine complex. A small blackboard, hung on the wall dividing the kitchen from the outer hallway, was used to list all manner of information related to food, such as kitchen work assignments and upcoming menus for the kami and people. (Occasionally, the names of upcoming visitors to the shrine would also be listed.) Whenever Fumiko was living in the shrine, she alone managed this blackboard, which gave her de facto control over the labor rhythms of the shrine community.

Significantly, unlike the mountain circuits of shugyō, usually performed alone, kitchen labor and cleaning require constant interaction and coordination with others. Even by Japanese standards those doing shugyō live and work in extremely close quarters with one another for many weeks or months at a time. Tension is unavoidable. Consider one example. Early on during my first stint of ascetic discipline, I inadvertently triggered a dispute between two of the dominant personalities at the shrine. One afternoon, when I returned from climbing the summit with Fumiko (on the second day of my shugyō), I was asked about the climb by Mrs. Takeda, the priest's wife and Kawai Mariko's granddaughter. I responded enthusiastically that the climb had been "Tanoshikatta!" ("I enjoyed it!") Mrs. Takeda, as it turned out, took great umbrage at this phrase, which she regarded as flippant. To her mind, my statement indicated that Fumiko had failed at properly supervising me. She severely remonstrated with Fumiko for this act of "irresponsibility" and for taking me on an unauthorized climb too far up the mountain, into its most sacred region. This minor dispute reflected long-running tensions in the shrine community between Mrs. Takeda's hereditary authority and the more charismatic influence of other kamisama mediums, including Fumiko's own spiritual advisor, Abo-sensei.

The next day, as we washed dishes after lunch, Fumiko remarked to me that her "real shugyō" was not climbing the mountain, which she enjoyed, but in the kitchen, for she found dealing and working with people the greatest of all possible trials. On that day, she was particularly angered at Mrs. Takeda for the previous day's scolding. As I soon learned, Mrs. Takeda and Fumiko frequently clashed over who would run the kitchen. Fumiko, who noted that Mrs. Takeda lived in town and never slept over at the shrine, found Mrs. Takeda's frequently expressed opinions about the kitchen preposterous. "What does she know about the mountain?" she asked.

As she angrily scrubbed out the rice cooker, Fumiko emphatically gestured to the hot water pot in front of us, noting that it had an outside (soto), which everyone could see, and an inside (uchi), which no one could see. Similarly, she explained, everyone saw her smiling and being very polite, but no one knew that inside she was on the verge of exploding with anger and frustration. The kitchen was truly, she declared, her *tesuto* (test).[10]

As this anecdote suggests, if the mountain in general serves as the mediating site between the worlds of gods and humans, then the kitchen constitutes one of the key mediating sites in the shrine itself, between "on the mountain" and "off the mountain," between the mundane and the sacral poles of the shrine complex itself. Divine water comes in from the mountain, and is mixed in the kitchen with offerings from the plain below; these combined offerings continuously move out to the shrine altars, where the gods consume them. As *gofu* (lit., a charm or talisman), they then return to the kitchen for further processing by women, so that they may be properly consumed by human worshipers. The kitchen is also a site where women engage constantly with intensified condensations of the labor processes of everyday female life. This seemingly conventional labor is valued as service to the kami, as it is pursued with the same concentration, efficiency, and grace as all other discipline during shugyō. Through these dense imitative acts, women transform the congealed labor of the lay worshipers—in the form of food offerings—into the cuisine of the gods, only to retransform it for human consumption afterward.

Sacred Sanctuaries: The Imitative Architecture of the Shinden and Reidō

Each morning, food and water prepared in the kitchen are reverently transported to two major sacred rooms of the complex, the Shinden and the Reidō, located at the farthest end of the L-shaped main building from the kitchen. Seen from the outside, the profane and ritual rooms form one continuous, interconnected structure, but the passage from residential to sacred space is overtly marked by performance cues and spatial indicators. For instance, a special vacuum cleaner, stored next to the Reidō, must be used to clean the two sacred rooms, in contrast to a "regular" vacuum cleaner used to clean the profane living and working quarters of the complex.

Virtually all my informants characterized the Shinden sanctuary as the most "beautiful" area of the shrine complex. Most report awe, fear,

9. The Akakura Mountain Shrine Inner Sanctuary building

and reverence while within it. The sanctuary (about twenty-five feet by sixty-five feet) provides the main setting of the morning and evening prayer services at the shrine. The front area, oriented toward the mountain summit, is given over to the altar. Large silk brocade curtains inlaid with silver and gold thread frame the visitor's view of the front wall, which is covered with various sacred objects and images. This front wall (actually a series of *fusuma*, sliding wooden doors) is opened up only once a year during the Great Summer Festival to reveal the Honden (usually glossed as the "holy of holies") behind it. At times, parts of the right connecting wall are pulled back, so that one can look from the Shinden into the slightly lower, adjacent Reidō. The rear and left walls, which consist of sliding fusuma doors (with wooden paneling on the bottom and large glass windows on the top), give expansive views of the route down the mountain and the forested banks of the Akakura River. During the day, the Shinden is thus the best-lighted and most "open" interior space in the shrine complex.

Many people reported to me that within the Shinden, the physically most elevated structure of the shrine complex, they "really felt on the mountain," sensing the power of the mountain and its resident divinities. "When we're praying in the Shinden in the rain," said Fumiko, "it's like we're out on the mountain, you can really feel the rain and

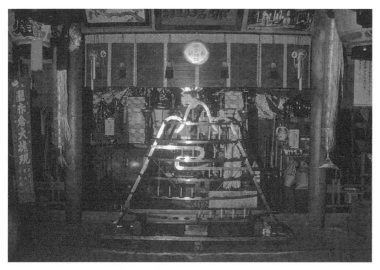

10. Altar of Akakura Mountain Shrine Inner Sanctuary

the wind." Another woman agreed: "There is something solemn and strange about the Shinden. You know, the kami are really coming right in there. It is their place, I think." During the July 1992 conversation in the Shinden, Narita implied that important revelatory events had happened to her and Kawai Mariko on the precise spot where the Shinden was constructed. "When you're in the Shinden, that's where you start to understand the mountain," she remarked.

Ritual paraphernalia at the room's front, which is saturated with imitative imagery, heightens this pervasive sense of the mountain's looming presence in the sanctuary. In the front center of the saidan stands a polished candelabrum, approximately six feet tall and eight feet wide at the base. As I was often told, this object "resembled" the shape of Akakura Mountain. It was composed of an external frame with six protruding horizontal crossbars, each holding a line of candles. (The six levels represent the six realms of transmigration, *rokudō*, through which all souls hope to pass in their journey through the universe.) Just beneath the fifth horizontal crossbar, an S-shaped strip of metal representing a cloud curls across the candelabrum, beginning on the left side, twisting down behind the fourth crossbar, and curving back to the right-hand outer frame. Immediately beneath this curved strip, superimposed over the second and third crossbars, one finds a metal Buddhist-style swastika. At the top of the candelabrum, another strip curves up in the shape of Akakura's top peak, flanked by the right and left lower peaks.

Immediately behind the candelabrum's "peak," on the rear wall of the shrine, hangs a sacred circular mirror of polished metal, one of the most important ritual objects in any Shintō shrine. It is linked to the great mirror at Ise Shrine and to the mythic mirror through which the goddess Amaterasu was lured back into the visible universe. About two feet above this mirror hangs a slightly larger circular metal mirror with the characters for "Akakura Mountain" inscribed on it.

This section of the Shinden, the closest point to the mysterious Honden (the formal home of the kami), constitutes a highly charged site of transaction between worshipers and divinities. Two long wooden shelves in front of the lower mirror span the width of the front altar area, and they are always richly stocked with offerings brought by worshipers and visitors. Bottles of sake, partially wrapped in special white papers that list on their front the names of each donor, make for the most common offerings. Foodstuffs, such as vegetable and fish, are also presented here to the kami, who "taste" and purify them, transforming them into gofu (護府) to be consumed by human worshipers. As discussed in chapter 4, women ascetics also present special offerings of water and food early each morning.

Various ritual objects are stored amidst the crowded offering shelves and trays behind the candelabrum in the dark front altar area, a rectangular space about ten feet deep and twenty-five feet wide. These include the sacred drum of Kawai Mariko, white paper *gohei* (御幣 purification wand), and a wooden sculpture of a hawk. When an ascetic who owns a pair of ritual oshirasama figurines resides in the shrine, her oshirasama will be stored on the altar, except during her morning ascents up the mountain, when she carries them with her.

The votive paintings that cover the room's upper walls further intensify the reported intimate resemblances between the sanctuary and the upper mountain slopes. These sacred images implicitly lay out the sacred topography of the mountainscape and the collective memory of the shrine community. Most of the paintings illustrate revelatory visions experienced by important members of the shrine, especially the founder Kawai Mariko herself. Members of the Akakura shrine community term these paintings hōnō (奉納 lit., offerings). Although

Kawai Mariko did not herself paint any such images, producing these paintings and drawings is understood as an act of disciplined reverence and service (otsutome).

In contrast to the Shinden sanctuary, devoted to the veneration of kami, the adjacent Reidō shrine room is reserved for ancestral memorialization. Its color scheme recalls the dark rich tones of Buddhist temples. If we think of the entire shrine complex as a rambling family farmhouse, the Reidō constitutes the structural equivalent of a house's butsudan, the domestic Buddhist altar at the heart of any home. Occasionally, worshipers would gather for conversation in the Shinden, but I never observed anyone engaged in conversation within the Reidō, which seemed to demand formal demeanor and hushed voices at all times.

Most worshipers found the Reidō an especially "strange" and disturbing locale, a feeling they often also expressed toward a regular butsudan. Here, more than anywhere else at Akakura, my informants found themselves conscious of their overwhelming obligations to the ancestors. "Of course I must go in there," Fumiko once remarked, "but it is not easy. It is heavy work, kuyō, after all." She continued quietly, "There is so much I don't understand about the ancestors. These things really are a mystery. It can be so frightening, don't you think?"

The Reidō's sense of opaqueness and mystery is heightened by the brocade curtains that partially cover the three deep alcoves in front of the room, including the dimly lit right alcove, in which sits a painted sculpture of the founder of esoteric Buddhism in Japan, Kōbō Daishi (Kūkai).

Living Images: Resemblance and
Co-residence between Kami and Humans

As in all Japanese religious institutions influenced by esoteric Buddhist traditions, this statue of Kōbō Daishi and the other consecrated sculptures found throughout the Akakura complex are understood not as "mere" representations but rather as living divine beings, due appropriate respect at all times from worshipers. Nonetheless, the statues exemplify the imitative logic of mitate that characterizes other human-made elements in the shrine. These images are linked to a vast chain of resemblances, tied into thousands of other carved votive images throughout Japan and wider Buddhist-influenced regions of Asia. As such they make for especially appropriate mediators between this world and the other world.

Although most shrine members insist that they lack detailed scriptural knowledge about Kannon, Fudō, Kūkai, Amaterasu, and other Shintō and Buddhist figures, worshipers report strong emotional and spiritual connections with these beings, largely emerging from encounters with multiple sacred images within the shrine and on the mountain. "I am not a very knowledgeable person," Fumiko told me one day as we placed flowers in front of the statue of Shōkannon, "but every day, just living in the shrine, I learn a little bit more. I see Shōkannon every day, and I know she is really for me. She really looks after me."

Fumiko, like other ascetics, had become intimately acquainted with two sequences of Thirty-Three Kannonsama stupas at Akakura. In the center rear of the shrine complex stands a large statue of Shōkannonsama (聖観音様), the most common form of the compassionate Bodhisattva, surrounded by thirty-three smaller Kannonsama stupas. Ascetics circumambulate this assemblage of statues during the winter, when the mountain paths are closed to ascetic climbs. From time to time nonascetic visitors make the circuit, depositing coins at each statue.

The entire congregation collectively circumambulates these Kannonsama statues twice a year, at the February Dragon Princess Rite and the October Ancestral Memorialization Ceremony. Each June, the Akakura Mountain Shrine congregation embarks on a pilgrimage along the Tsugaru region's Thirty-Three Kannonsama route, which begins at Kudōji Temple in southern Hirosaki and covers most of the Tsugaru peninsula. Thus, once every four months, the congregation undertakes Thirty-Three Kannonsama performances, spaced out evenly through the annual cycle.

During the open season of the year, advanced pilgrims may climb along a line of thirty-three Kannon statues that stretches all the way up the mountain on its left ridge to the summit, culminating in another large Shōkannonsama image. (This route is described in detail in chapter 5.) In so doing, they come into renewed contact with the shrine's microhistories and experience deepened connections with fellow worshipers. As I was often told, each Kannon statue was carved by a member of the congregation and carried up the mountain as a meritorious act of service (お勤め otsutome). As ascetics climb the mountain, they pray to each Kannon stupa in turn; each Kannon, it is said, has the power to bless the worshiper with revelatory visions or strength. During one famous mountain climb, for example, a group of pilgrims led by Mrs. Okuda observed the third stupa (the Jikyō or "sutra-holding Kannon") miraculously spin around many times in response to their prayers and offerings. Some ascetics even claim that the Kannonsama statues detach themselves from the ground and walk up and down the mountain on their own.

Immediately to the right of the circle of Kannon statues stands the small Mieidō subshrine, which houses an important life-sized statue of a sitting Kawai Mariko, carved with startling verisimilitude.[11] The pupils of the foundress are painted black, to give them a lifelike appearance. Her right hand holds a prayer stick. In her lap sits an actual cloth bag with a drawstring top, of the sort carried by older Japanese women as a purse. Cloth flowers adorn both sides of the statue. The names of shrine donors are written on white paper hung near the ceiling on the side and back walls of the shrine.

A glass window sliding door that opens up into the sacred *ofuro* (bath) of Kawai Mariko constitutes this room's right wall. The bathtub's dimensions equal those of a regular Japanese bathtub, but no one ever uses it for bathing or ritual cold-water discipline. Filled with water from the Akakura River once a year during the Dragon Princess ceremony in February, it is the source of kami no mizu in the shrine. A bright silver metal gohei is permanently enshrined within this water.

Although the maternal figures of Kannon and Kawai Mariko are commemorated immediately next to one another, they carry different emotional valences for most worshipers. Many perceive Kannon as unconditionally accepting and nurturing, and even first-time visitors to the shrine will willingly give offerings and pray in front of her stupas. In contrast, most apprehend the "Great Mother" Kawai Mariko as a somewhat frightening figure; her shrine seems the least inviting place in the whole complex to most worshipers. Such contrastive reactions to maternal images are common in the Akakura system as a whole. As we shall see in chapter 5, ascetics experience important features on the maternally coded mountain landscape as alternately soothing and terrifying.

11. Central Shōkannonsama statue

12. Statue of Kawai Mariko in her shrine

13. Fudō Myōō painting in the Godaimyōō subshrine

Fudō, the fierce male Buddhist divinity of fire, also constitutes a tangible presence on the mountain. At Akakura Shrine, he is especially associated with the most common destination of shugyō, "Fudō-taki." A red-painted stone statue of Fudō, carved by a prominent shrine member, stands to the right of the waterfall's pool. Revelatory dreams and visions of Fudō are not uncommon in the shrine community, especially among those undertaking shugyō. Several important collective ceremonies invoke Fudō during the annual cycle, including the 1 May pilgrimage to the Fudō Waterfall and the four performances of the Sword of Fudō healing rite.

The pervasive gender complementarity between the male Fudō and the female Kannon is reiterated in the important Godaimyōō or Five Fierce Lords building, the center-rear subshrine of the shrine complex. On the left wall of the shrine hangs a painting of Fudō sitting to the right of a waterfall, seated in the lotus position. As usual in Japan, he holds in his right hand a sword, to slash away impurities and worldly attachments, and in his left hand a rope, to bind up evildoers. Flames sprout from his head. His right eye looks down to hell, while his left eye looks up to heaven; his right fanglike tooth is pointed up, his left tooth is pointed down. A Sword of Fudō (Fudō-ken), stored in the rear altar of this building, is used in the special healing rite conducted in this small shrine four times per year.

To the right of Fudō hangs an elaborate painting of a *tennin* (angel or celestial maiden) floating through a blue sky above green tree branches. Her hair is garlanded in lotus-shaped jewelry, in her right hand she holds a lotus flower, her translucent garments trail behind her. On the ceiling are painted seven more tennin, also floating through air. Four of the figures face the front of the shrine; three face its rear. The two deities closest to the shrine's entrance carry lutes.

Other sacral figures in statuary form are venerated through the shrine precincts. In the front courtyard the visitor first sees a covered, life-size standing statue of the founder Kawai Mariko, which once a year (at the Great Summer Festival) worshipers carefully dress in fine brocades. To her left stands a stone pillar around which is twined the Dragon Lord (竜神様 Ryūjinsama), honoring the dragon that flew out of Akakura's left-hand peak to summon Kawai Mariko. Further off to the left stands a statue of Kōbō Daishi, the founding figure of Japanese esoteric Buddhism. Also to the left of the Shinden stands a statue of Sakanoue Tamuramaro, the alleged Yamato conqueror of the Tsugaru region.

Finally, worshipers are vaguely aware that secret images of the divinities are stored within the Honden, the subshrine located behind the Shinden that formally houses the kami. The Honden is an undecorated, modest structure, about ten feet high. So far as I know, worshipers approach it only once during the year, at the Great Summer Festival, when the raised concrete platform on which it stands is connected by a bridge to the Shinden. To the right of the Honden one finds the small shrine for the dragon deity Ryūjinsama, an enclosed miniature shrine on a four-foot high foundation, containing a small sculpture of the dragon.

Taken together, the statues, the hidden sacred objects, and the votive paintings—depicting the mountain avatar Akakura Daigongen, Fudō Myōō, Kannonsama, the Dragon Lord Ryūjinsama, the Dragon Princess, and other divinities—constitute the extended cosmological

14. Statue of Sakanoue Tamuramaro

family of Akakura. In Fumiko's words, "We are not far from the kami when we are living here. They are letting us all live with them here, all in the same family." Okuda elaborated, "The kami see us every day, they walk with us on the path, and they watch over us when we sleep. We are just their children, here, and they are our parents. You must not forget that."

The Cosmological Architecture of Akakura: Transpositions and Resemblances between the Mountain and the Shrine

Taken as a whole, the spatial organization of these living votive images, which resemble so many other sacred images throughout Japan, produces a tangible image of the entire therapeutic Akakura mountain-scape. Worshipers conceptually divide it between the two principal paths of shugyō: the "left" route past Thirty-Three Kannon up to the summit, and the "central" (or "right") route up to the Fudō-taki in the "center" of the mountain. Each of these sites on the upper mountain slopes corresponds to sites in the shrine complex. The rear line of sacred sites reproduces the three sacred peaks of Akakura (which were concretized in the three sacred scrolls given by Akakura Daigongen to Kawai Mariko). The Dragon Shrine on the left is associated with the left peak, the central Shōkannonsama statue is associated with the central summit, and the Kawai Mariko Shrine on the right is associated with the right peak.

Just as the waterfall of the fierce deity Fudō Myōō is believed to be at the center of the upper mountain, so the small shrine of Fudō (the Godaimyōō) is located in the center-rear of the compound. Just as a line of thirty-three Kannon statues marks the high ridge path up to the ultimate Shōkannon statue at the summit, a half-circle of thirty-three Kannon stupas is located in the outside rear of the shrine, visibly dominated by a Shōkannon statue. In turn, the sacred ofuro in Kawai Mariko's shrine recalls the great sacred pool at the base of the Fudō Waterfall, in which Kawai Mariko performed *mizugyō* (water discipline) and beheld revelatory visions.

The gorge of Fudō and the Shinden sanctuary may be understood as transformations of each other. The walls of the Shinden, decorated with votive paintings of the mountain, recall the high banks of the gorge. In turn, the snow-covered floor of the gorge, covered with offerings and incense presented by pilgrims, recalls the Shinden's altar. In both spaces, worshipers reverently face the mountain summit.

Collective ceremonials, undertaken by the entire congregation over the course of the annual cycle, ritually emphasize and reconstitute these correspondences between the shrine complex and the mountainscape. During the Great Summer Festival in July, the bridge over the Akakura River, which takes worshipers from the shrine precincts up the path to the realm of the kami, duplicates a special bridge that runs from the front of the Shinden to the Honden. Similarly, at the Mountain Opening Ceremony (Yamabiraki) on 1 May, the congregants climb to the gorge of the Fudō Waterfall, buried deep in snow. Flanked by the steep walls of the gorge, they hang a new sacred rice straw rope over the gorge, make offerings, and pray to the kami, before returning to pray in the Shinden sanctuary below.

Six months later, at the October Ancestral Memorialization Ceremony (Senzo Kuyō), the last collective rite of the year held on the mountain, the congregation collectively reenacts a mountain pilgrimage up the other mountain route, the Thirty-Three Kannon path, by marching thirty-three times around the shrine's outer precincts, centered on the shrine's thirty-three Kannon statues. As they march, ritual specialists burn three pyres, each associated with one of the mountain's three volcanic peaks, respectively in front of the Dragon Shrine, the Shōkannon statue, and the Kawai Mariko Shrine.

Chapter 3 considers these ceremonies, and the larger ritual cycle in which they are located, in more detail. In addition to intensifying the general transpositions between the human-made shrine and the divinely created mountain, these collective rites function both as models of and models for the daily practice of ascetic worship by individual worshipers. As in shugyō, sustained bodily labor during the major ceremonies allows human worshipers to constitute themselves and their immediate environs as progressively more and more like the gods and their dwelling places. These coordinated efforts, conceived of as physical and symbolic mountain ascents, gradually reform the interior and exterior states of individual worshipers' bodies and of the extended shrine complex, reclassifying human devotees as intimate kin to the mountain kami. As a united family, mortals, gods, and ancestors work together to reproduce key regenerative cycles, ensuring biological and agricultural fertility throughout the year and safeguarding the collective health and well-being of the mountain and all of its children.

3

l a b o r   a n d   r e b i r t h

Cosmological Kinship in the Annual Ritual Cycle

Mythic Kinship in Ritual Performance

Thirteen times a year committed members of the Akakura Mountain
Shrine congregation gather to perform collective ritual action, on or
off the mountain. Through these coordinated exchange transactions,
the transformative capacities of the gods and ancestors flow back into
the human realm and make possible continued human traffic with the
"other world" (あの世 ano yo). As in the shrine's other domains, these
ritual exchanges between worlds depend on a set of imitative and representational practices through which mortals fabricate and manipu-
late tangible images of their dynamic relationships with divinities and
ancestors.

In analyzing the ritual symbolism of this annual performance cycle,
I concentrate on two imitative complexes, the Cooking Pot Ceremony,
performed three times each year, and the Mountain Opening Ceremony, performed once a year. As we shall see, these rites anchor a
year-long exchange system that mediates between two orders of kin-

15. Dragon Princess Ceremony (15 February): Climbing
toward Akakura Mountain Shrine

ship—practical, conventional kinship, associated with regular human households, and what may be termed "mythic" or "cosmological" kinship, through which living worshipers, ancestors, and the mountain divinities are linked as members of a ritual family, commonly oriented toward the mountain. Through careful ritual interaction with the cosmic womb of the mountain, members of shrine are reborn each year as "children" of the divinities. In principle, this periodic rebirth should allow the faithful to return rejuvenated to their conventional kin networks in the plain below.

As is the case with the landscape and architectural features examined in the previous chapter, this mediation between kinship on and off the mountain depends on a set of homologies between ritual practices at Akakura and those in a typical northern Tōhoku agrarian household. As elsewhere in Japan, conventional household ritual structures in Tōhoku are principally oriented toward kuyō (供養) of family ancestors (仏様 *hotoke-sama*). At domestic ancestral altars and in related sites, living family members present concrete tokens of their labor in the form of offerings to ancestors, and in turn they receive life-giving blessings from the honored dead. As Ruth Benedict (1947) long ago observed, these ritual offerings, like all labor for the family line's enterprises, are motivated by an overpowering sense of obligation (*giri*) to those who gave life to their descendents. Although the debt owed to ancestors, in Benedict's words, "can never be repaid one ten-thousandth," this debt relationship necessitates continuous exchange transactions between the living and the dead through formal ceremonies and intimate gestures (114–32).

Rather like members of a regular household presenting offerings to the family domestic altar (and, by extension, to the family line as a whole), the members of the shrine congregation embed tokens of their dedicated labor in the mountain of Akakura. Over time, they withdraw or reaccess from the mountainscape these invested energies in the enhanced forms of blessings, physical health, bountiful harvests, and fiscal prosperity. By investing value in the cosmological family of the mountain, mortal worshipers secure spiritual, financial, and therapeutic benefits for their regular human families.

Like members of an ordinary household, the mortal members of the shrine community must contribute to this regenerative cycle by conscientiously performing collective ceremonies in a timely fashion. Appropriately, given that the goal of these rites is to multiply the value invested by worshipers in a manner that recalls human kinship and descent, these rituals deploy the symbolism of marriage, procreation, and gestation, binding together mortals, ancestors, and gods through periodic prestations and counterprestations.

The successive performance of thirteen annual collective rites spread through the year accomplishes this overall exchange cycle: (1) The Dragon Princess Rite in February; (2) the New Year's rite in March; (3) the Mountain Opening Rite in May; (4) the Sword of Fudō rite in May; (5) the Thirty-Three Kannonsama pilgrimage in June; (6) the Sword of Fudō rite in June; (7) the Mount Taihei pilgrimage in July; (8) the Great Summer Festival in July; (9) the Mount Hakkōda pilgrimage in August; (10) the Ancestral Memorialization Rite in October; (11) the Sword of Fudō rite in September; (12) the Sword of Fudō rite in October; and (13) the Autumn Festival in November.[1] Taken as a whole, this ceremonial sequence constitutes the shrine association as a classificatory family organized according to symbolic linkages of adoption, filiation, affinity, and lineal descent. At the same time, these rites in principle allow worshipers to redirect the blessings of the cosmological family back into the mundane domestic sphere.

The Cooking Pot Ceremony: Linking the Household and the Mountain

Most forcefully, the important *kamado* (竈 cooking pot) rite, a ceremony long associated with kamisama spirit mediums throughout the Tsugaru region, accomplishes the intimate linkage between cosmological and domestic domains (Ikegami 1987). In one sense, the cooking pot is a tangible icon of Sumeru, the world mountain that rises out of the cosmic sea, and of the volcanic mountain of Akakura itself. At the same time, the kamado is widely recognized as a sign of a regular human household. In Tsugaru, the word *kamado* is frequently used as a synonym for "house" or "household." Many Japanese households honor the divinity Kamado no Kami (竈の神) by a miniature shrine in the kitchen (Herbert 1967, 498; Bocking 1997, 83). In rural northern Tōhoku households, the kamado has especially close associations with the traditional hearth and center house pole.[2]

The Cooking Pot Ceremony is performed three times each year at Akakura, during the New Year's festival in February, the Great Summer Festival in July, and the Autumn Festival in November. A special cooking pot decorated with five purified paper *shide* strips (zigzagged white paper strips), is heated on an elaborate brazier. I have been told, but have not been able to confirm directly, that a special volcanic rock from Akakura is placed within the barrel prior to heating. As the water in the pot begins to boil, the shrine's senior spirit medium drums the shrine's sacred drum and leads the congregation in a long performance of "Saigi, Saigi," the song of mountain ascent. If all goes well, the pot begins to emit an unearthly hum, a sign of the kami's beneficent presence. As soon as the humming begins, all members of the congregation are rapidly assembled in line and must each toss raw rice grains and salt into the boiling water, shouting "Isshin!" (一心 one heart/mind; wholeheartedly) as they do so. The partially cooked rice will be returned to worshipers as divinely purified substance (gofu) in small white paper envelopes stamped with the shrine's seal. My informants referred to this cooked rice as protective medicine (*kusuri*) that would safeguard their family.

The loudly humming rice barrel serves as an icon of the miraculous conjoining of the realms of the visible and invisible, a pivotal moment in which the uninterrupted, perfect beauty of the kami flows out in unobstructed, audible waves to refashion the bodily beings of every single worshiper. These are precisely the qualities (openness, lightness, and purity) that every ascetic struggles for during shugyō, and which the rite should ideally transmit to each and every worshiper present.

In many senses, the Cooking Pot Ceremony, officiated by women who have performed extensive stints of shugyō, recapitulates the process of mountain asceticism. It is presented as a symbolic ascent up the mountain, signaled by the singing of "Saigi, Saigi," the song performed during the 1 May Mountain Opening Ceremony and sung each day by those undertaking shugyō. As in the ascetic offering practices discussed in chapter 4, the Cooking Pot rite condenses and elevates the domestic labor of women in preparing and processing food, especially the sacred, pure food of rice. Rather like the passage through the narrow tunnel of the Ubaishi Boulder, discussed in chapter 5, the Cooking Pot plays on female reproductive processes, compressing and heating the rice offerings and the water of the gods, so as to "give birth" to the sound of the gods and cooked rice. Just as the great rock may produce a mysterious sound as a powerful ascetic crawls through it, so should the cooking pot (widely believed to contain a small rock itself) emit a miraculous noise. Similar energy transactions characterize the heating of the ascetic's body in shugyō, when the "hot breath" of the god "burns away" unnecessary encumbrances, impurities, and passions (Blacker 1975, 164–85). Through exposure to the therapeutic sound waves of the cooking pot, lay worshipers partake in the divine blessings that the dedicated practitioners of shugyō have gained.

Just as food offerings move back and forth between human and divine realms, the Cooking Pot Ceremony may be understood as an aural exchange transaction between human worshipers and the kami. While singing "Saigi, Saigi" and performing austerities high on the mountain, the dedicated worshiper may hear mysterious noises emanating from stones and statues. Similarly, the Cooking Pot rite establishes a reciprocal connection between the production of sound by human worshipers and the miraculous production of sound by the

16. Great Summer Festival (28 July): The cooking pot and drum

17. Great Summer Festival: Offerings and prayer
in front of the cooking pot

gods. The senior kamisama spirit medium beats a sacred drum and chants, then leads the congregation in the "Saigi, Saigi" chant. At the song's conclusion, human voices cease and are responded to by the "voice" of the gods, manifested as the otherworldly humming emanating from the barrel.

The rite's two musical instruments, the drum and the barrel-shaped

18. Great Summer Festival: Line of worshipers
offer rice and salt before cooking pot

pot, both of them hollow cylinders, also suggest this linked contrast
between human-made and god-made sound. The hollow drum sits
horizontally on its side, to the medium's left as she beats it, while the
barrel stands upright, to her right front. The sounds on the left half
of the altar are visibly human-made, produced through vocal chords
and by the rhythmic beating of the large drum. In contrast, the sound
produced on the right half of the altar is produced invisibly and not
considered human-made.

The configuration is a familiar one. In votive paintings hanging in
the Shinden (where the kamado rite usually takes place), the female
medium is depicted on the left side of the mountain, below the male
god of the mountain, Akakura Daigongen, who stands above her on
the mountain's right side. Similarly, during the kamado rite, the medium (facing the altar and the mountain) sits on the altar's left side,
while the cooking pot, into which the many mountain kami enter,
stands elevated on the platform's right side. This aural exchange transaction produces the effects sought in shugyō and in the "Saigi, Saigi"
chant—bodies beautifully free of all obstructions. As the true voice
of the kami radiates out through the shrine in a continuous, unobstructed fashion, the kami's sound seems to ripple through the wor-

shipers' bodies. As the gods "speak," all members of the congregation must hurriedly stand in line and give an offering into the resonating barrel. With determined effort, each worshiper throws in a handful of raw rice and salt, intoning her or his quiet requests to the kami. At the ceremony's conclusion, each worshiper receives a small stamped packet of this semicooked rice to take home, to be consumed by all members of the household. Within the boiling barrel, the individual rice grains commingle and transform, just as the worshipers commingle and transform within the shrine over the course of the ritual. Each worshiper takes home, in effect, a sample of this symbolic commingled congregation as a protective substance to be incorporated into the bodies of the entire shrine community.

In her study of Japanese mediumship, Blacker (1975) argues that during her initiation, the novice medium must "become" the hot male divinity (usually, Fudō or the dragon deity Ryūjinsama) to whom she is ritually married. In this respect, each Cooking Pot Ceremony evidently reenacts the performing kamisama medium's initiation into mediumship. The boiling pot evokes the fiery god, Fudō Myōō, and stands as an externalized image of the medium's body, intensely "heated" by conjugal alliance with her tutelary divinity. The pot also seems to recall the rice cooking and rice serving instruments Japanese mediums bring to their initiation—as they would to a conventional marriage. By praying in the presence of this rite, the worshipers vicariously coparticipate in the trials and blessings of the kamisama medium filled with the spirit of her tutelary consort.

The three Cooking Pot Ceremonies occupy important structural positions in the annual calendar, especially in relation to the 1 May Mountain Opening Ceremony. One Cooking Pot Ceremony is held each season, with the exception of the spring. The most important Cooking Pot rite is performed at the late-July Great Summer Festival (赤倉山神社夏季大際), precisely 275 days (the traditional northern Japanese period of human gestation) before the Mountain Opening Ceremony. A ritual act of conception, the July Cooking Pot rite inaugurates a symbolic pregnancy that culminates nine months later in the ritual rebirth of the mountain divinities.

Mountain Opening Ritual: Marriage and Rebirth

As on many other Japanese sacred mountains, a special yamabiraki or mountain opening ritual marks the start of the official mountain climbing season.[3] The Akakura Mountain Opening Ceremony is fixed to the solar calendar 1 May. By this point in the spring, the shrine itself is easily accessible by automobile, although the middle reaches of the mountain are still covered in deep snow. About one hundred people participate in the celebration each year.

After a blessing from the priest in front of the Shinden, the congregation climbs from Akakura Mountain Shrine to the Fudō Waterfall. Most years, a group of about a dozen men who carry the 250-foot rice straw rope, tied up with small strings, accompany the ascetics most of the way up the mountain. The climbers follow the standard route of mountain shugyō to the Fudō Waterfall.

As the worshipers hike up the mountain, traditional musicians (hired for the day), who lead them in a rousing performance of "Saigi, Saigi," also accompany them. In 1991 the climb took about two hours. When we came out of the forest and reached an open snowfield (several hundred yards down stream from the still obscured Fudō Waterfall), a stop was called, the small strings were untied, and the rope was stretched out so that all the pilgrims could help carry it. The priest Mr. Takeda emphasized that every person must help carry the rope. He and his helpers attached sacred zigzag paper shide streamers to the rope before we recommenced. After five minutes, we could look directly up into the great narrow gorge of Akakura, to see several other great rice straw ropes, hung by other congregations, stretching across the ravine. Above us we could see the great domes of volcanic rock that dominated the gorge, and glimpsed the (usually forbidden) path leading up to the obscured summit.

Just over Fudō-taki, deeply encased in snow, the climbers paused, keeping the rope aloft and taking care not to let any of it touch the snow-covered ground. Two groups of experienced men clambered up the two steep slopes of the gorge with mountaineering equipment. The climb in the thick snow was difficult, and it was not unusual for a man to loose his footing and tumble down the snowbank. Eventually, men on the left slope secured a guide rope—which extended from one end of the *shimenawa* (sacred rice straw) rope—to two trees high on each

19. Mountain Opening Ceremony (1 May): Congregation prays at shrine before climbing the mountain

20. Mountain Opening Ceremony: Congregation carries the unfurled shimenawa rice straw rope

slope and flung the line down. The other group on the right slope slung another guide rope around another high tree growing out of the slope; a few minutes later, they tied the guide rope to the rear end of the rope when it was brought forward. The men worked capably and efficiently, with no more talking than absolutely necessary.

After about five minutes, those holding the front end of the rope advanced forward up the left slope and began to feed the front of the rope up toward the four men high above them, who gathered around the tree and yanked on the guide rope as hard as they could. The same process was repeated on the right-hand side as the rope was pulled up to the other tree. As the groups around the trees secured the lines, another group of men held the bulk of the rope aloft in the small canyon, careful for it not to touch the snow. Then, with a great collective effort, as they shouted out "Yosh! Yosh!" (Heave! Ho!), the two crews slowly pulled up the rope in jerks, making it rise up dramatically and eventually stretch straight between the two trees, about fifty feet above the kneeling worshipers. The national Rising Sun flag hung down from the rope's center, directly over the snow-covered Fudō Waterfall. The men removed the tattered remnants of last year's rope, tossed them down to their helpers below, and then carefully descended back into the canyon.

The rope will hang over the Fudō falls for a year, marking off the most dangerous, spiritually charged upper precincts of the mountain. As the men hauled up the rope with loud, rhythmic, and exultant shouts, women quietly prepared offerings in the snow below.

Once the rope was safely hung, the shrine priest led the assembled group in prayer and song as they faced uphill, toward the summit. The remnants of the old rope were ritually burned; the ashes of this rope would later be distributed to the congregation, to be placed around the boundaries of each person's house as a protective substance during the coming year.

After the services at the snowbound waterfall were completed, the worshipers joyously descended the mountain. During the descent, the men raucously drank the *omiki* (お神酒 divinely purified sake) that had been "consumed" by the divinities at the falls. All gathered for a feast in the shrine.

The performance of this rite officially "opens the mountain," so that the ascetic exercises of shugyō may take place on its slopes for the next

21. Mountain Opening Ceremony: Lifting up the shimenawa

22. Mountain Opening Ceremony:
Attaching the shimenawa

23. Mountain Opening Ceremony: Hoisting the shimenawa

24. Mountain Opening Ceremony: Raising the shimenawa to
its final position across the gorge (another congregation's
rope and flag hang in the foreground)

six and a half months. The worshipers may now enact the Sword of Fudō rite on the twenty-eighth day of each month of the open season (except during July and August, when the congregation must participate in the Summer Festival and the Hakkōda pilgrimage).

The Rice Straw Rope: Establishing
Productive Distinctions and Resemblances

To appreciate the significance of the Mountain Opening Ceremony, it is helpful to review the symbolism of the shimenawa rice straw rope (注連縄), a ubiquitous ritual device throughout Japan. Beyond their manifest function of creating a purified, demon-repelling boundary around a sacral space or element, shimenawa in Japan have long been associated with the production of life-enhancing visibility. In a famous early passage of the *Kojiki,* one of Japan's most important mythological texts, the sun goddess Amaterasu, appalled at the defilement of her brother Susa-no-wo, retreats into a cave (or rock tomb), causing darkness to descend, dangerously, on the universe. Other gods lure her out of the cave by a mirror, which seems to present to her an image of a female deity as beautiful as she is. Once she has ventured a little out of the cave, a god quickly hangs a shimenawa between her and the cave opening, establishing the boundary beyond which she cannot cross. He thus ensures her inability to return to the cave and the continued presence of light in the universe.

My informants sometimes glossed the term *shimenawa* as "rice straw on which the roots are visible." In gathering rice straw for this ritual rope, they said, one should try to pull up the plant by its roots before it has produced rice grains; the shide of folded white paper that usually hang from a shimenawa reflect the shape of these root-tassels. The rope, in other words, makes visible the root structure associated with the sacred rice plant's germination and early development—a growth that, not insignificantly, sunlight and the coming of spring make possible, all of which emanate from the annual return of the sun goddess Amaterasu. Appropriately, the most common use of the shimenawa in Japan is at New Year's festivities, as communities look forward to the return of light, warmth, and agrarian fertility. These ropes establish a visually obvious boundary between pure and impure spaces, repelling evil and creating visible frames for proper visual perception (Brandon and Stephan 1994).

In a similar fashion, the rope hung at Akakura gorge each May helps transform the enormous Akakura gorge into a purified ritual gateway. In accordance with common practice, the old shimenawa is burned just after the new one is hoisted, removing the pollution of the old year and purifying the congregation and its environs. As in the *Kojiki*, the shimenawa rope spanning Akakura gorge signals the return of the sun goddess Amaterasu into the world. It celebrates the coming of spring and light; the soaring span centers on the Rising Sun flag, an image of the goddess herself.

Of the year's thirteen rites, the 1 May Mountain Opening is the only one that has the congregation collectively climb Akakura Mountain. In addition, it is the only ceremony held at Akakura that includes neither a Thirty-Three Kannon circuit (like the Dragon Princess and Ancestral Memorialization Rites), nor a Cooking Pot rite, nor a Sword of Fudō performance. These unusual features reflect the special function of the Mountain Opening. It must undo and reverse the spatial distinctions established half a year earlier at the Great Autumn Festival that ritually "closed" the mountain by a performance of the year's final Cooking Pot Ceremony. Carrying the great shimenawa rope up into the sacred precincts of the mountain, the worshipers transgress on the previous boundary between gods and humans and thus enable a half-year period of productive, intimate traffic between mortal and divine realms.

Unlike the three Cooking Pot Ceremonies, the Mountain Opening does not summon the kami to descend to a site inhabited by people; instead, the congregation ascends to encounter the deities of the mountain directly in their own abode. In striking contrast to the female-organized gestational symbolism of the Cooking Pot Ceremonies in summer, fall, and winter, this ascent is presented as a sexual transgression by men, who alone are authorized to raise the rope at the base of a vagina-like gorge.

In some respects, one may regard the Mountain Opening Ceremony as a ritual marriage between the male and female dragons of the mountain. Just as the two flying dragons featured in the votive paintings in the Shinden shrine face each other above or within the forested slopes of the mountain, the great rice straw rope is hoisted skyward and links the mountain's left (female) and right (male) sides. In the votive paintings, the heads of the two dragons peer out from either side of Akakura gorge, near the points from which each end of the rope is hung.

Each year, the shimenawa is fabricated in the town of Kuroishi during the same month, February, that the core worshipers gather on the mountain to perform the Dragon Princess Rite, initiating the annual ritual cycle. Now, three months later, a male-coded ritual image of the dragon is brought up the mountain to the waterfall, considered the source of the Dragon Princess's water. In effect, the female-coded "dragoness," associated with the waters of the high mountain slopes, is conjoined with the male-coded dragon. The great rice straw rope stretched over the gorge is thus a fluid signifier, simultaneously evoking the mountain domain of the gods, the rice fields of the plain below, and the vital linkage between these two realms.

Like other such ropes, the 250-foot-long shimenawa has extensive phallic associations. It begins the ascent coiled up and gradually is extended during the climb. First a dozen men carry it slung together in sections (or in some years, the whole congregation helps carry it, also keeping it slung together in bunched sections). Once they reach the open snowfield just below the gorge's opening, the entire congregation hoists up the rope on their shoulders and stretches it out in a long line. As it advances, the front end of the thick rope points directly at the narrow gorge in front of the worshipers. Just below the vaginal canyon, the front end of the rope is lifted in rhythmic spurts by the combined effort of the men up the left (female-coded) side of the gorge. As it is raised, the rope quickly changes from being low-slung and flaccid to being stretched out as tautly and as high as possible.[4]

The Mountain Opening thus recalls the mythological marriage between the indigenous Dragon Princess and the stranger male god. Yet the Akakura version of this marriage differs significantly from mainstream understandings of this ancient union. For example, at the standard Shintō Iwaki-san Jinja on the omote side of the mountain, the marriage is usually referred to as a conquest of the goddess. Each September at the public Ōyamasankei ritual on the "front" of the mountain, hundreds of men gather at the mainstream Iwaki Shrine carrying enormous phallic gohei or ritual poles. At midnight, they raucously ascend to the mountain summit, reenacting the mythic act of consummation with the indigenous mountain goddess. Significantly, on re-

turning to the shrine at the mountain's base, the men immediately retrieve their phallic poles and return with them to the plain below. As
conquerors, they should only have fleeting contact with the goddess.

In contrast, the shimenawa rope brought up the Akakura slope by
the mixed-sex Akakura Shrine congregation is only partially phallic.
Unlike the immediately retrieved ritual poles on the mountain's front
side, the great rope remains hanging for an entire year, below the great
vaginal gorge, deep in the domain of the indigenous Dragon Princess.
While the rope makes its advent as a male conqueror, it is assimilated
into the realm of the native princess and her divine kin.

The ritual marriage enacted at the Akakura Mountain Opening thus
recalls the special form of Japanese marriage known as mukoyōshi,
son-in-law adoption. Families often deploy this practice when a house
lacks a suitable male heir. They recruit a husband for one of the daughter's of the house from outside (usually from a poorer or lower-status
family) and legally adopt him into the line. He takes on his adopted
family's name and in principle abandons all fealty to his biological parents and to his natal ancestors, becoming a full member and heir of his
new family. In a sense, the adopted husband and his wife are classified
as siblings, children of the same parents.

The semi-animate rice straw rope brought up the Akakura slope
occupies the ambiguous structural position of an adopted son-in-law.
Having married the daughter of the mountain gods, he cannot take his
bride home with him, but instead must remain within her domain as a
loyal son of her parents. In turn, the entire congregation (closely identified with the rope by having helped fabricate and carry it) similarly
comes to occupy the structural position of an adopted spouse of the
mountain divinities. Having climbed from their conventional home in
the plain, they are reborn as adopted kin of the kami.

Partially for this reason, hanging the shimenawa rope over the gorge
is also structured as a cosmologized act of birth from the great mountain gorge, a feature explicitly likened to a vagina or onna no koto
(女の事). Like a curled fetus, the rope is carried in tight coils up the
mountain, to be extended only once the worshipers reach the open
field beneath the gorge.[5] The men of the congregation then attach
guide ropes around trees on opposite sides of the gorge. Some informants explicitly compared the great demanding spurts of energy required to lift the rope to the rhythmic contractions of birth. Appro-

priately, this rite of generative congress and fecundity takes place in mid-spring, amidst mating, birth, and growth in the mountainscape's animal and vegetable realms.

As noted above, the Mountain Opening rite takes place precisely 275 days—the traditional period of gestation in Japanese folk belief— after a performance of the Cooking Pot rite at the previous year's Great Summer Festival. This act of giving life to the previously slack shimenawa also "gives birth" to the young, virile, and vigorous black-haired incarnation of the mountain deity Akakura Daigongen, associated with the summer season, when the mountain is covered in thick, dark forest. This incarnation will, in effect, reign for a half-year until the young god-image is succeeded by his elder, white-haired incarnation, associated with the winter season, when the mountain is covered in white snow, at the Great Autumn Festival in November. In a sense, then, the hanging rope is structured as a ritual battle between the old year and the new, in which the men of the congregation triumph on behalf of the young incarnation of the god. Indeed, after accomplishing the difficult, athletic task of hanging the rope, the men congratulate one another on their "victory." (Significantly, the term is not used in reference to any of the other annual rituals.)

The Mountain Opening Ceremony thus epitomizes Kawai Mariko's balanced synthesis of relatively indigenous and alien cosmological forces. The fecundity of the mountain is controlled through purposive human action in a manner that bridges the two aspects of Akakura Daigongen, fusing the left and right, female and male, and natural and cultural dimensions of the divinity. As the congregation mystically participates in this ritual process of fusion, it further grafts itself into the great cosmological family of the mountain.

Death, Rebirth, and the Structure of the Year

Having considered the symbolism of the Cooking Pot and Mountain Opening rites, let us now turn to the overall structure of the ritual year at Akakura. Taken together, the year's thirteen collective rituals bind the congregation in a cosmological cycle of death and rebirth, constituting them as part of a great family made up of mortal worshipers, ancestors, and the immortal divinities. In some respects, the entire year-long ritual cycle at Akakura recalls the foundational ritual process that underlies Japanese structures of kinship and descent, the transmigration of the honored dead through cycles of death and rebirth. The classic Japanese family is defined as a group of persons linked together through repeated acts of memorialization oriented toward common ancestors. Similarly, through commonly honoring the okāsan Kawai Mariko, the shrine congregation is united as a family linked together through ties of mythic kinship.

At one level, the annual progression of rites at the shrine can be understood as a grand sequence of kuyō memorialization for the charismatic founder, Kawai Mariko, reenacting her exemplary life. This life narrative parallels the entire seasonal cycle of the mountain and also recalls the life of the Buddha, which serves as a frequent model for esoteric Buddhist rites (Inagaki 1988). At the same time, the ritual sequence binds worshipers into the mountain's invisible cosmological family by involving them in ritual dramas of repeated union, separation, and development. Spread over the course of the year, these rites reiterate the basic pattern of the human life cycle, emphasizing key moments in the reproduction of the domestic unit. The Dragon Princess Rite in February emphasizes the symbolism of initial conception, the Mountain Opening in May conjoins the symbolism of birth and of marriage, the Great Summer Festival in July evokes the triumphs of a coherent household and the conception of a new generation, and the Ancestral Memorialization in October evokes death and ascent into ancestorhood.

To begin with, the 15 February Dragon Princess Rite reenacts Kawai Mariko's spiritual conception in her mother's womb. The essence of the mountain's life-giving water is carefully confined and concentrated within an enclosed pool in a secluded room in Kawai Mariko's sub-shrine at the back of the complex. A human chain composed of about thirty-five of the shrine's most important members gathers in the depth of winter to transport water from the sacred Akakura River to the ritual bathtub. After the bathtub has been filled, the silver-colored, large metal gohei wand is once more lowered into the tub, and senior spirit mediums pray and drum to the gods to make the water pure. As they do so, the rest of the worshipers outside march in a clockwise direction around the outer boundary of the shrine complex thirty-three times, performing a miniature pilgrimage of Thirty-Three Kannonsama.[6]

The next morning, a barrel of this water is taken into the Shinden, and a willow branch (柳 *yanagi*) is placed in it. After some drumming and chanting, worshipers pour this water back into the ofuro in the Kawai Mariko shrine. As of this moment, the bathtub's water is considered to have become the "seed water" (種の水 *tane no mizu*) of the "water of the gods."

This rite reiterates the ancient Tsugaru myth, discussed in chapter 1, of the marriage between the conquering male god (variously identified as Okuninushi, Utsushikunitama no mikoto, or Sakanoue Tamuramaro) and the native Dragon Princess (variously identified as Tastubihime no mikoto, Anjuhime, Onigamisama, or Akakurasama). In the Edo-era *Iwaki-san Engi,* the "shining dragon goddess" emerged from a pool to present the conquering male divinity with a sacred jewel (see Kodate 1980; Liscutin 2000, 193). Appropriately, in the Dragon Princess Rite, indigenous water from the upper reaches of the demoness's mountain must be fertilized by the male priest, who uses a metal staff that recalls the one obtained from the demoness by the conqueror Tamuramaro. The water, in turn, is subjected to a female procreative force the next morning when a long willow branch is inserted into it.[7]

A ritual womb, the carefully enclosed ofuro of Kawai Mariko contains and concentrates the liquid (and female) essence of the mountain to bring forth new life. In this respect, the ofuro recapitulates in microcosm key qualities of the mountain itself, which serves as a repository of life-giving water for the human communities of the plain. By producing the seed water of the water of the gods, this act of ritual irrigation ensures that the merit generated by this small group in the labor of shugyō will flow equitably to all lay members of the extended congregation.

Two weeks later, the congregation performs at *Shōgatsu* (New Year) the first Cooking Pot Ceremony of the year. This symbolic birth purifies the congregation for the coming year and honors Kawai Mariko's spiritual and physical birth. Next comes the Mountain Opening Ceremony, in which worshipers raise the dragonlike rope high on Akakura mountain, thereby recalling Kawai Mariko's initial vision of the flying-dragon manifestation of Akakura Daigongen. It also honors her initial ascetic climb to the Fudō Waterfall, where she beheld the wild male form of Akakura Daigongen.

As we have seen, the Mountain Opening rite also constitutes a kind of spiritual marriage, as the phallic rice straw rope is brought up to the vaginal gorge midway up the mountain. The female Dragon Princess, associated with the upper waters of the mountain river, is conjoined with an image of the male dragon, in the form of a rope produced from the rice fields of the plain below. Like a marriage bond, the unified rope then spans the "male" and "female" sides of the mountain, connecting them for the coming year. As we have seen, this marriage closely resembles the practice of son-in-law adoption, through which an incoming male is fully grafted into the bride's descent line. Not insignificantly, Kawai Mariko insisted that her own daughter, Takeda Kimiko, marry an adopted husband, ensuring that Kimiko would become preeminent heir of her mother's house. Kimiko, in turn, arranged for her own daughter to marry an adopted husband, who in time became the shrine priest.

In a sense, the ceremony also recreates the symbolic "marriage" between the kamisama medium and her male tutelary deity, as well as the mythic liaison between the indigenous demoness and the male foreign conqueror. After the Mountain Opening rite has accomplished this conjugal symbolism, four subsequent performances of the Sword of Fudō ceremony spaced through the rest of the year further reiterate it. Like Kawai Mariko before her, the leading female spirit medium is entered by the flaming power of her spirit husband, Fudō Myōō.

In turn, the Thirty-Three Kannonsama pilgrimage throughout the entire Tsugaru peninsula in mid-June reenacts Kawai Mariko's pilgrimage on this same holy route after she had accepted the calling of the kami and begun her many years of dedicated service. The mid-July pilgrimage to Mount Taihei reenacts Kawai Mariko's subsequent southward extension of her shugyō to Akita prefecture as her fame and religious authority grew.

The 28–29 July Great Summer Festival, which includes the second and most important Cooking Pot Ceremony of the year, commemorates Kawai Mariko's founding of Akakura Mountain Shrine after the postwar constitution guaranteed freedom of worship. In turn, the 28 August Mount Hakkōda pilgrimage honors the development of Kawai Mariko's following, as the congregation retraces the pilgrimage of her leading disciple, Sugiyama Junko.

The final pair of major rites, the October Ancestral Memorialization Rite, devoted to the separation of the soul from the world of the living, and the Autumn closing ceremony, performed down on the

25. Ancestral Veneration Ceremony (October): Priest and
two kamisama spirit mediums pray at central pyre

plain, commemorate Kawai Mariko's death and her accession to the
status of ancestor. The Memorialization Rite takes place as the mountain foliage is visibly dying: the lower slopes are a profusion of red,
yellow, and gold, while the upper reaches are already barren and gray.
The community burns the three ritual pyres, associated with the three
peaks of Akakura Mountain, as it once again circumambulates the
shrine's precincts thirty-three times, sings "Saigi, Saigi," and prays for
the peaceful repose of the honored dead. As mortals prepare to withdraw from the mountain for the deep winter months, the ancestors
are, in effect, respectfully returned to their elevated abode.

The rite conjoins the beatific Bodhisattva Kannonsama, who com-
passionately guides souls toward enlightenment, and the fierce deity
Fudō, who burns away the attachments that prevent spiritual ascen-
sion. As noted above, at Akakura, Kannon is strongly associated with
the relatively indigenous female figure of Onigamisama (the Mountain Demoness) or Yama Hime (the Dragon Princess). Fudō, in turn,
is linked to the aggressive male figures of Bishamon (Vaisravana) and
the foreign conqueror Sakanoue Tamuramaro. The year began with a
rite capturing the first trickle of local water, associated with the female
dragon divinity and her gift to the alien male god. The year continued
with a ritual marriage between these male and female dragon prin-

26. Ancestral Veneration Ceremony: Worshiper circles pyre

ciples at the Mountain Opening in May. Now the year ends with the couple's return to their mountain abode.

In many respects, the ritual constitutes a transformation of the ancient fire rites of the deity Acala (the inspiration for the Japanese divinity Fudō) described in ancient Sanskrit texts. It follows the basic format of the *goma* rituals of yamabushi mountain priests, in which requests to Fudō, the fierce representative of Dainichi and the Amida Buddha, are written on wooden staves that are burned during the recitation of chanted prayers (see Reader 1991; Inagaki 1988, 51–52). The flaming pyres thus serve as visible manifestations of Fudō, who in the Five Lords Shrine painting immediately adjacent to the Kannonsama statues is shown wielding a flaming sword that burns away evil, passion, and pollution. As the flames blaze and the smoke billows heavenward, the head priest must rapidly recite multiple prayers dedicated to Fudō. Appropriately, each pyre is composed of twelve layers of four wooden sticks, each in turn comprising forty-eight pieces, recalling

27. Ancestral Veneration Ceremony: Kamisama medium
at pyre in front of Kawai Mariko's shrine

the forty-eight vows of Amida Buddha, of whom Fudō Myōō is the
earthly representative.

In addition to recalling the three volcanic peaks of Akakura Mountain and the three sacred scrolls given to Kawai Mariko by Akakura
Daigongen, the three burning pyres recreate Fudō's mythic, flaming
sword, an instrument often shown surrounded by a spiraling dragon.
Appropriately, the left-hand pyre stands in front of Ryūjinsama's
shrine, honoring the dragon form taken by the god when he emerged
from the mountain's left-hand peak. The right-hand pyre stands in
front of Kawai Mariko's shrine, commemorating the ancestral Great
Mother of the shrine community.

The central wooden column of fire, into which the priest places the
written names of each memorialized ancestor, stands directly in front
of the central statue of Shōkannonsama and recalls her great statue
on the mountain's highest, central peak. Shōkannonsama, to whom
the ceremony is officially dedicated, is made supremely beautiful by a
brocade kimono and the surrounding chrysanthemums, the flowers of
autumn and imperial splendor. As in other esoteric Buddhist rites, the
conjoining of the fearsome male Fudō and the female Kannonsama is
necessary for the souls of the departed to ascend heavenwards toward
the universal mountaintop.

As in the offering trays discussed in the next chapter, these ritual events inhabit a simultaneously macrocosmic and microcosmic scale. Although the overall structure of the ritual evokes the soul's transmigration up the world mountain, the ritual officials go to great lengths to compress the performance frame down to the immediate environs of the shrine. They are careful, for example, to improvise new lines to the "Saigi, Saigi" song of mountain ascent, referring to the precise features of the shrine that the marching congregation happens to be passing at any given moment. They thus conjoin the immediate setting of the shrine with the overarching architecture of the cosmos through which participants and their deceased relatives must travel.

The parallels and contrasts between the Ancestral Memorialization Rite in October and the Dragon Princess Rite in February prove instructive. Like the paired Dragon Princess and New Year's rites at the start of the year, the Ancestral Memorialization and Autumn Festival at the year's end are only a few weeks apart from each other. Both the Dragon Princess and the Ancestral Memorialization Rites incorporate thirty-three internal Kannonsama circuits around the shrine, and both precede a Cooking Pot rite by a few weeks. The two rites, which frame the year of performance on the mountain, also frame the cosmic cycle of life: the Dragon Princess Ceremony is oriented toward the beginning of life and emphasizes the healing power of water, while the Ancestral Memorialization ritual is oriented toward life's conclusion and emphasizes the cleansing power of fire. In this sense, the annual cycle fulfills the observation in the Akakura Prayer that "all things in the universe, everything, may be compared to water and fire."

Appropriately, the six-and-a-half-month period from the May Mountain Opening to the November Great Autumn Festival, during which the shrine community ritually reenacts the many decades of Kawai Mariko's ascetic discipline, is precisely the period during which worshipers themselves may perform mountain shugyō on Akakura, literally following the founder's steps along the rocky mountain paths. During the alternate half-year period, the one that does not commemorate Mariko's years of shugyō, the worshipers are confined to the shrine's precincts and do not perform the Sword of Fudō.

At the same time, each annual sequence also traces the journey of the soul through the six transmigratory realms of the Japanese Buddhist universe (rokudō). Not counting the three summer pilgrimages performed away from Akakura (the Tsugaru Thirty-Three Kanonsama pilgrimage in June, the Mount Taihei pilgrimage in July, and the Mount Hakkōda pilgrimage in August), the congregation enacts six major collective rites each year in the vicinity of Akakura Mountain itself. The sequence of six rites—the Dragon Princess Rite, New Year's, Mountain Opening, Great Summer Festival, Ancestral Memorialization, and Autumn Closing—corresponds to the soul's progress through the six cosmic realms. The transmigratory process as a whole is facilitated through three ritual performances of the Thirty-Three Kannon sequence, the pilgrimage route that throughout Japan reenacts the soul's journey toward enlightenment. Significantly, one Thirty-Three Kannon circuit takes place every four months, spaced out evenly through the annual cycle.

Appropriately, the collective singing of "Saigi, Saigi" marks all the major rites through which the worshipers seek to cleanse their six "openings of perception" as they move themselves, their ancestors, and especially the shrine's founder through the six transmigratory phases of existence, classically envisioned as the world mountain, Sumeru. Indeed, some worshipers explicitly compare the entire annual cycle to movement up and down a mountain. "The hardest part," explained Mrs. Takeda, "is getting to the 'top' of the year. That's the Great Summer Festival, which is the hardest thing. After that, it is much easier, like going downhill!"

The general principles of symmetry and reversibility, emphasized in the organization of each day of shugyō and in the preparation of offerings, also informs the basic organization of the ritual cycle. Each of the first five rites during the first half of the "open" season, before the Great Summer Festival, appears to be paired with a corresponding rite after the Great Festival: The Mountain Opening Ceremony with the Mountain Closing Ceremony; the May Fudō-ken with the October Fudō-ken; the June Thirty-Three Kannonsama Rite with the October Ancestral Memorialization Rite (also oriented around a Thirty-Three Kannonsama circuit); the June Fudō-ken with the September Fudō-ken; and the pilgrimage to Mount Taihei in July with the pilgrimage to Mount Hakkōda in August. The Great Summer Festival, the culmination of the ritual year, in effect stands alone at the "summit" of the year.

Making Kinship

In collectively moving the soul of the Great Mother Kawai Mariko through the great world mountain of rokudō, the congregation effectively constitutes itself as a coherent, albeit mythic, family line. As we have seen, this process partly recalls the distinctive northern Japanese mechanism for establishing kinship—bridegroom (or son-in-law) adoption (嫁養子 *mukoyōshi*). Through this process, repeatedly used by Kawai Mariko's own descendants, spouses are transformed into structural siblings, common "children" of the same house. Similarly, each and every member of the congregation helps to carry the male-coded rice straw rope up to the Dragon Princess's pool, where they are commonly assimilated into her domain. In turn, just as an adopted son-in-law cleaves to his new family line by undertaking kuyō for his bride's lineal ancestors, members of the Akakura Mountain Shrine community enter into their new family by venerating the gods of Akakura and memorializing a common ancestor, Kawai Mariko.

Significantly, over the course of the ritual year, marriage is evoked from both the male and female perspective. In hanging the great shimenawa rope above the Fudō Waterfall, the congregation primarily takes the conquering male part, as they marry the male Dragon Deity to the relatively indigenous female Dragon Princess. In contrast, the female perspective on marriage seems to be emphasized each time the congregation gathers to perform the ancient shamanic Cooking Pot Ceremony. These rites of spiritual marriage and symbolic sexual congress in turn enable a vital relationship of filiation or consanguinity between successive annual cycles, as each year, in effect, "gives birth" to the next.

To review our discussion thus far: the twin pivots of this overlapping structure, which span two annual cycles, are the 29 July Great Summer Festival, at which the most important Cooking Pot rite is performed, and the subsequent 1 May Mountain Opening Ceremony, at which a great shimenawa rice straw rope (associated with a fetus, its umbilical cord, and the phallus) is hung over the mountain gorge. The July Cooking Pot performance (in which all members of the congregation are expected to participate) is structured as a cosmic act of conception, which productively fuses mortal and divine as well as male and female elements. This union is brought to fruition during the next year's cycle, precisely 275 days later, in a great ceremony of symbolic birth at the next 1 May Mountain Opening Ceremony. (As noted above, 275 days is the traditional Northern Japanese reckoning of the length of human gestation.)[8]

The overall effect of this ritual of magical rebirth each May is to reinvigorate both orders of kinship, on and off the mountain. The new rope is made of rice straw from the previous year's harvest, while the old rope (made from the products of the year before last's harvest) is ceremonially burned and its ashes distributed for placement around the corners of each worshiper's home. Just as the rope guarded the borders between the realms of humans and kami, so do the purified ashes guard the borders of each household of the congregation. In such a manner are the macrocosmic ritual dynamics of the mountain transacted down to specific households in the plain below.

The annual ritual cycle thus coordinates between the dynamics of the worshiper's kinship group and the macrocosmic kinship scheme of the mountain. Serious engagement with the cosmological family of the mountain ideally prepares the worshiper to return, purified and rejuvenated, to her or his family's affairs. Having honored the divinities and the shrine's collective "mother," the worshiper may productively concentrate on serving proximate family ancestors and living relations. This balanced pattern also characterizes a typical day of shugyō on the mountain: each morning the ascetic climbs the mountain to honor the kami and then, that afternoon, back at the shrine, the believer memorializes her or his own family ancestors.

The Spiraling Dragon: Kinship and the Power of Mythic Recombination

The complex ritual image of the dragon deity Ryūjinsama, which informs nearly every ceremony of the annual cycle, accomplishes the periodic movement back and forth between conventional and cosmological kinship. Although this precise symbolic deployment of the dragon is peculiar to Akakura Mountain Shrine, the imagery stays consistent with broad themes in Japanese and East Asian dragon symbolism. If the mountain (山 yama) is the basic mediator between this world and the other world (Yamaguchi 1991), then dragons function as exemplary mediators for mortals between the mountain base and the mountaintop. This results in part from the fact that dragons are mobile models of mountains, one of their principal abodes. Their scaled surface is as hard as rock, and their layered scales recall the accumulation of boulders in a volcanic gorge. Like volcanoes, they emit fire, and like the world mountain that contains the cosmos, they frequently play with an orb, jewel, or "gem" (tama) containing the entire universe, which is also associated with the human soul (Blacker 1975, 43; Smyers 1999, 124–25, 167–68).

The mediating capacity of the dragon derives from its status as a manifestly human-made composite mythical figure. The dragon is composed of qualities appropriated from truly existing animals, such as the horns of a stag, the face of a camel, the neck of a snake, the stomach of a huge mollusk, the claws of an eagle, the scales of a carp, the paws of a tiger, and the ears of a bull. In many East Asian artistic and religious traditions, the dragon embodies the human capacity for creative bricolage and symbolic action.[9]

At Akakura, the recombinatory capacities of the dragon have been put to the service of mythic kinship. As a manifestation of Akakura Daigongen, the doubled dragon fuses the conquering male figures of Sakanoue Tamuramaro, Bishamon, and the yamabushi priest with the relatively indigenous, feminine demoness Onigamisama. The paired dragons emphatically represent hybrid products of human labor. The female dragon emerges out of the Dragon Princess Rite in February, during the same period that her companion male dragon image (the shimenawa rope) is fabricated in the plains below. At any time of year, painting or carving a votive image of a dragon is considered an especially meritorious act at Akakura.[10]

By building these icons of the mythical species, the biologically unrelated congregation members constitute themselves as "kin" with one another and with the gods. The dragon image, a synthetic construct, is a particularly appropriate mechanism for representing and producing new relations of kinship, inasmuch as kinship itself is the fundamental human process of arbitrary synthesis and recombination.[11]

As individual human beings create and guide this composite mythic dragon couple toward a ritual marriage, they, too, become forged together as members of a collective family. This process depends on appropriating another common theme in East Asian religious thought —the dragon's spiritual ascent up Sumeru, a flight which in esoteric Buddhist traditions commonly represents the soul's passage into enlightenment (Blacker 1975, 177–79; Stein 1990, 232–41). Several paintings of spiraling, flying dragons adorn the central Shinden shrine room. Outside, to the immediate left of the Shinden's main entrance, visitors confront a standing stone pillar around which is twined an upwardly ascending dragon. The shrine's founder Kawai Mariko was first summoned to Akakura by her vision of Akakura Daigongen in the form of a flying dragon that spiraled out of the mountain's left peak, an image represented in a votive painting over the front door of the Shinden. As we have seen, this founding dream narrative is also concretized in the left-hand rear subshrine of the complex, dedicated to the Dragon Deity.[12]

In addition to fabricating the dragon in material and architectural form, worshipers also enact the dragon's mythic movement with their ambulatory, physical bodies. The year begins on its first full moon with the Rite for the Powerful Mountain Dragon-Princess's Great Deities' Medicine (Dragon Princess Rite), at which the dragon's river water is collected to serve for the year as the "seed water" of the kami no mizu, the medicinal water of the gods. The core worshipers transporting the holy water stretch out in a line from the river to the Kawai Mariko Shrine, forming with their bodies a tangible image of the dragon's elongated shape. Immediately afterward, the group performs a collective spiral of ascent, marching in single file as they circle the shrine precincts thirty-three times and singing the mountain ascent song. Like the composite dragon spiraling toward heaven, their queued individual bodies wrap around the symbolic circuit of the cosmic mountain to form a single synthetic "body."

Two weeks later, at the New Year's festival, the congregation again performs a rite of ascent, with the year's first performance of the Cooking Pot rite, which will be repeated at the summer and autumn festivals. Although the dragon god Ryūjinsama is not explicitly referred to in the Cooking Pot Ceremony, it conforms to the basic structure of a miraculous, fiery ascent usually associated with dragon flight. As noted above, the kamado functions both as a miniature mountain, especially the world mountain Sumeru, and as a living model of the fierce fire deity Fudō, the tutelary guardian of most kamisama spirit mediums. The heated barrel within which trapped steam rises recalls the common image of Fudō as a sword around which spirals a great, fire-breathing dragon (Stein 1990, 256–58; Blacker 1975, 177–79). Indeed, Fudō's ritual sword, the *Fudō-ken,* is carefully placed on the Shin-den altar on the morning of the Great Summer Festival, just before the most important Cooking Pot performance of the year. A long line of worshipers, who must rapidly snake around the shrine room, recipro-cate the miraculous appearance of the god.

Implicit flying dragon symbolism also characterizes physical hu-man movement during the 1 May rite of Mountain Opening. Not only does the congregation transport the long, serpentine shimenawa rope; it must also walk in single file up the mountain to the Fudō falls, the source of the Dragon Princess's medicinal waters. As my friends and in-formants often told me, the act of carrying the shimenawa each year re-united the worshipers as a family (*kazoku*). Significantly, a ritual image of the male-aspect dragon, itself woven by the congregation from thou-sands of disparate rice straw stalks, creates this symbolic unity, as does the fact that every member of the congregation must hold the rope as it stretches out in a long line toward the waterfall. United at the Mountain Opening Ceremony, the integrated image of the male and female dragon couple will span the great gorge over the waterfall for the coming year.

In turn, the two summer mountain pilgrimages each begin with a short climb to a dragon shrine, where the worshipers importune the guardian dragon deities for permission to climb each mountain. (The Mount Taihei pilgrimage is itself preceded by a short dawn ritual in the Kawai Mariko building at Akakura, where the congregation is blessed by water in the tub filled during the February Dragon Princess rite.)

The year's final ritual observance on the mountain, the October An-cestral Memorialization Rite, reiterates the theme of fiery, dragonlike ascent. Three pyres are constructed—in front of the Dragon Shrine, the Shōkannon statue, and the Kawai Mariko Shrine. As the worship-ers pray to the fire god Fudō, fire and smoke billow heavenward. Even more dramatically than the three heated cooking pot rituals of the an-nual cycle, these three memorial pyres resemble the familiar image of the blazing Fudō Myōō, the earthly representative of Dainichi who manifests himself as a dragon and burns away all the ties that prevent enlightenment. As the three pyres burn, the congregation once again enacts an upward spiral through its parading bodies by circling the en-tire shrine area thirty-three times. In so doing, the worshipers perform

28. Pilgrims from Akakura climb Mount Hakkōda

29. Akakura pilgrims praying on Mount Hakkōda at
the gorge also known as "Akakura"

the most important obligation of Japanese kinship—venerating their ancestors and praying for their safe repose.

Labor, Sexuality, and Gender in the Annual Ritual Cycle

As in regular structures of kinship and lineal descent, the dragonlike ritual mechanisms for producing cosmological kinship emerge out of the careful management of labor, gender, and sexuality. The Mountain Opening Ceremony constitutes an erotically charged ritual of marriage and birth centered on a great shimenawa rice straw rope produced by many persons' coordinated labor. The dedicated worshipers carrying the rope are bound together as cosmological kin through a ritual image of a conjoined dragon pair, which itself is fabricated out of thousands of disparate rice straw stalks into a single entity. Like human-made bonds of kinship, the composite shimenawa rope appears naturally whole and unitary. An embodied image of the congregation's collective, pure-hearted agrarian efforts of the previous year, the rice straw rope helps establish for the coming year a productive, semi-permeable boundary between the upper, rain-giving mountain and the fields of the plains below. Produced out of the plant stalks of the previous year's rice harvest, the rope thus safeguards each household's agricultural efforts.

Similarly, the venerated products of rice cultivation are deployed in the Cooking Pot rite, which is itself a transformation of women's daily domestic labor practices. As she partakes of the ritual's upward spiraling heat, each worshiper forcefully throws grains of rice (and salt) into the pressurized boiling pot, evoking processes of insemination and gestation. Nine months later, the womblike pot, a miniature version of the sacred volcanic mountain and the fire-breathing dragon, will give birth to next year's rice straw shimenawa as it is hung high over the waterfall of Fudō.

In a comparable fashion, the Ancestral Memorialization Rite exhibits pronounced conjugal symbolism that leads to the enhanced valuation of the labor energies which the community has collectively invested within the mountain "storehouse" (倉 *kura*). In front of the statue of the female Bodhisattva Kannonsama, a pyre evoking the male fire god Fudō and his flaming dragon incarnation is burned. Meanwhile, the worshipers march energetically in the Thirty-Three Kannonsama circuit, performing a symbolic ascent of the world mountain. The combination of this symbolic labor and conjugality helps move ancestors through the cycles of transmigration.

Like labor and procreative efforts invested in family enterprises, these generative rites should return with interest the labor effort invested by worshipers. The Mountain Opening rite reestablishes a productive separation between the realms of mortals and immortals, allows the congregation to feast on food and rice wine blessed by the mountain divinities, and produces ashes (from the previous year's rope) that guard the boundaries of each worshiper's house. The ritual of the Cooking Pot (an instrument that in other contexts represents the prosperity of a household) produces small packets of partially cooked rice distributed through the congregation as prophylactic medicine that will safeguard each family's health and welfare for the coming months. In turn, as it closes a year of conscientious ritual participation, the Ancestral Memorialization Ceremony brings special benefits back to the human kinship order. As the three pyres burn, the worshipers hope to have accumulated sufficient spiritual potency that their prayers will be fully efficacious and that their properly venerated ancestors will bring blessings to their living families.

The annual cycle at Akakura Mountain Shrine is composed of overlapping narrative sequences elegantly coordinated through the year's major ritual observances. These sequences include: (a) the exemplary life of the charismatic founder Kawai Mariko; (b) the cyclical passage of the seasons on Akakura Mountain; (c) the related alternation between the elderly white-haired incarnation of Akakura Daigongen and his youthful black-haired incarnation; (d) the discipline of shugyō; (e) the conception, gestation, birth, adoptive marriage, and rebirth of the mythical dragon couple, which evokes the proliferating strands of human kinship; (f) the repeated death and rebirth of souls as they travel through the realms of transmigration (rokudō); and, finally (g) the union of relatively indigenous and foreign cosmological forces, as evoked in the paired dragon couple, the union of Kannonsama and Fudō, and the mythic link between the demoness Onigamisama and Sakanoue Tamuramaro. The long-term effect of these interlaced symbolic processes is to unite the disparate worshipers into a mythic, composite family at one with the divinities and ancestors that inhabit the sacred mountain.

As in human biological reproduction and conventional kinship, successful movement through this annual cycle of ritual kinship depends on careful coordination of male and female efforts, exemplified by the comingled presence of male and female elements in both the single Mountain Opening Ceremony and the three Cooking Pot rites. Unlike the thrice repeated and female dominated Cooking Pot rites, the singular Mountain Opening rite climaxes in a dramatic act performed solely by men, who hoist up a great rice straw rope in a cosmic act of male sexual arousal and penetration. Yet even this seemingly "male" rite depends on partnership between hard-working men and women and recalls the process of birth itself. In turn, the New Year's rite, the Great Summer Festival and the Autumn Festival all culminate in ritual action by women, playing on the symbolism of marriage, conception, gestation, and birth. As it happens, performances of a Thirty-Three Kannonsama circuit, venerating the female deity that safeguards pregnancy and childbearing, directly precede each of these three rites of symbolic birth. Spaced out along the 275-day period that runs from the Great Summer Festival to the Mountain Opening, the three Cooking Pots initiate and nurture the gradual passage of a cosmological pregnancy, culminating in the simultaneous birth and sexual union of the 1 May ascent. Yet even these quintessentially "female" rites depend on careful ritual purification of the performance space by male Shintō priests.

The entire mountain of Akakura may thus be regarded as a womb of cosmic proportion, which embodies the opposing principles—autochthonous and foreign, female and male, living and ancestral—necessary to its reproduction. Year after year in this vital androgynous space, dedicated, hard-working worshipers are collectively reconceived, nurtured, and reborn as a mythic family, united as pure "children" of the gods.

4

m i n i a t u r e   m o u n t a i n s

Offerings and Exchange

To offer and humble oneself to the supreme deity Amaterasu. To turn one's face to heaven and offer precious things. —Opening lines of the Akakura Prayer

I asked the kami, although my body was very tired, and the kami replied, "Yes." I made the offerings to the kami, you know, and I said, "Kamisama, Kamisama, this is a bit impolite, but I have many children. Please grant me your power so that my children will be outstanding in other people's eyes and may I work for this." And I said to the kami, "If I work with these hands, let there be money." And I went alone, and I cried to the kami, "Wai, wai, wai." That was all I could say. —Narita Emiko, 28 July 1992

The Art of Offerings: Labor, Exchange, and Beauty

This chapter explores the fabrication and presentation of offerings at Akakura, the foundational practices through which worshipers estab-lish and maintain productive relations with divinities and ancestors. A novice worshiper at the shrine is first taught the skill of making offerings, which condenses the basic principles and aesthetics of all other ritual and labor actions within the Akakura tradition. As veteran worshipers instruct her in the representational and imitative practices of offerings, the apprentice is believed to become increasingly open to the transformative capacities of the kami, entering into a state of attentive readiness that will serve her well as she performs solitary disciplinary exercises on the rugged mountain slopes.

Akakura worshipers emphasize that a well-presented offering alters the "heart and mind" of the donor. Many friends and informants have told me that as they arranged offerings, they would nervously wonder about the presented elements' sufficiency, and that their minds were full of anxious thoughts about difficulties at home and at work. Like Mrs. Narita quoted above, supplicants at times cannot even bring themselves to articulate their wishes and may simply cry out to the divinities as they begin an offering. However, worshipers note that once the offerings have been properly laid out, presented, and accepted by the kami, these worries tend to fade away. Many describe a feeling of "warmth" and "quietness" after a successful presentation. Some even compare this sense to the pacific contentment experienced by a small child in the presence of its mother. As one friend told me, "Gofu is the purest food; it is like milk from one's mother."

By projecting varied sentiments and concerns into the offering and submitting it to a force external to herself, the Akakura worshiper is able to reenter the state of unconditional dependence associated with early childhood; she becomes able to receive *amae* (甘え indulgence) from the kami and in turn becomes better able to indulge other worshipers. The learned choreography of service and offerings emphasizes skills of imaginative reversibility, of subordinating one's immediate human desires so as to anticipate the needs and perspectives of the divinities. Great efforts are taken to ensure that these offerings are visually pleasing and eye-catching to the gods. Succulent vegetables and fruits should be clean and shiny. Fish should be fresh and glistening, the tail tied back in a beautiful arch. By giving such offerings, worshipers seek to become "beautiful like the kami."

The graceful ritual presentation of *sakaki* branches, performed several times each year in the Inner Sanctuary, exemplifies this aesthetic of flexibility and reversibility. At the climax of a service, one worshiper at a time is called up to the altar to present a green sakaki branch decorated with a white paper shide streamer. First, the priest hands the leafy branch to the worshiper who cradles it in her outstretched left hand, her right fingers balancing it on the top, so that the outer edge of the leaf faces the worshiper and the branch portion faces the priest (or, more precisely, the altar and the divinities). As she presents the branch to the altar, the worshiper must carefully turn it 180 degrees in a clockwise manner. She rotates her right and left hands around an invisible vertical axis in the middle of the branch so that its base no longer faces her, but instead confronts the priest and the implied vantage point of the divinity. In so doing, she redirects the root of the branch to the kami, the source of all life and growth.

As Mauss (1954) argues, the gift's capacity to mediate between persons is enabled by the manner in which it embodies in its material form the persons and the overall social relationship signified. Appropriately, the evergreen sakaki leaf branch shares qualities with both human donor and divine receiver. It approximates the size of the human hand that presents it, and has serrated edges and visible veins that recall the fingers and palm lines of humans. Just as a human hand and arm project from a body, the leaf and branch project from a tree trunk. Like the kami who eternally preside over the realm of nature, the sakaki remains perpetually green and shiny. Furthermore, the sakaki branch's partial reversibility embodies the mirrored relationship between human giver and divine receiver and allows for a mutual transposition between them. In such a manner, the sakaki effectively mediates between person and divine being. A condensed image of the donor's projected body and selfhood, the branch is rearranged to take on qualities (including directional orientation) of the kami, so that the human donor may, by extension, take on broader qualities of the divinity. In performing the aesthetic labor of presenting offerings, the worshiper is believed gradually to take on more and more of the gods' luminous, streamlined qualities.

As mediating operators between human and divine structural domains, these offerings should bear the traces of their human presenters' disciplined labor. They are often the products of agrarian and domestic work and must be prepared with great care. Mrs. Narita recalled that in order to determine where she should perform ascetic discipline, she would offer rice to the kami each morning, pleading with them to write their instructions in the sacred grains: "Because I offer rice like this, in the morning on this [tray], please write on this rice where I should go for gyō, and first of all, first what I should do. Please write on the rice that I have offered, on this, like this" (she gestures as if writing on an uncooked pile of rice).

Although standard Shintō and Buddhist offering practices are often followed at the shrine, the best style of offering, worshipers often told me, comes directly "from the heart," under direct inspiration from the divinities. When making an offering, Narita would speak the following words, which she explained had been taught to her by the kami themselves: "'The kamisama of three reigns . . . come down from heaven. Let them come down from the heavens. And with sake, candles, and the seven grasses [grains]. We offer these things to the kami, please receive these offerings!' That's how the kami said I should pray."

When the labor put into these objects or media is insufficiently directed, not of one "heart-mind" (*kokoro*), the offering will fail. If the giver is distracted from total purposefulness, the presented substances will not embody the proper relationships between persons and mystical forces and thus have diminished or negligible efficacy. Conversely, when worshipers make their offerings with proper discipline, the latter are "beautiful" and come to the full attention of the kami.

Rice, Labor, and Being "Seen by the Gods"

During the important July 1992 conversation in the Shinden sanctuary, the spirit medium Mrs. Narita articulated the basic principles governing exchange and offering in the Akakura system, with particular emphasis on the transacted medium of rice.[1] She began her autobiographical narrative with her childhood in a rice-poor fishing village. Unable to feed her, her family placed her as a komori (nurse-maid) with other families from the age of nine. As an adolescent, she first came to the gods' attention through her disciplined involvement with the production of rice itself, in the fields of wealthy landlords:

> You know, this house [kamado, lit., cooking pot] had no one to do the job. So that's why they asked me to work. So I finished the job quickly. I like to make them happy. I only think like that. I only think like that. I worked with that feeling in the fields, and the kami saw this, the kami from the heavens, the kami from the mountains,

also they saw this, and they saw my feelings. I was not tired at all. Then suddenly the job was done. The job was done, and I was not at all tired. I could run and walk, and during rice-cutting season, all I did was eat rice, go to the toilet, and cut rice again. And I would quickly cut 140 *shima* [bunches of rice] and stand them up, and pile it into a forty-six–*kan* [3.75 kilogram] pile, and then turn it over, carry it, and pile and tie it like this, and carry it like that.

During this period, she proudly told us, she never got ill, and she made more money than anyone else. Absolute concentration, dedication, rapidity, and efficiency characterized her work in the rice fields, the very same qualities that she and other kamisama mediums emphasize must govern the performance of ascetic discipline on the sacred mountain:

> Then we cut rice, and kept on cutting, and cutting, and cutting, and cutting. The rice fell down with a thud, you turned it over, and on like that, and soon it's dinnertime. You put a stack of rice down and immediately turn it over here, finish, and stand them up in a line, and then it's all ready to put on the stick. So how quickly the job is done depends on how much effort you put into it. It will be clear whether you make rapid progress or no progress.

Rice constitutes a "pure" medium of communication because of its self-evidence. The amount of work done in the rice field immediately registers in the size of one's pile of cut stalks. Such "authentic" hard work becomes its own reward, and stood in contrast to the conventional alienated peasant or factory labor familiar to her listeners. In Narita's words, "I love to work. I never thought [in the rice fields of the landlord] that I was working for anyone but myself."

Having apprehended her diligence and her "true feelings" working in the rice fields, the gods then commanded her to labor for them on the mountain by writing in her rice. She recalls, "Every morning, I found written on the rice [the words]: 'Worship the kami.'" Subsequently, each time she wondered how to perform ascetic discipline, she would beseech the kami to write her instructions in her rice. Guided by the messages in the katakana syllabary that subsequently appeared in her rice each morning, she went on to have numerous revelatory visions and dreams on the mountain. Rice, the product of her dedicated labor and her sincere kokoro, functioned as a supreme medium of knowledge and consciousness through which she gained access to deeper truths.

This intimate linkage between rice, labor, and mental life also informed Narita's repeated contrasts between the "good" kami of Akakura and the "bad" Inari deity and its familiar, the feminine fox spirit, kitsune. Inari and kitsune, she stressed, are prone to possess people in an unproductive fashion, filling their mind with false images, offering only the illusory appearance of wealth and pleasure. Seduced by Inari in the form of a beautiful woman, a man may dream a whole life of riches and worldly success, only to wake up in a ditch, naked, impoverished, and bereft of all hope. The deceptive Inari, Narita insisted, is "of different mouth and heart," whereas the Akakura divinities are straightforward, "of one heart, one mouth."[2] Ascetic discipline on the mountain, she reiterated, demanded the consistent genuine labor that characterizes good work in rice fields. In contrast, since the benefits promised by Inari are not gained through real labor and do not contribute to the growth and redistribution of rice, they do not lead to a virtuous cultivation of mind and spirit.

Narita's passage into the deep knowledge of senior mediumhood was, in turn, anticipated by a miraculous gift of rice. One evening she discovered that the futon mattress that she kept at the mountain shrine had mysteriously filled with small bundles of rice, sent by the gods as a reward for her devoted service: "there were many little bags, like this one, full to bursting, that were in my futon where I sleep. When I was beginning to get ready for bed and unfolding my futon, it was folded in four parts like this, you know. There were absolutely no wrinkles in it because it was full of rice."

Significantly, this miraculous gift appeared inside her shrine futon, on which she slept when receiving important revelatory dreams at night. In the past, arising each morning from this mattress, she would find divine messages written in rice. At that point, rice, the medium of pure labor and transcendental knowledge, entered into her immediate space of sleep and productive dreaming.

Narita's narrative of the futon anticipated the structure of the shamanic Cooking Pot rice-cooking ceremony that she would perform the next morning in the Inner Sanctuary. This performance would publicly signal her new status as the shrine's preeminent medium. In both the Cooking Pot rite and the futon narrative, the gods work miraculously to fill a container to absolute capacity with a communicative medium. (Suggestively, Mrs. Narita characterized the futon with the Tsugaru-ben dialect term, *pan,* which means "filled to a bursting, rounded extent.") During possession episodes, kamisama spirit mediums are expansively filled with the divine spirit and speak for the gods in a strange, unearthly voice. Similarly, during the Cooking Pot Ceremony, the boiling rice pot emits an animated hum, considered to be the ineffable "voice" of the gods in their mysterious language, which also expands out into space, permeating all precincts of the shrine. Symbolic miniature mountains, the cooking pot, and the futon function as models of the medium's mind and body, into which the communicative forces of the divinities stream, building up pressure until the gods' messages must burst out into the human world.

At the end of the rite, the partially cooked rice, folded within white paper envelopes, is redistributed to all members of the congregation. Similarly, instead of sleeping in her futon (and thereby selfishly exploiting its contents), Mrs. Narita insisted that this precious futon rice, a gift from the gods, remain undisturbed in the mattress just as she found it, until she could redistribute it to everyone in the shrine:

> When it's rice made by the kami, you can't eat it alone, you have to give it to other people. As you can see, if you try to be greedy, it's bad, it's no good if you don't share with everyone. If something is done for me and I just take it, it's no good. I'm an old-fashioned kind of person, I come from a fishing family, and if you have enough to eat for yourselves, then you give the rest to others so they can also eat. Then, if you, or even you over there, receive something rare and precious from a friend, then, the next time, when it's time to return the favor, you dare not simply buy something and bring it. I hate that, and I want to ask, "Why did you just buy something to bring?" I am that kind of person. The kami see and understand my feelings.

Narita's narrative exemplifies a basic hierarchical logic of exchange in the Akakura Shrine community and in similar kamisama-oriented networks in modern Tsugaru. Wage labor and a pervasive commodity culture threaten to disrupt extended kinship-based networks of production and distribution, isolating the person from kin, ancestors, and the gods. Purchased food items threaten to alienate interpersonal relations and productive links to the divinities. In contrast, disciplined regular labor by a person may open her or him up to more fundamental exchanges with the kami, in which concretized tokens of one's labor are offered to the gods and plentifully returned, often in the form of miraculous vision, insight, and knowledge. Mrs. Narita's hard physical labor in the rice fields allowed her inner mind and emotions to be "seen" by the gods, who granted her magnificent revelatory visions as she performed austerities on their mountain. As a later sign of their blessings, the gods placed in her futon abundant amounts of rice, the very substance she had labored to produce and the very medium through which they had made her conscious of their presence. Like the spiritual blessings of her possessed body, the freely circulating rice from the ritual barrel and from the mythic futon bursts out from concealed spaces to be consumed in the light of day by human worshipers.[3]

Suggestively, Mrs. Narita summed up her life-long involvement with rice by observing, "If you work honestly, and believe in the kami, then I am the mirror, am I not?" She delivered these words in the shrine's Inner Sanctuary below the sacred mirror found in most Shintō shrines. This divine instrument recalls an important episode in the ancient mythological text, the *Kojiki* (chapters 15–17). Since, as we shall see, this story deeply resonates in the collective imagination of many Akakura worshipers, it is worth considering in some detail.

The rice god Susa-no-wo and his sister, the sun goddess Amaterasu, commit incest and bear children. Having violated the principles of exogamy, the male god enters into a destructive rage, violating the integrity of the agricultural and livestock resources that he had previously protected. He breaks down the ridges between rice paddies, covers up their irrigation ditches, defecates in the palace hosting the harvest festival, and skins a pony backwards. Each of these acts, like incest itself, violates a set of oppositions and boundaries necessary for the continued survival of the community. Offended and terrified (and perhaps having undergone a symbolic death), his sister flees into a cave, leaving the world in darkness. As in the depth of winter, no crops can grow. Light is only restored to the world when the gods devise a trick to fool Amaterasu into leaving her hiding place. Fashioning a great mirror and setting it before the cave, they laugh and play uproariously, claiming to worship a goddess greater than Amaterasu. Amaterasu, tricked into believing she sees a rival sun goddess in the mirror, emerges from the cave. The gods block her return into it by hanging a magic rope between her and the cave entrance. They also exorcise Susa-no-wo. The magic mirror thus restores sunlight and the growth of rice plants to the universe (Phillipi 1968, 76–86).

We will return to the pervasive metaphor of the mirror in the final chapter, but for the moment, let us note that in comparing herself to "the mirror," Narita in effect argues that her life devoted to dedicated labor in the rice fields has also helped bring divine blessings into the domain of agricultural production, restoring violated balances and oppositions. In the Cooking Pot rite and in the rice-filled futon episode, she distributes life-giving rice to all worshipers. Like the ritual processes that she supervises, Narita herself continuously makes visible the invisible qualities of the divinities, encouraging them to move from their hidden quarters atop the mountain to the proximate environs of shrine, rice field, and village. As her narratives emphasize, she makes the gods' vivid mental images and life-giving energies accessible to ordinary humans through her tireless physical engagements with the material landscape that the gods themselves have created and by giving back to the gods offerings that encapsulate her labor and their blessings.

In short, offerings and exchange transactions place labor and transcendence in a positive dialectical relationship to one another. Dedicated work should allow the worshiper to project her sincere kokoro into the great "storehouse" of the mountain and its resident divinities; their blessings, in turn, should stimulate further productive human work, enabling images and qualities of this sacred landscape to reenter the worshiper's mind and body.

The Water of the Gods as Categorical Solvent

Along with rice, kami no mizu constitutes one of the most important symbolic media in the shrine complex. As the novice quickly learns, there exist two different kinds of kami no mizu at Akakura. The most common kind comes from a special tap in the central kitchen sink (to the front right as one enters from the main living quarters). This is the only water that human worshipers are supposed to drink, and the only water presented to the kami and to ancestors. The second kind of water of the gods is stored in the rear Kawai Mariko Shrine in a deep basin called the ofuro. As noted in chapter 3, ascetics hand-carry this water from the mountain stream during the Dragon Princess Ritual in February, when the priest and major spirit mediums bless it as seed water with a special metal gohei. This water is bottled and distributed to all members of the congregation as "medicine." Three times a year, this water is boiled in the Cooking Pot Ceremony, as a senior spirit medium summons the kami to manifest their presence audibly.

Older worshipers approvingly noted my frequent thirst for kami no mizu during shugyō as evidence that I was leaving my old ways behind and striving to become "more like the kami." Fumiko often told me that learning to present divine water was the first, and perhaps the most important, lesson of shugyō. "When we give this water back to the kami, everything changes. We are becoming different, closer." She then elaborated, with reference to the bridge the pilgrim crosses each morning to begin ascetic climbs on the mountain, "That is why giving the water is such important work. It is just like crossing the bridge." Her linkage of kami no mizu and ascetic circuits on the mountain was highly suggestive, for the disciplinary pathways of shugyō are in many respects modeled on the basic flows of this divine liquid, which functions as a complex symbolic solvent and mediator in the shrine system. Kami no mizu breaks down conventional categorical distinctions between gods and humans, the living and the dead, above and below, and it helps enhance fruitful affinities between persons and supernatural beings. The effectiveness of shugyō, like the shrine's annual ritual cycle, depends on worshipers, priests, and spirit mediums carefully mobilizing these dissolving and recombinatory potentials of divine water.

Commensality with the Kami

In addition to water, worshipers give great attention to their food consumed during shugyō. Every food item consumed is first presented to the kami on an altar, so that they may partake of it and transform it into gofu. I here briefly note some of the key qualities of these foodstuffs. To begin with, one should eat and drink only that which meets the divinities' standards. Once, when I was working in the shrine's kitchen during my first phase of shugyō, I asked Fumiko why no one ate red meat at the shrine. Was it because it was healthier not to? She looked at me momentarily puzzled, and then replied that it had nothing to do with health as such. It was because the kami wanted the worshipers' bodies to be "cleansed/beautiful" (*kirei*). She added that such "beautiful" bodies would give greater pleasure to the gods.

The kami continuously receive "pleasing" food offerings, given by members of the congregation during individual visits or during large festivals and collective ceremonies. It is taken as self-evident that these more "pleasing" foods were water, sake, rice, vegetables, fish (especially auspiciously colored red fish), and other seafood. Chicken, pork, beef, garlic, and onions were nowhere to be found. No one ever articulated why some foods were acceptable and some unacceptable. Beyond the general Shintō aversion to blood and "unclean" foods, I surmise that "good foods" serve as icons of the basic boundaries and regenerative cycles instituted and managed by the gods. Rainwater and snow flow down the mountain, creating rice fields and rice, and ultimately they flow down to the sea. The most appropriate offerings to the kami are thus condensations of various moments in this basic cycle: rice and watery vegetables (such as radishes or melons) irrigated by this water, wine made from rice and water, or fish, squid, and seaweed from the sea itself.

Some of the consumed substances may be regarded as especially potent "condensed transposers" (Munn 1994) that embody the complex relationships between humans, their offerings, and the gods. Worshipers ultimately consume all the contents of the various morning offerings presented on the trays. After the morning services, the rice presented on the five trays returns to the kitchen to be mixed into the communal rice cooker and eaten by everyone at breakfast.

Similarly, the only drink consumed by worshipers at mealtimes is an herbal tea brewed from water emptied out of the altar containers and small bowls on the offering trays. As gofu, this water has been consumed by the kami the day before humans drink it, and it is therefore considered medicinal. (Indeed, on one occasion a group of worshipers became convinced that they could see gold dust, considered especially therapeutic, within the tea as they drank it.)

These purified substances effectively link together consecutive twenty-four-hour cycles. Water that has rested on the altars from one dawn to the next dawn is mixed with water presented to the gods the next morning, and then imbibed as tea throughout the next day by human worshipers. Significantly, this tea is brewed on the wooden stove around which shrine members spend most of their free time, relaxing, smoking, and telling stories. In this sense, the herbal tea has associations with communal relaxation and sociability. As in the daily singing of "Saigi, Saigi" the assembled community internalizes a tangible icon of itself and of the cyclical processes of service.

The offerings make manifest the aesthetic principles that the worshipers themselves strive to embody. Pared down to the absolute essentials, the bowls are presented with a sparse minimum of quantity, decoration, or embellishment. Similarly, the worshiper undergoing shugyō gradually becomes "hard" as she loses fat, solidifies her muscles, and eliminates all extraneous movements from her daily comportment.

The Early Morning Circuits of Shugyō:
Presenting Water and Food to the Divinities

The deep homologies between edible prestations and the body of the worshiper become particularly evident in the offerings presented early each morning during periods of ascetic discipline. After awaking at 4:00 A.M., the novice worshiper quickly puts away her futon and gets dressed. She then faces her first task of shugyō, preparing water and food offerings for the kami and carrying them out to the five shrines. These first circuits of the day force the human ascetics to partake of the peculiar temporality and spatiality of the divinities, in a manner that anticipates the more dramatic spatial and temporal features of the subsequent mountain circuits. It is often stressed that the kami are early risers, who eat once at the start of the day.[4] Their worshipers follow this example by rising before dawn, promptly presenting offerings to the gods, and then consuming pure and simple foods in moderation. Immediately afterward, the mountain climb, the most demanding effort of the day, should take place as quickly as possible during the early morning hours.

The shrine members placed great emphasis on the bodily discipline of preparing the presentation trays each morning. The more experienced women supervising the process insisted that each bowl be placed in accordance with a precise pattern, that each bowl be neat and "beautiful," and that utmost care be taken in transporting, presenting, and collecting the trays.

The morning's very first circuit is usually reserved for the most junior ascetic currently residing in the shrine.[5] On rising, the novice must fetch, clean, refill, and replace the water jugs containing kami no mizu on the five altars. Each morning, the worshiper first retrieves a special red tray, used solely for this purpose and stored in the kitchen, in a small space between two cabinets for the "trays of the kami." She then collects each water jug from the altars, proceeding in precisely the same fixed sequence each morning. First she collects water from the front two shrines, beginning with the Shinden, and then proceeding rightward to the Reidō room. She then empties the water in each jar into the herbal tea pot in the kitchen (extra water goes into a special jar), rinses each jar with water from the special divine water spigot in the central sink, and then dries the jars with the special kami towel. She then refills each jar with divine water from the appropriate spigot and places the containers back on the tray before proceeding in the same sequence to put the water jars back on each altar.

Once finished, she goes outside and back under the connecting "bridge" that links the two major shrine rooms to the rear row of subshrines. She walks directly to her left, to the Ryūjinsama Shrine, then to the central Godaimyōō Shrine, and then to the Kawai Mariko or Mieidō Shrine at the furthest right (and rear) end of the shrine complex. This sequence conforms to regular Shintō practice, giving precedence to left over right and to front over rear (Herbert 1967, 118, 395).

During these rounds, it is especially important that the adept light incense (*osenko*) for the Kawai Mariko Shrine in back, since Kawai Mariko only gets water, no food. Incense is considered the "steam" of the kami's food, alerting them to the presence of an offering and calling them down to the human realm. As suggested by the characters for *osenko* (お線香 lit., revered line of fragrance), incense mediates between matter and spirit, establishing a direct path from this visible world to the other, invisible one.[6]

This same sequence—left to right, front to back—will also be repeated by the priest and worshipers during the morning and evening prayer services, at which worshipers begin their prayers in the Shinden, then move to the Reidō, and finally to the Five Lords Shrine. The

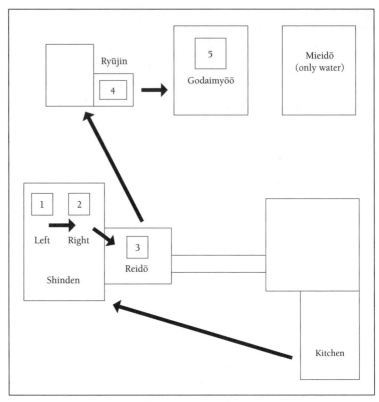

30. Sequence of presenting the five morning trays

ascetics also follow this pattern of movement at the rock "shrine" of Ubaishi during mountain climbs, when they climb through the cave tunnel in a clockwise fashion.

The presentation practices also impose a specific mode of bodily comportment. Like other processes of physical movement during shugyō, the process of carrying the trays from the kitchen and presenting them to the kami should be smooth and continuous, free from fumbling, hesitancy, or mistakes. In this, as in so many other domains, the worshiper carrying the jugs and trays strives to become more and more aligned with the Akakura kami, who like light and water move without hesitation. Thus, in the early morning darkness, the worshiper carrying water jars and trays must move with speed, sure-footedness, and efficiency through the twisting hallways, rooms, and rocky outdoor paths of the shrine complex, just as she must subsequently traverse the twisting and treacherous pathways of the mountain itself. As in

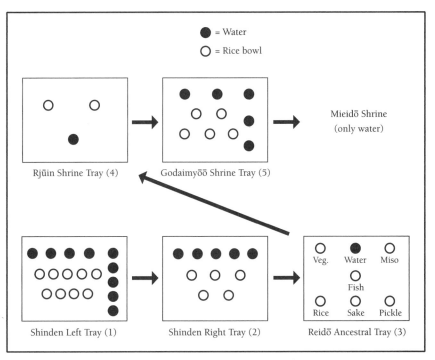

31. The organization of the five morning offering trays

mountain ascent, the water and food carrier is continuously oriented toward the summit of Mount Akakura: she leaves the kitchen facing the mountain top, and she faces the summit as she places each water jar and tray on its appropriate altar.

After having made the water offerings, the adept then returns to the kitchen to assist a more experienced worshiper with preparing the food and water trays for the kami. On most days, all trays, except the Reidō one, consist only of rice and water, served in small bowls and cups. However, special days demand the preparation of elaborate food trays for particular altars.[7] I here discuss the standard presentations of the five trays, considered an extremely important and distinctive aspect of worship at Akakura.

Each of the five simple food trays is arranged differently: The "left" Shinden tray contains nine small water bowls, lined along its rear and right edge, and nine rice bowls in the front area. The "right" Shinden tray (placed under the sacred mirror and behind the candelabrum on the central altar) contains five water bowls lined against the rear edge, three rice bowls in the middle row, and two rice bowls at the front. The Reidō Ancestor Room tray, presented as a conventional full meal, consists of rice, water, sake, miso, fish, and pickles, arranged in standard Japanese culinary fashion. The Ryūjinsama (Dragon) Shrine receives a simple tray with two cups of rice in the rear and one cup of water in front, positioned in between the two rice bowls. The Godaimyōō (Five Lords) Shrine's tray must have three water bowls in a back line, two water bowls along the right side, three rice bowls in front, and two rice bowls in the center. (As noted above, the Kawai Mariko Shrine does not receive a food tray, only water.)

The Rice and Water Tray Offerings as Images of the Mountain

At the most basic level, the organization of the four trays to the kami seems rather straightforward. The tray comprised of five pairs of rice and water bowls presented to the Godai Myōō in the rear of the shrine complex surely serve the Five Lords themselves, including Fudō Myōō. The pair of trays in the central shrine room, the Shinden (nine pairs of rice and water offerings on the left tray, and five pairs on the right tray), are presumably offered to the fourteen most important kami residing in the closed Honden shrine immediately behind the Shinden. The Honden kami encompass those mentioned in the Akakura Prayer, including the sun goddess Amaterasu, the Dragon Princess, the Mountain Princess deity, and Kōshin Deity. The right tray of five pairs of bowls "belongs" to the male (right-hand) aspects of the god, associated with the violent male foreign conqueror and the "Fierce Five Lords" enshrined in the rear Godaimyōō subshrine. The left tray of nine pairs of bowls is offered to the female (left-hand) aspects of Akakura Daigongen, related to the appropriated spirit of the demoness Onigami-sama in the form of Amaterasu, the Dragon Princess, and the Mountain Princess deity.[8] Similarly, the two rice bowls presented to the Ryūjin-sama Shrine refer to the male and female aspects of the dragon and of Akakura Daigongen more broadly. Evidently, as one divinity with two aspects, the dragon kami requires only one bowl of water.

For the following further speculations on the four trays, I ask the reader to bear in mind that the interior spatial organization of Shintō shrines is laden with mystery and is invariably governed by complex mathematical and astrological patterns, patterns not always fully intelligible to anyone, even the shrine's senior ritual specialists (Herbert 1967; Nelson 1996; Inoue 1994; Uryū and Shibuya 1999). With these caveats in mind, I suggest that the trays are mimetic spatial and geometric representations of the sacred mountain and of the shrine community. First of all, note that the layout of offerings in each tray incorporates the basic triangular shape of the mountain, a shape also depicted in the great candelabrum in the Shinden and in multiple votive paintings. For example, the three bowls of the dragon tray form a single triangle. The rice bowls in the left Shinden tray could be read as composed of seven overlapping triangles (or three distinct triangles) of three bowls each. We could interpret the rice bowls in the right Shinden tray and the Five Lords tray as each constituted of three overlapping triangles of three bowls each.

Viewed more carefully, the shapes formed within the various trays appear to be geometrical transformations of one another, according to principles of inversion and reversibility. Trays 1 and 5 share a double triangle layout (pattern A): One diagonal triangle is formed out of their water cups, which form two perpendicular lines along the rear and right edges, while a second (partial) triangle is formed out of their rice bowls (which themselves contain internal triangles). Trays 2 and 4 share the same single triangle layout tapering toward the front (pattern B), formed out of their rice and water bowls. Tray 3 (in the Reidō) exhibits a unique layout (pattern C) in the form of the standard full Japanese meal. The five trays in this respect manifest a reversible sequence: A-B-C-B-A. Such a sequence would be encountered climbing the mountain, if "A" represented the base, "B" the midpoint, and "C" the summit. As noted above, a similarly reversible structure characterizes each day of shugyō.

In turn, each paired set of kami trays constitutes a partially inverted image of the other. As we have seen, trays 2 and 4 are similarly structured as single triangles that taper toward the front. However, they invert the order of their constitutive elements, rice and water. The second (right) Shinden tray has water in the rear and rice in the front. Conversely, the simpler dragon tray consists of rice in the back and water in front. Similarly, the first and final trays invert an aspect of each other. The first (the left Shinden tray) contains a partial triangle

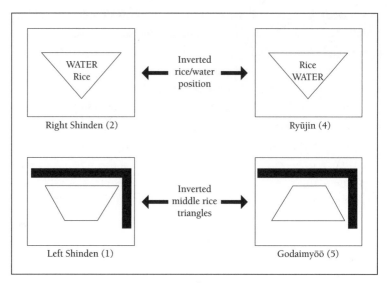

32. Inversions in the morning trays

formed of rice bowls that tapers toward the front. In contrast, the final tray (in the Five Lords Shrine) contains a partial triangle of rice bowls that tapers toward the rear.

The trays are thus exemplary, iconic models of the domain of the gods and other important sacred sites. Like the mountain and the sacred mirror, the trays exhibit overall reversibility but are only partially symmetrical. In presenting daily offerings, the worshipers thus align themselves with the sacred shape of the mountain in its mysterious manifestations and transmutations.

The Trays and the Experience of Alignment

The unexplained nature of these presentation practices may constitute their most important quality. The compulsory and mysterious acts of carefully arranging the bowls and cups on the trays typify the shrine community's basic aesthetic of putting "each thing in its proper place," even if the motivation for this order has never been intellectually clarified to the worshiper. The repeated sensation of submitting to external rules and hidden aesthetic patterns hardly ever articulated might well be regarded as the experiential foundation of shugyō. One's body and heart should gradually come into ever greater alignment with the kami, who configure themselves and the universe in complex patterns beyond the immediate apprehension or understanding of mortals.

The minute scale of these delicate bowls, less than one-tenth the size of bowls that humans would use, appears to deepen the processes of transposition and alignment. The small bowls appear as condensed projections of the worshipers themselves. As we have seen, the trays are placed on the altars following the same sequence that the human worshipers proceed along during worship, from left to right and front to back. In addition, the worshipers have carefully arranged these elements within the confined rectangular tray, just as they carefully arrange their own bodies within rectangular shrine rooms during worship services and mountain ascents.

As evidence for this interpretation of an intimate correspondence between the congregation and the material offerings, consider a vision experienced by Kawai Kenji. While cleaning the Shinden room with the help of forty-one people in preparation for the annual Great Summer Festival some years ago, Kenji looked into the water jug and saw precisely forty-one pieces of the *mannengusa* (万年草) plant (a medicinal mountain moss) floating in the water.[9] As we have seen, the total number of rice and water bowls presented to the divinities on the four kami trays is forty-one. (This figure is the sum of twenty-eight bowls on the Shinden trays, three in the dragon tray, and ten bowls in the Five Lords tray.) In this sense Mr. Kawai's vision appears to have been an apprehension of the united group of worshipers projected into the forty-one symbolic miniature mountains presented to the gods' altar.

Similarly, I suggest that during each morning service the congregation projects aspects of itself into the offering water jugs and the trays, both simultaneously icons of the worshipers and of the sacred mountain. Like the sakaki branch, the offerings embody human and divine qualities. The rice they contain is an agrarian product of human labor, carefully arranged through the delicate work of worshipers. This arrangement of the tiny bowls, as noted above, incorporates geometrical shapes and symmetries of the mountain. Condensed expressive signs of the community of worshipers who have aligned themselves to the shape of the mountain, the contents of these minute bowls are consumed by the mountain gods during the morning prayer session. In so doing the kami transform the water and food into purified gofu that is, in turn, consumed by the worshipers.

Hence, by transposing their bodies into the offering trays, the worshipers help transpose the kami's qualities back into their human subjects. The minute amount of rice and water offered in the small bowls exemplifies the kami's much-remarked on capacity to use everything to its fullest extent; they would take offense by an offering too large or too extravagant. (Early on in shugyō, I was roundly scolded when I filled up the water bowls to the brim. This was unseemly, I was told, as the kami only wanted and needed just the right amount of water.) Thus the human worshiper internalizes the fundamental value of efficiently maximizing everything down to the last drop of water or the last grain of rice.[10]

Symbolic intimacy between the worshiper and the kami is further established by the manner of the trays' transport. When carrying the two trays to the Shinden, the worshiper must hold the "left tray" (which will be placed on the left-hand altar) in her left hand. She carries the "right tray" (which will be placed on the center altar, immediately under the water jug and central mirror) in her right hand. The devotee, in effect, adjusts her bodily comportment to anticipate the contours of the shrine room. Similarly, in the morning ascent that follows these offerings, the worshiper will adjust her bodily comportment to the contours of the sacral mountainscape.

Speculatively, the offered trays may also align worshipers with the basic temporal processes of the shrine. The twenty-eight bowls contained together in the two Shinden trays may evoke the twenty-eight days of the lunar month or the female reproductive cycle, or the twenty-eight chapters of the Lotus Sutra. As discussed in chapter 3, the twenty-eighth day of each month marks the performance of an important ceremony during the mountain's open season. In turn, the two rear trays (dragon and Five Lords) contain a total of thirteen bowls, perhaps representing the thirteen lunar months of twenty-eight days that comprise a solar year, and recalling the total of thirteen collective rites performed each year. The kami trays could thus be understood as condensed representations of the annual cycle, embedding the worshiper ever more intimately within the cosmic mountain womb through which the congregation is "reborn" each year.

A worshiper may undertake kuyō for one, two, three, or four deceased relatives, and these may include ancestors in her husband's line whom she has never met. During any given period of shugyō the worshiper continues to memorialize the same set of ancestors.

The priest assigns each worshiper a special tray, along with one plastic, foil-lined cup for each ancestor memorialized. The tray and cups are then stored under the central kitchen sink, directly below the kami no mizu spigot. As soon as she picks up her kuyō tray and cups from their special place in the kitchen, the ascetic must become absolutely silent and remain so throughout the entire hour-long circuit of kuyō. Although the general prohibition on talking was often broken during morning mountain shugyō, I never heard anyone utter a word during afternoon memorialization. The worshiper carefully filled her cups with kami no mizu and walked directly to the Shinden, placing her tray on a shelf well below the tray on which the food offerings had been presented that day. Bowing, she chanted prayers for about half of an hour before moving herself and the tray to the adjacent Reidō room to repeat the procedure with the special prayers appropriate to that shrine. Still maintaining strict silence, she then carried her water tray outside down the path to the stream. Just upstream from the wooden bridge, she carefully emptied each cup of water into the flowing stream water. She walked back to the shrine kitchen, and placed the tray and cups under the sink, careful to turn the cups upside down. Only once she had returned these implements to their storage place was she considered to have completed kuyō and was thus free to speak aloud again.

Significantly, none of the elaborate patterns or symbolic transpositions characterizing the morning offerings to the divinities mark ancestral memorialization. In contrast to the water offered to the kami in the morning, later consumed by the worshipers in the form of herbal tea, the water offered to ancestors is emphatically not consumed by mortals. Instead, it is returned promptly to the mountain stream. Worshipers seek commensality and intimate identity with the kami through emulating the complex configurations of the endlessly proliferating divinities. In contrast, they seek to establish productive separation between themselves and the dead of their family line.

Just as a conventional Japanese family draws a distinction between the kamidana shelf (through which the kami are honored) and the butsudan (the domestic Buddhist altar through which the family's ancestors are memorialized), so worshipers largely preserve the distinction between kami and ancestral veneration at Akakura. All devotees pray and make offerings to more or less the same assembly of kami, but each worshiper memorializes the distinct ancestors of her or his family line. All the faithful wish to become "like" the divinities, but they strive to differentiate themselves from the honored dead.

The Power of Categorical Distinctions:
Differentiation and the Dynamics of Generational Progression

The two kinds of ritual orientations do not, ultimately, stand in contradiction to one another. As she develops the important capacity to establish stable categorical distinctions between the realms of the living and those of the dead, the worshiper becomes more and more like the kami, the ultimate source of all divisions and distinctions. An experienced worshiper especially gifted at controlling categorical distinctions between different realms may in time become a kami-sama (lit., a divine being), capable of moving productively between worlds, healing the sick, imploring the gods through especially efficacious prayers and other offerings, and teaching the skills of offerings and asceticism to her disciples—who will come to regard her as their "mother."

Thus there is a curious double edge to the craft of making and presenting offerings. On the one hand, as we have seen, offerings potentially reduce the donor to a state of primal dependence. In giving an offering, the worshiper can become like a small child, utterly open to the omnipotent indulgence or power of supernatural and superordinate beings. However, deepening skill in fabricating and presenting offerings intensifies the worshiper's capacity to establish meaningful distinctions and correspondences in the universe. The power to establish effective resemblances between worlds through careful imitative practice makes one more than a mere child and propels one into a senior generational position in relation to other disciples of the kami.

The promise held out to worshipers by the mountain of Akakura can be thought of in Durkheimian terms as the collective potential of society itself. The mountain is explicitly understood as an enormous, potential repository of value for those who labor in the plains beneath it. For countless generations, human worshipers have striven to embed mimetic tokens of their work, their imagination, and their emotional lives within the mountain's complex landscape in the form of material offerings, aesthetic representations, ascetic discipline, and ceremonial performances. In turn, through collective and individual ritual undertakings, worshipers have struggled to reaccess these deposited energies and mental images, which they hope the mountain's beneficent divinities have enhanced. Meaningful encounters with the mountain landscape, the domain of the gods and of the honored dead, are therefore equivalent to accessing the collective achievements of society itself. To become more knowledgeable of the mountain thus means to move up the symbolic generational hierarchy, taking on the position of elder and ancestor relative to one's followers.

As a living image of the social experience of its primarily female worshipers, the mountain serves as a tangible icon of generational progression and thus proves especially resonant for senior local women. As we have seen, worshipers are often compelled to participate in processes of projection and internalization through profound, painful crises in their psychic lives and in their social milieu. At the relatively impoverished periphery of one of the world's wealthiest societies, many Tsugaru persons find themselves deeply torn by contemporary circumstances. They follow privatized accumulation strategies, moving among small-scale agrarian enterprises, part-time service businesses, and semiskilled wage labor, yet continue to operate within kinship and social networks that emphasize broad redistributive obligations to kith and kin. Older women, who make up the vast majority of Akakura worshipers, feel these heavy obligations especially keenly. Senior women, charged with looking after the health and emotional and financial welfare of their immediate family, also have broader obligations for the spiritual welfare of living and deceased members of their natal or affinal descent group (Lebra 1984; Lock 1996; Long 1996). The fear of failing to meet these material, affective, and ritual obligations often manifests itself in ambivalent encounters with maternal figures.

As the idealized guardians of familial propriety and continuity, mothers, mothers-in-law, and grandmothers (or symbolic substitutes thereof) may forcefully possess a woman or visit her in a dream vision, demanding the dreamer make extensive sacrifices on the sacred mountain. Such a visitation was experienced by Kawai Mariko in her founding dream, and by her daughter Kimiko a generation after her. As we shall see, this potential fate still haunts Yuko, Kimiko's daughter.

In some cases, these fraught mother-daughter relations prove fictive or classificatory. Many kamisama mediums, including Kawai and Narita, worked as komori during late childhood and adolescence. Mrs. Kurita, an elderly kamisama, told me that the kami first spoke to her when she was a thirteen-year-old komori, giving her advice on how to care for her young charges who had been crying inconsolably. For many decades, Mrs. Kurita's charges, their children, and grandchildren continued to honor Kurita as their spiritual guide. At the age of ninety-three, bedridden in a hospital, this medium still conversed with the divinities, requesting that they care for the souls of all her "children." As Tamanoi (1990, 1991, and 1998) has argued, although child nursemaids were extensively exploited in prewar Japan, they did have recourse to alternate forms of power and were often enmeshed in long-term struggles over the loyalty and love of their structural children.

Ascetic discipline at Akakura offers potential solutions to these internalized conflicts over biological and classificatory kinship, allowing access to powerful experiences of shared heart-mind with fellow worshipers and the all-understanding (yet also all-demanding) kami. This solidarity comes at a severe price. As we shall see in the next chapter, the dislocating habitus of mountain shugyō that causes ascetics to recapitulate certain formal features of early childhood development, leads them to encounter the mountainscape as a powerful maternal being, both loved and feared. Paradoxically, ritual practices, often undertaken out of a sense of failure vis-á-vis one's mother and all she stands for, may lead a worshiper to much more intimate, traumatic engagements with symbolic maternal figures in the form of mountain divinities and demonesses. At the same time, these practices also hold out the possibility that in time the worshiper may move into a new, exalted position, becoming a "great mother" in her own right as she moves up the generational hierarchy of the world mountain.

5

m y   m o t h e r ' s   g a r d e n

Ascetic Discipline on the Mountain

The Mother of the Mountain, her power is in you. You have that power because
Mother [Kawai Mariko] made you climb the mountain. — Okuda Setsuko, quoting Narita Emiko, 28 July 1992

A well-crafted offering potentially expands and enhances the selfhood
of the donor, increasing her spiritual and social standing and rendering her more like the divinities she serves. Through a lifetime of effective offerings to the mountain divinities, a worshiper gradually ascends
the generational hierarchy embedded in the sacred mountain and becomes increasingly identified with the exalted position of the mountain summit. Yet each act of offering also contains within it the destructive potential for the diminution of the self. A badly presented offering
may cause physical illness or deep distress in its donor, limiting her
mastery and sense of accomplished seniority. In effect, poor or insincere offerings (which are themselves conceived of as miniature images
of yama, the mountain) limit the worshiper's capacity to ascend the
hierarchy of the cosmological mountain.

Even greater potential for good or ill is embedded in the task structure of individual ascetic discipline on the literal slopes of Akakura Mountain. Through active physical engagement with the mountainous landscape, which contains the great social tableau of generational progression, the pilgrim may become even more intimately involved in the cosmologized kinship network of the mountain, and may develop a deeper understanding of her human family and her position in the wider social world. Through bodily action, she may dramatically encapsulate her personal history and the predicaments of her loved ones and may thus open herself and them to blessings from the invisible world.

Yet this process of spiritual maturation and exchange with supernatural forces is fraught with uncertainty and danger. There is no guarantee that those participating in the annual ritual cycle or shugyō will necessarily come to terms with the divinities, with their ancestors, or with their living relations. Novice worshipers may be caught in a state of excessive dependence and may never attain a state of mature autonomy. They be "lost" forever on the treacherous paths of the mountain, unable to find their way home. Yet, if all goes well, the drama of cosmologized kinship on the mountain may impel spiritual and psychological maturity and allow the worshiper to return to her conventional family better able to cope with the obligations of everyday life. She may even develop an abiding relationship with a tutelary deity and become recognized as a powerful kamisama spirit medium.

This chapter explores the ambiguous potentials of shugyō, with particular attention to the complex familial relations projected onto and encountered within the mountainscape. The chapter's title, "My Mother's Garden," is taken from an enigmatic comment made to me by Sakurai Fumiko, one of my closest friends and informants as I began training in ascetic discipline at Akakura in 1991. An hour before dawn on a cold October morning, Fumiko led me and another novice up the steep slopes of the mountain, along a path leading to the sacred Waterfall of Fudō, nestled in the high central gorge. In principle, pilgrims are enjoined to silence as they undertake mountain ascetic discipline, but as we rested, Fumiko began to recount the first climb she had taken that year up to the sacred waterfall. When she arrived at the falls and began her prayers she had been freezing, but she then felt the "warm breath" of the deity Fudō-sama (不動さまの暖かい息 Fudō sama no atatakai iki), which warmed her body and spoke reassuring words to her heart. She then immediately explained that her late mother had often undertaken ascetic discipline on this very mountainscape, with which she had been intimately familiar. "Akakura," remarked Fumiko with a wry smile, "is my mother's garden" (母さんの庭 kāsan no niwa).[1]

I take Fumiko's evocative reference to the mountain as "my mother's garden" as my point of departure for considering the social and psychodynamic ramifications of mountain ascetic discipline at Akakura. The literature generally treats shugyō as a rather autonomic affair, the enactment of a prescribed liturgical or textualized cosmological scheme on a given landscape (e.g., Blacker 1975, 2000; Hori 1968; Earhart 1970). Yet in the course of my participation in, and observation of, shugyō, I have noticed that although it involves extremely demanding physical labor, entailing repeated bodily engagements with the material world, this form of religious discipline also occasions remarkably creative flights of imagination. These include acts of calligraphy and votive painting, elegant offerings to the ancestors and divinities, marvelous stints of storytelling and oral narration, and the graceful choreography of traversing the mountain. These practices do not simply constitute enactments of a prior structure followed without questioning or innovation. They are, in many respects, creative acts of self-discovery and self-fashioning that necessarily vary from person to person. Worshipers generally begin intimately linked to antecedent figures—their literal and metaphorical "mothers"—even as they struggle to establish degrees of separation and autonomy from these maternal beings and begin to function as "mothers" to new disciples.

It is in this light that I approach Fumiko's puzzling characterization of the mountain as her "mother's garden." In many respects, the comment expressed her well-known ironic sense of humor; how, in effect, could something as wild and enormous as a mountain serve as a "garden"? This apparent contradiction points to a deeper set of paradoxes at the heart of mountain asceticism. Through dedicated labor to the divinities, the worshiper simultaneously comes to experience the mountain as an object of devotion and dread, as both intimately known and profoundly alien. The worshiper should constantly feel enormously dependent on the mountain and its divinities—who are the source of all life, beauty, and blessings. As in any form of amae, this deep love is hedged about with anxiety and potential aggression, for the power of the nurturing beloved threatens to overwhelm the subordinate receiver of the superior's indulgence. Learning to give and to receive amae, ultimately, is the process of learning how to produce one's own personhood through careful relations with the personhood of others. It is necessarily a perilous process, potentially heralding the expansion or diminution of the emerging self.

"Understanding with the Body and Heart":
The Bodily Space-Time of the Mountain Circuits

To a significant extent, shugyō resembles the condition of physical affliction. Those undergoing ascetic discipline continuously discuss with one another the pain and fatigue of the experience, and they are expected to look forward to the date of their release from confinement at the shrine. Like some forms of illness, shugyō is marked by repeated, occasionally painful episodes of varying intensity. The first days of shugyō are expected to be particularly difficult, as one's body adjusts to the new sleep cycle and gradually detoxifies. When I complained about the headaches I usually got during the first days of ascetic discipline, people would respond that this was not uncommon; people were often sick when they began shugyō.

Toward the end of my first stint of shugyō, Takeda Yuko and others remarked approvingly that I looked very tired, and even appeared "tired on the inside." They interpreted my fatigue as a sign that I had done a good shugyō, with "all my might" (*isshōkenmei*). Ultimately, the temporary "disease" of ascetic discipline is held to heal more fundamental breaches between the self, the ancestors, and the gods. Severe austerities cleanse and purify the body's "six roots of perception" and reform the tired and battered body.[2]

During the July 1992 conversation, the experienced ascetic Mrs. Narita described a day of mountain climbing in these terms: "I woke up and put on my white socks, and I went up [the mountain] and returned, and I walked in dirty water, and as far as I was concerned, that was nothing, wasn't it, because when the kamisama took me walking, my feet did not touch the earth." In "teaching through the body," the mountain does not only impose itself by means of its physical contours; it also works through its distinctive climactic conditions. Significantly, Akakura is the particular face of the larger Iwaki Mountain that has been most visibly gouged out or contoured by the very forces of the kami that the worshipers seek to emulate—the repeated long-term operations and flows of lava, wind, rain, snow, cascading waterfalls, and streams. As the worshipers often noted, Akakura receives the highest amount of rain of any area on the mountain: on otherwise clear days, clouds, mist, rain, hail, or snow would concentrate around its slopes.

Rain on the mountain during shugyō is auspicious and purifying. The medium Mrs. Okuda recalls that just before she and her fellow pilgrims crawled through the Ubaishi tunnel, midway up the mountain, they were soaked in a sudden rainstorm:

> We went up to the shrine of Ubaishi. And it was very good that it rained in large drops. It was great weather, the rain fell in big drops, and these raindrops restored us, and this was a purifying rain, you know. So then it was first a purifying rain, so then, this time . . . we were being purified. . . . Afterwards, we went and entered Ubaishi *yashiro* [shrine] and were forced into the Ubaishi hole. . . . Then, we crawled through [Ubaishi] three times. When we were done, everyone said, "The kami have heard our prayers! [Goriyagu da!] Banzai!"[3]

At the end of my first period of shugyō, just as I was departing the shrine, the sun finally came out. "You did a really good shugyō," everyone told me. "It never stopped raining!" At the time, I assumed this was simply an observation that I had triumphed over adversity. In retrospect, I believe all were expressing their approval at my proper exposure to the dramatic, tangible flows through which the kami announce their purifying presence. Although I never stood under the waterfall, I had evidently undergone an alternate form of mizugyō (water discipline) by unreservedly subjecting myself to the cleansing force of falling water.

As such comments suggest, the shugyō practitioner strives to produce and reproduce a particular kind of "bodily spacetime" (Munn 1986; see also Comaroff and Comaroff 1992), which makes her person progressively more like that of the divinities whom she serves. This "service" (otsutome) makes her body (karada) and heart (kokoro) increasingly acceptable, apprehensible, and aesthetically pleasing to the kami. I was often told, for example, that the kami "like" it when one works hard, wears white during shugyō or pilgrimage, and refrains from eating red meat and chicken. In turn, these related practices help to reconstitute the mountainscape as a vital mediating site where human worshipers may gradually embody the powers and qualities of the kami, further aligning human devotees, as individuals and as a collectivity, with the gods. Each disciplinary circuit within the shrine or on the steep mountain slopes thus entails complex "transpositions" and realignments between the visible body of the human worshiper and the invisible "bodies" of the divinities. Rather than sedentary or static one-to-one mappings, these circuits enable dynamic coordination between human and divine bodies in motion, so that the "moving center" constituted by the mobile human subject may partake of the various mobile and flowing qualities of the kami themselves. These complex effects are not limited to the realm of the gods, the mountain, and the shrine, but may dynamically reorient the worshiper's subjective and practical engagement with their home life and with the wider social, economic, and cultural field of modern Japan. The complex discipline of shugyō on the mountain, which silently "teaches" the worshiper's body to labor productively without encumbrance, may refashion the subject's experience of labor in domestic, informal, and formal economic spheres.

Repeated disciplinary movement by the ascetic worshiper up and down Akakura's craggy mountain slopes during shugyō gradually allows her to partake of the "cleansing" and "beautiful" mountain flows of lava, wind, and water that have constituted the terrain on which she labors. Her service to the kami thus progressively "beautifies" her body, purifying the perceptual apertures that link her bodily interior to the surrounding world. Significantly, much of her effort is oriented toward physical apertures in the mountainscape itself. Every day she climbs toward the forbidding Akakura gorge, formed over the centuries by the mountain's volcanic eruptions. She crawls through a tunnel under an enormous rock overlooking this gorge and should pray at a waterfall emerging out of the rock face at the gorge's base.

These dramatic landscape features figure prominently in the dreams, revelatory visions, and memories of all who undertake shugyō, and they constitute the principal subject of votive paintings produced by ascetics. It is at these sites, where the hidden interior potentialities of the mountain have been externalized and concretized for uncounted human generations, that the most profound transpositions between landscape and bodily form occur, and that important transformations of the worshiper's interior and exterior spiritual states come into effect.

The ascetic should also strive to incorporate microcosmic elements of the mountain. During shugyō novices are instructed to search for a special kind of elongated mountain slug and to eat it with purifying salt. Like serpentine dragons and snakes, long slugs (which resemble tiny snakes) are considered auspicious manifestations of the mountain divinities. Indeed, devotees say that the kami only make this particular kind of slug visible during gyō, as a reward to their dedicated servants who are thus allowed to partake of the mountain's essence.

The Mountain Routes: Following the Paths of "the Mother"

In addition to sensing the omnipresent mountain kami, all ascetics at Akakura are deeply conscious of their human spiritual "mothers" as they perform ascetic austerities on the mountain. To this day, worshipers follow the disciplinary patterns laid down by Kawai Mariko and her early disciples in the 1920s and 1930s. While undertaking shugyō, they reside at the mountain shrine, awake at 4:00 A.M. each morning, perform prayers, and prepare meals and offerings for the mountain divinities before climbing up the mountain along designated pathways.

These climbs, which generally take between four and nine hours round trip, proceed along three long-established routes, known to have been followed by the founder Kawai Mariko and the other great kamisama spirit mediums associated with the shrine. These routes are: (1) most frequently, up along the banks of the Akakura gorge stream to the sacral waterfall of Fudō, about one third up the mountain (a strenuous two-hour climb); (2) somewhat less frequently, and only during longer periods of shugyō, up along a high ridge overlooking the Akakura stream, following a line of Thirty-Three Kannonsama (三十三 観音さま Sanjūsan Kannonsama), thirty-three statues of the compassionate female Bodhisattva Kannon, to a sacral boulder known as Ubaishi (a four-to-five-hour climb); or, (3) much less frequently, continuing along the entire Thirty-Three Kannonsama path to the mountain summit, where there stands a special statue, Shōkannonsama (a six-to-nine-hour climb). Although Akakura Mountain Shrine members have followed these major routes for at least six decades (and other local pilgrims may have followed them for centuries or even millennia), the meaningful qualities and narratives attached to specific features along these paths are subject to continuous alteration, year to year. Although the mountain is in principle eternal and constant, the specific collective experiences accessed through the standard task structure of shugyō would appear to be in gradual flux, as new narratives and sensory experiences accrue onto this dynamic landscape.

Having said this, we can note certain general features of the topography. To begin with, all pilgrims are constantly oriented to the Akakura-gawa stream, which flows down the "middle" of the mountain past the shrine. Flowing from the vaginal great mountain gorge, this river provides the source of the water of the gods, gathered each year during the Dragon Princess Rite. The river marks the most common mountain route of ascetic discipline, from the shrine up to the Fudō Waterfall, the only route undertaken by those doing a three-day shugyō. In addition to linking the celestial domain of the gods to the human-inhabited plain below, the stream constitutes the key medial site between the environs of the shrine and the realm of the kami. As soon as she crosses over the stream bridge each morning, the ascetic must throw purifying salt and address the mountain gods, requesting safe passage through their domain.

The forceful and flowing qualities of the stream also provide a tangible model for the moving devotee. Through unceasing, disciplined effort, she attempts to enter into and be carried along by the lines of power believed to flow up and down the mountain. Like the stream itself, the worshiper strives for unhesitating, flowing movement. All my teachers continually stressed the importance of purposeful, unidirectional locomotion: the climber's attention should be directed straight ahead, overcoming all temptation to glance off to the side or to the rear.

Although worshipers attempt to keep up a steady pace as they climb and descend, they do not conceive of the route as entirely homogeneous. Those doing shugyō frequently discuss the varied physical and spiritual topography of each section of the mountain. For example, devotees consider a deceptively easy section of the path up to the waterfall, covered with bamboo, one of the most spiritually dangerous sites on the mountain; demons are believed to conceal themselves within the grove, readying themselves to attack unwary worshipers. Positive beings, however, are also associated with this space: once, as the powerful spirit medium Mrs. Okuda traversed this section climbing up to the Fudō Waterfall, a magical snake began to follow her. (Mrs. Okuda could not see the snake, since she observed the strict prohibition against looking back. Yet worshipers regarded this creature as an auspicious manifestation of the mountain deity Akakura and interpreted its presence as a sign of Mrs. Okuda's extraordinary spiritual potency.)

These sorts of testimonies, it is important to note, constantly circulate throughout the shrine community, especially when worshipers gather at teatime or in the evening to chat and reminisce. Narrating miraculous visions and revelatory knowledge of the mountainscape is one of the most important responsibilities of the senior members of the shrine, who carefully supervise and mediate novice's experiences of the mountain.

For example, during my very first climb with Fumiko and another novice, Mrs. Hirata, Fumiko managed not only the physical, logistical side of our training, but also exercised considerable narrative control over the experience, recounting in advance the history of key sites before we physically encountered them. She told us stories about feeling Fudō's warm breath and seeing the vast green dragon at the falls before we reached the waterfall itself. In this sense, she actively guided and mediated our first shugyō encounter with this sacred natural site. She explained, as we crossed the spiritually dangerous bamboo field, that the kami had sent her dreams of dangerous sites on the mountain before she climbed them.

There is, in other words, a deeply accretive quality to the paths of mountain shugyō. One walks along a path not merely physically carved out of the mountain by natural forces and by the countless feet of those who have walked before, but suffused with the collectively held remembrances of the shrine community, gleaned through decades of repeated devotional climbs. With each climb, as the worshiper learns more and more of this lore and gradually experiences visions of her own, the mountain takes on greater and greater meaning.[4] Over time, each section of the path comes to be densely associated with particular person's visions as well as with particular spiritual forces. In this sense, no worshiper ever travels alone along a mountain path, for the collective presence and memories of her human antecedents are tangibly inscribed in the complex terrain that she traverses. To an even greater extent than participation in collective ritual, repeated movement through the pathways of shugyō grafts the worshiper into the extended family of Akakura.

The Social Intimacy of Mountain Asceticism

Although they avidly share and listen to stories of the mountain, worshipers insist that verbally derived knowledge alone is insufficient for understanding the mysterious topography of Akakura. As I was often told, the only way to learn about the mountain and the kami is to climb the mountain and learn for oneself. Although in principal each worshiper is said to encounter the sacred mountain on her own, in practice, during the initial stages of shugyō, a more experienced ascetic usually accompanies the novice along the mountain paths. Throughout their spiritual careers, most veteran worshipers closely associate powerful landscape features with their early guides who first alerted them to a given site's power and mysteries.

In order to convey how one pilgrim imparts this geographical and spiritual knowledge to another as they traverse the mountainscape, I give an account of my second morning of shugyō, when I was guided by Fumiko up the Thirty-Three Kannonsama route to the mountain summit.

At 5:30 A.M. I looked out into the gloomy rain and asked Fumiko if we were really going to head out up the mountain under these treacherous conditions. She replied simply, "Ikanakereba naranai." ("I *must* go.") So off we went; since we had a long way to climb, we were excused from attending services, preparing water and food trays for the kami, or eating breakfast. After making the usual quick obeisance within the shrine, we crossed the Akakura-gawa stream over the wooden bridge. As we had the day before, we paused, clapped, threw salt, and greeted the gods. We then explained to the gods that we would be traveling along the Thirty-Three Kannonsama route today and begged their protection.

Since we could barely see anything in the early morning obscurity, we used our flashlights as we climbed up the slippery first section of the path. After a half-mile, we came to the small grouping of minor shrines; here we cut off to the left, away from the path we had taken the day before up to the Fudō Waterfall. Instead, we began to climb up a steep incline heading toward the ridge running along the lower Akakura gorge. As we began to climb this upper path, usually restricted to those pursuing "serious" stints of shugyō, Fumiko said that I should not worry excessively about memorizing prayers and chants, but should recite them from the "heart." If I did that, she explained, the mountain would "become your friend." She also warned me not to talk too much along the climb on this route; we remained generally quiet throughout the ascent.

We stopped at each Kannonsama, stone statues about four feet high of the various incarnations of the compassionate Bodhisattva Kannon atop a stone pedestal. At each statue, we clapped and bowed, and asked for protection along the climb. After about ninety minutes, at the eighteenth Kannon station, we reached an enormous triangular-shaped boulder, about twenty feet high. Fumiko said that the boulder was called Ubaishi, and without further explanation, she lit candles and incense and placed out food offerings. Kneeling in the pouring rain, we then recited a full set of prayers for about twenty minutes.

When we finished with the services, Fumiko announced that we now had to climb under the rock. She abruptly ducked and crawled into a long dark tunnel, emerging at the other side of the boulder a minute later. Next was my turn. Following Fumiko's example, I took off my rain gear, and then, with considerable trepidation, began to crawl into the dark space. No light came from the other side; the rock walls were wet and muddy. I was sure I would encounter a venomous snake. The tunnel seemed to head uphill, and it rapidly narrowed, so that I could no longer crawl on all fours, but had to rest on my belly, awkwardly propelling myself forward through the mud with my arms clutched tight to my side. Halfway through, for a terrifying moment, I was sure my body was too large to fit through. I thought that Fumiko might relent and declare that I should back out of the tunnel. But she said nothing, and I continued forward, my anxiety mounting. Finally, I saw a glimmer of light and pushed myself along for the final yards before emerging, completely mud-covered, back into the rain.

For a moment I assumed that we had finished with Ubaishi, but Fumiko cheerfully announced that we each had to crawl under the boulder three more times, although normally we would each crawl through six times. She did her three circuits first, with her usual dispatch. I followed, increasingly anxious and exhausted with each passage through the rock. At this point, I thought that we would descend the mountain and return to the shrine, as the head priest Mr. Takeda had instructed the night before. To my surprise, Fumiko stated that since we had the "chance," I should accompany her up to Shōkannonsama, the highest Kannonsama statue, all the way up to the mountain summit. (As matters turned out, I was never again to ascend higher than Ubaishi. As I was to learn much later, only those undergoing shugyō for over a year are allowed to take the higher paths up to the Akakura summit.)

As we climbed on, the path disappeared and we navigated around large boulders to our left, while to our immediate right the mountain slope fell off abruptly in a steep drop for several hundred feet to the gorge below. A visible steep dirt path eventually reappeared, leading us up to one of the many "demon-inhabited" sites on the mountain, a place known as *Oni no Dohyō* (Sumo Ring of the Demons). Here, three Kannonsama faced out into a stretch of the long, multisectioned Akakura gorge.

The next hour of the climb proved the most difficult; at moments, I felt sure I was going to collapse. Fumiko, who seemed to know just how far she could push me, allowed us brief rests at selected intervals. She finally allowed us twenty minutes rest at a wide flat plateau that held three Kannon statues and shared her canned coffee drink and rolls with me.

As we approached the highest reaches of the mountain, the rocky terrain underfoot gave way to a smooth heather-covered surface, crisscrossed by a network of paths. Banks of clouds obscured our view down the mountain and mist swirled around us. As we turned west toward the Sea of Japan, a heavy wind nearly knocked us down. The mist seemed to boil up from the exposed western slope as we skirted below the entire western edge of the Akakura summit, moving in the direction of the middle summit of the three-peaked mountain. Turning back toward the Akakura summit (still about seventy-five feet above us), we saw the Shōkannonsama statue, carved in white stone, a little larger than life-size and dressed with a brocade pouch around its neck. It had, Fumiko quietly explained, been carved in situ during Shōwa 30 and 31 (1954–55) by Kawai Hisao, the brother of the shrine's founder, Kawai Mariko.

We made an offering of two buns, sake, and several Yakult yogurt drinks in their distinctive tiny plastic containers. After lighting incense and candles, we performed prayers (including Hannya Shingyō), then ate the buns, drank the Yakult, and poured the sake over the rocks at the statue's base. Fumiko then immediately turned around and began to lead us back down the mountain along the confusing upper paths.

The temperature dropped abruptly as we descended. A third of the way down it began to look like it would snow. The gray sky seemed to be enveloping us, as cold wet wind beat our exposed faces. Fumiko careened down the mountain ahead of me, half flying, sometimes disappearing altogether around a curve in the path. Her eyes never seemed to glance down; it began to seem to me as if she were moving on the wind itself. As before, Fumiko stopped occasionally to allow me to catch up. I would arrive panting, out of breath, always more awkward in my negotiation of the slippery rocks, marveling aloud that Fumiko managed to make it look so easy.

As we set off again after one of these catch-up stops, Fumiko began to reassure me that I, too, would learn how to walk on the mountain the way she did, without ever letting her feet rest on the ground for more than the slightest instant. She said, "The mountain will teach [you] through your body" ("Yama ga karada de oshiete"). With that she leaped effortlessly over the boulders and turned back, demonstrating how easy it would become for me. Just at that moment it began to snow. As the snowflakes swirled around us, the clouds above us shifted rapidly in the wind, casting alternating patterns of darkness and brightness on the rock face. In spite of the bitter cold, it was one of the most beautiful sights I had ever seen. Fumiko suddenly became very still. Looking back at me, she declared solemnly, "Always remember this moment, all right?" ("Ima itsumo oboete, ne?"). She gestured skyward to the falling snow and shifting rays of light. Once more looking back at me she said: "I hope you will never forget."

We quickly descended the rest of the mountain, arriving at the main shrine around noon. Mrs. Takeda, the wife of the priest, was there to greet us at the door. I could hear Fumiko suck in her breath anxiously before we reached her. Mrs. Takeda asked me how my shugyō was going that day. I explained that it had been wonderful because Fumiko had taken me up to Shōkannonsama: "It was really terrific, I enjoyed it!" ("Totemo tanoshikatta!"). We quickly gave thanks to the kami in the shrine, changed clothes, and began to prepare the lunch meal.

"The Mountain Will Teach You through Your Body":
The Social Dimensions of the Mountain's Pedagogy

As even this abbreviated account suggests, the patterned daily ritual of disciplined movement through the richly contoured landscape operates as a complex "switchpoint" between received, collectively held knowledge about the kami and the idiosyncratic personal experiences of the individual worshiper and her immediate guide or guides. Every morning the pilgrim moves through a densely narrated territory, apprehending and accessing various tangible qualities and features of the sacral mountainscape. As she forces her body to conform to the mountain's rocky paths, crevices, inclines, and passageways, she physically and morally internalizes important revelatory and cosmological schemes that have been, in effect, handed down from the mountain divinities through elder members of the shrine community. Some of these narratives are passed on explicitly from worshiper to worshiper, through guided "tours" up the mountain the first few times a novice climbs these routes or through informal evening conversations down in the shrine's living areas. In a more subtle but perhaps most pervasive fashion, these standardized narrative schemas are silently reproduced through the required task structure imposed by the mountain's tortuous, minutely detailed geography.

In turn, the worshiper's specific sensory encounters with this highly meaningful landscape (including her personal revelatory visions, aural experiences, and memorable sensations of extreme heat, cold, or wetness) may eventually be incorporated into the more commonly held oral narratives that continuously circulate within the larger shrine community. For instance, a particular boulder field becomes known as the place where the calls of demons tempted Mrs. Okuda; a twist on the path may become imbued with the story that Mr. Kawai witnessed a great mouth opening and closing there; the pool below the waterfall of Fudō may become intimately associated with Fumiko's widely recounted sensation of a hot wind blowing from the falls. The tunnel under Ubaishi Boulder becomes linked to the mysterious sound ("Pon!") it produced when Mrs. Okuda and other ascetics emerged from it.

In some respects, then, the mountain constitutes a profoundly social space in which the dedicated worshiper is engaged in symbolic interactions with her living and dead antecedents, with the divinities that safeguard her on her dangerous travels, and with those that may come after her. At the same time, worshipers are made continuously aware (through spoken narratives and by the sheer physical awe inspired by the massive contours of the mountainscape) that they are only temporary sojourners, perhaps even trespassers, in an alien and frightening territory. The mountain, one is reminded again and again, belongs to the gods, ancestors, and demons; it is not the natural abode of human beings who traverse it at their peril in order to partake of its life-giving flows and qualities. As guests on the mountain, we must not stay there indefinitely; we must, when the time comes, leave the mountain and return to the world below.

This double quality of mountain shugyō, which entails both proximate sensuous encounters with the mountain terrain as well as separation from this powerful object of nurturance, was pointedly evoked by Fumiko during our long climb to the summit, when she counseled patiently, "The mountain will teach you through your body." At one level, Fumiko's advice may be understood as a poetic rearticulation of the inchoate folk theory of shugyō. Just as the topographical contours of the mountain direct a stream along its course, so should the worshiper surrender to the higher forces of the benevolent kami and follow the true pathways the mountain has laid down for her. As we have seen, the attainment of this unusual subjective state, the spontaneous capability and expertise that transcends the conscious, hesitant, or segmented nature of quotidian difficult activity, constitutes a vital aspect of "becoming more like the kami," who themselves walk up and down the mountain. The gods and the media in which they manifest themselves move across space in an irresistible, nonsegmented, continuous manner—like wind, blowing rain, the flow of a river, or the steady waves of the sea.

Yet even as she was urging me to let the mountain teach me, Fumiko herself, of course, functioned as a skilled instructor, emulating in her own spontaneous, graceful leaping the flowing qualities of the mountain and its resident divinities. Inevitably, to be "taught by the mountain," is also to be taught by one's human guides, who are intimately associated with this strange, intermediate landscape. Just as the novice worshiper is both compelled by and fearful of the mountain's dramatic landscape features, she also develops ambivalent relations to her human guide, who simultaneously encourages and scolds her, opening up remarkable mysteries while subjecting her to demanding and terrifying physical austerities.

Kannonsama and Ubaishi: Separation and Rebirth

Not one's human "mothers," but the thirty-three "living statues" of the female Bodhisattva Kannon that line the high Akakura ridge mediate movement along the most important path of shugyō. The worshiper on this demanding route stops at each statue of Kannonsama to bow, pray, or make offerings, and then moves up higher along the path to repeat the process at the next Kannonsama station. This sequence exemplifies the basic logic of shugyō: movement toward increasing spiritual purity and individuation is achieved through the compassionate intervention of a maternal being, from whom the worshiper is in turn separated so as to cleave to a new mother figure, only in turn to be separated from her as well. Like maturation during early childhood, shugyō entails a cyclical alteration between intensive attachment to and detachment from the principal object of love and nurture. This process at times proves joyous, even transcendent, for the worshiper, but she can also experience it as profoundly disturbing and terrifying. Although most ascetics report feeling greatly comforted by the statues of maternal Kannonsama, these figures also have "uncanny" characteristics. Many worshipers recall that as they pass the five stupas that lead to Ubaishi Boulder, the statues or the stones nearby produce a mysterious, frightening noise that sounds like "gura, gura." Some pilgrims report having seen the Kannon statues miraculously turn themselves around, or even detach themselves from their foundations and walk up and down the mountain on their own.

The great Ubaishi Boulder, encountered a little more than halfway up the Thirty-Three Kannonsama route, at the eighteenth Kannonsama statue, exemplifies these ambivalent encounters with maternal forces. Although my informants never spoke of it as such, I surmise that the Ubaishi Boulder is intimately associated with the eighteenth Kannon, "Rock or Cave Door" (岩戸 Iwado in Tsugaru-ben, Iwato in standard Japanese). It is also sometimes referred to as "Ubaishi Yashiro" (Shrine of Ubaishi), or simply "yashiro."

On reaching this twenty-foot high triangular shaped boulder, circled by a large shimenawa rope, worshipers pray for about twenty-five minutes, then and crawl three, four, or six times through a long dark tunnel beneath the rock. Worshipers consider the crawl through the dark wet tunnel physically and emotionally demanding.

As in so many other instances of East Asian ascetic cave crawling (e.g., Hardacre 1983; Stein 1990; Blacker 1975), the Ubaishi route has pronounced uterine symbolism. Like a newborn infant emerging from a womb, a worshiper should utter a cry on emerging. With each traversal, the ascetic undergoes a "rebirth," entering into a higher purified plane of consciousness. Novices are told that by crawling through the Ubaishi tunnel, "*sanshō* [the three hindrances] are taken from you." In classical Buddhist thought (with which most Akakura worshipers have only passing familiarity), the three hindrances are (1) *bonnōshō,* evil passions; (2) *gōshō,* evil karma; and (3) *hōshō,* the painful retributions of being reborn through each of the six realms rokudō (Inagaki 1988, 274). It is presumably for this reason that novices are told that they must crawl at least three times through the tunnel and that they ideally should crawl six times through it.

However, these disciplinary circuits are more than the enactment of an intellectually conceived cosmological schema. The demanding practice of repeatedly navigating through the narrow tunnel viscerally imprints the boulder's massive compressing weight onto the physical body of the worshiper. The inevitable terror of the experience (a terror that I vividly recall and that other worshipers privately confirmed to me) may temporarily cause the devotee to lose control of her bodily functions and of her appendages. But out of this bodily "dismembering" emerges a powerful state of "re-membering" (Comaroff and Comaroff 1993), which remains permanently lodged in the corporeal being of the worshiper.

Like other shugyō practices, one can regard the Ubaishi circuit as a "condensed transposer" (Munn 1994), a set of bodily encounters with material forms or elements that create a tangible, felt image of the general experience and hoped-for effects of the entire shugyō process. Significantly, this tunnel narrows to just the width of the adult human body. As other ascetics remarked, the worshiper has the powerful bodily sensation of just "fitting into" and filling a space. This visceral, embodied experience of spatial, corporeal adjustment constitutes a basic component of the shugyō process; the worshiper's body learns to transpose itself from its usual expanded comportment into confined disciplinary spaces created for it by the kami, and it thus adjusts itself to their more perfect contours. In this respect, the Ubaishi crawling exercise exemplifies recurrent parallels between shugyō, biophysical illness, and death encountered by worshipers at Akakura. The terrifying sense of compression, danger, and enforced immobility, so reminiscent of illness, is immediately followed by the joyous sensations of openness, expansiveness, recovery, and new life. Significantly, several prominent ascetics reported that as they emerged from the tunnel, they heard a miraculous sound issue forth from the boulder, the same sound produced when the kami's healing breath enters a patient's body and gives her or him "new life."

Crawling six times through the narrow tunnel under the "wet nurse" boulder, the worshiper is thus "reborn" in a nurturing, feminine space.[5] Informants state that this action is, and should be, terrifying to the novice. This coincidence of nurturing dependency and primal terror proves significant: submission to the will of the divinities demands a frightening rupture from one's previous attachments and from one's conventional way of existing in the world.[6]

To summarize, the compassionate intervention of a nurturing mother figure makes possible the ascetic's ritual movement through the great cosmological cycles of death and rebirth on the mountainscape. Yet since this movement depends on successive separations from multiple incarnations of the "great mother," ascetics experience the maternal being ambivalently, as both soothing and potentially violent.[7]

Demons on the Mountain

These dangerous aspects of the maternal mountain are dramatically condensed in the image of the demons (鬼) believed to inhabit Akakura's deep-set pathways. Undomesticated relatives of the ancient indigenous demoness Onigamisama, these creatures can easily lead any ascetic astray. Indeed, many aspects of the mountainscape encountered during shugyō recall Melanie Klein's concept of the "phallic mother," in which aggressive impulses are projected into the mother and maternally coded objects (Klein 1975a; Segal 1979). Shugyō opens the adept up to general dependence on parentlike forces, which may both nurture and overwhelm the dependent subject. Many of the most charged landscape sites encountered by the ascetic have ambiguous gender qualities, evoking a maternal presence that has potentially dangerous masculinized undertones.

This tension or duality is especially evident at the Fudō Waterfall. On the one hand, the falls present a soothing, nurturing face. Here worshipers may feel the warm breath of Fudō and find great comfort as they pray kneeling before the sacred pool at the fall's base. At the same time, the site is replete with phallic and aggressive masculine associations. Like many other Japanese sacred waterfalls, the shape of these falls resembles Fudō's sharp, flaming sword. Worshipers here may encounter frightening visions of menacing dragons and hairy, virile manifestations of Akakura Daigongen. From the falls, the worshiper gazes up at the most dangerous part of the mountain, the barren upper reaches of the great Akakura gorge. Ascetics often told me that there was a path leading directly from the Fudō falls to the summit through the upper gorge area, but that it posed extraordinary physical and spiritual dangers to all who ventured along it. Considered the heart of the mountain, this awe-inspiring zone is the most visible and exposed part of the vagina-shaped onna no koto that dominates the mountainscape's northeastern face.

A commonly told story in the shrine community recounts how a violent demon possessed the "honorable mother" Kawai Mariko at the Fudō Waterfall in the 1930s. Her disciple Mrs. Narita recalled the event six decades later in these terms: "[Kawai Mariko was] possessed [lit., ridden by] a demon, and she became a demon, and she foamed and foamed at the mouth, and then she opened her mouth this wide [Narita gestures with her hands], and a horn sprouted [on the top of her head]. . . . And you see [Mariko's face] turned purple, and oh, [she] was exactly on the border between life and death."

To this day, veterans warn every novice that oni will often tempt her by shouting out her name on the path behind her in a familiar or pleading voice; an undisciplined pilgrim who turns to look, may be possessed and transformed into an undisciplined, monstrous demon herself. Like the libidinal Titans in Freud's myth, these long-buried creatures reemerge undiminished out of the rock face from time to time and confront the conscious self with long-denied drives and fantasies. Hearing her own name shouted on the mountain, a worshiper usually flees in panic in the opposite direction.

The fear directed against these "demon" figures recalls Freud's insight that antagonism toward one's interior drives is generally redirected toward an externalized force: "By means of the sole defensive mechanism thus set in action, a projection outward of the instinctual danger has been achieved. The ego behaves as if the danger of a development of anxiety threatened it not from the direction of an instinctual impulse but from the direction of a perception, and it is thus enabled to react against this external danger with the attempts at flight represented by phobic avoidances" (Freud 1959, 184).

Oni, the "bad mothers" of the mountain, appear as an externalized image of the worshiper's self; significantly, they always deceive by calling out the adept's own name. They tempt the worshiper traversing a psychic topography that recalls her own childhood to return to a primal state of libidinal, narcissistic self-indulgence. Often in Japan, when oni appear in masked form during the February *setsubun* or "bean throwing" rite, children are expected to chant, "Oni wa soto, fuku wa uchi!" (鬼は外！ 福は内！ "Demons out! Good fortune in!"), in effect expelling excessively infantile qualities from within their emerging sense of selfhood. Demons display comic, perverse exaggerations of ordinary body parts, including grotesquely wide noses, horns that sprout through uncombed, matted hair, enormous bulging eyes, and voracious, long-toothed mouths. These unlicensed projections of teeth, hair, and nose, which emphasize the infantile oni's inappropriate penetration of proper social space, are profoundly at odds with the highly constrained, disciplined, and graceful modes of bodily comportment to which all ascetics aspire.

It is for this reason that ritual specialists at Akakura take special pains to warn novices against the temptations posed by the demons, which can prevent the ascetic from ever "coming down off the mountain." Having reentered the psychological landscape of early childhood, the new worshiper is at particular risk of being frozen in an infantile state and never achieving the necessary spiritual and psychic distance from the nurturing mountain.

Not insignificantly, the three Kannonsama of the Oni no Dōhyō oversee the zone of highest spiritual purity on the mountain—normally attained by only the most disciplined ascetics—and carefully guard the final route to the summit. Only once the adept has been judged to have put all childish things behind her, will she receive authorization to enter the mountain's greatest heights. Yet even at the summit, I was told, the most powerful ascetic may be possessed and "lost" in the mountain's shroud of fog and confusion. Fumiko's transcendent "Mother's Garden" in effect stands in the shadow of another garden, the *Oni no Niwa* (Garden of the Demons), which continually threatens to trap the dependent worshiper.

Fumiko's Shugyō

With these dynamics in mind, let us now return to the case of Fumiko herself. As noted in chapter 1, Fumiko, like many women drawn to Akakura, felt burdened by a pervasive sense of unfulfilled familial obligations. At the time she called Akakura "my mother's garden," Fumiko was forty years old and unable to bear children. Her infertility had for years been a source of considerable tension with her husband's family with whom she resided and for whom she worked in the small resort hotel they ran in the Japanese Alps.

Some years earlier, plagued by worries and arguments with her in-laws, Fumiko had been advised by a kamisama spirit medium to undertake an extended, ten-year period of shugyō at Akakura Mountain Shrine. When I met her, Fumiko was about halfway through this period. During each winter she worked with her husband in the family hotel and for much of the summer and autumn would be based at the mountain shrine.

In Fumiko's case, general obligations coalesced in her sense of specific obligation to a pair of oshirasama (オシラ様) ritual objects, which had been passed down from mother-in-law to daughter-in-law in her husband's family line for many generations, and which she in turn had received from her mother-in-law on marriage to her husband. As discussed in chapter 2, oshirasama are simple carved wooden figurines wrapped in many layers of silk, representing the mythic couple of a young woman and her male horse lover who were sacrificed and reborn as divinities. Oshirasama are used by itako spirit mediums as they enter into trance and are regarded as deities that they must serve (Sakurai 1970; Blacker 1975; Schattschneider 1996a). Many northern Japanese agrarian families also own such figurines, which may bring good or ill fortune (depending on how well they are cared for).

Fumiko carried her pair of oshirasama on her back each morning as she climbed the mountain, and restored them to their resting place on the shrine's main altar as soon as she returned from the mountain. Although she never explicitly spoke of the dolls as her children, she often talked of their needs and desires, and of her unbreakable responsibility to care for them.[8]

In addition to her kinlike relations to the *oshira* figurines, the immediate social world of the shrine presented an alternate tableau of familial psychodynamics. Like many worshipers, Fumiko often spoke of the core members of the Akakura Shrine congregation as her family. In many respects, these immediate relations proved as complex as those she experienced with her natal and affinal kin, and they were marked by close affection, conflict, and resentment.

Fumiko's fraught relationship in the shrine community was with the local "honorable mother" figure Mrs. Takeda, the granddaughter of the shrine's founder, Kawai Mariko. This relationship was complicated by the fact that although Mrs. Takeda had decided not to follow her mother's and grandmother's spiritual healing practice as a kamisama at Akakura, she was actively involved with the day-to-day management of the shrine, in which her husband (adopted into Mrs. Takeda's mother's line) served as the official Shintō priest. Although Mrs. Takeda was formally referred to as an okāsan of the shrine, she refused to sleep there and had never undertaken ascetic discipline.

Mrs. Takeda often came into direct conflict with Fumiko, who managed the kitchen during her extended periods of shugyō. The two often disagreed about just what ought to be cooked, by whom, and when food should be served. Fumiko remarked to me one day while cleaning up in the kitchen that her "real shugyō" did not involve climbing the mountain, which she deeply loved, but instead took place in the kitchen, where working with people, and especially with Mrs. Takeda, presented the greatest of all possible trials.

In many respects, Fumiko's relationship with Mrs. Takeda recalled her fraught relationship with her own mother-in-law. The shrine kitchen resembled the hotel, managed by her husband's parents, in which she worked when not undertaking ascetic discipline. In contrast to her affines' hotel, the shrine offered her a daily escape up the mountain. As she often told me, it was only when she gazed into the frothy waters churning at the base of the Fudō Waterfall, underneath the great gorge of Akakura, that her rage against Mrs. Takeda dissipated. "Only on the mountain," she would tell me, "do I feel at peace."

During the initial years of her shugyō, Fumiko had spent much of her time on the mountain thinking of her difficult, childless marriage and the excessive expectations placed on her by her mother and mother-in-law. Over time, she came to see these figures in a more benign light. In this sense, Fumiko's ability to conceive of the mountain as her "mother's garden" signaled a mature capacity to sublimate her longings for dependence into a complex aesthetic enterprise. Calling the mountain a "garden" emphasized the controlled beauty of its landscape and of its resident divinities. Like other veteran ascetics, Fumiko strove to emulate these gods by making her own laboring body "beautiful," even as she became increasingly aware of the inevitable disparity between her mortal existence and the gods. Finally, like other experienced worshipers at the shrine, Fumiko reported that her life at home and at work had become much easier as she had come to know the divinities and had become assured that they were benevolently watching over her.

During my apprenticeship on the mountain, I became one of the many beneficiaries of Fumiko's deepening serenity and mature ease with the mountain's spiritual and psychic topography, which she sought to transmit to novice ascetics in many ways. In distinct contrast to less experienced worshipers, she became increasingly adept at improvisation and experimentation, and although she maintained the common mode of expectant silence on the mountain, she became willing to speak aloud at profoundly significant moments.

For both of us, the most moving such moment was just after we had climbed to the summit and gazed at the falling snow and shifting rays of light. "Ima itsumo oboete, ne?" ("Always remember this moment, all right?") Fumiko told me, "I hope you will never forget." Fumiko had just taken me on an extraordinary journey into the higher realms of the mountain. As I was to learn later, she had taken a considerable gamble in bringing a novice along on this spiritually dangerous path. At the very least, she risked the legendary anger of Takeda Yuko. (As it happened, Mrs. Takeda castigated Fumiko for days afterward for this act of "irresponsibility.") Although I did not fully realize it at the time, Fumiko had given me an extraordinary gift, a tangible expression of the deep knowledge of the mountain's mysteries that she had wrested out of three hard, long years of shugyō. After years of repeated ritual transpositions between herself and the mountain topography, she had, relative to novice worshipers, taken on the structural position of the mountain and the kami themselves. She had chosen to impart fundamental knowledge to me, not simply through words, but through the grace, simplicity, and skill with which she moved up and down the mountain.

How appropriate, then, that the moment after she told me that the "mountain will teach you through your body," she herself gracefully leapt up onto a rocky outcropping; like the mountain kami that she served, she was educating me through a tangible example of dynamic, flowing movement. How deeply appropriate, as it began to snow and the transcendent beauty of the mountainscape revealed itself to us, that Fumiko solemnly declared her hope that the two of us would forever share the memory of this moment. For this, too, represents an enduring theme of shugyō: that the transformations and consequences of ascetic discipline are never simply a matter of individual self-betterment or even of personal enlightenment. Most of the time, mountain climbs are undertaken on one's own. Yet truly productive and transformative encounters with the mountain and the kami must be constantly shared, continuously transposed from individual acts of discipline and individual experience into collective acts of "beauty" and collective memories, which will in turn guide the next generation of worshipers as they serve and honor the kami.

Kinship, Labor, and the Path of Maturation

Like the ritual and exchange practices explored in the preceding chapters, ascetic discipline on Akakura may be understood as an attempt to negotiate the complex ambivalence generated by structures of kinship, conventional gender-role expectations, and familial obligation. Through the performance of demanding disciplinary labor and ritual action on a sacral mountainscape, worshipers give objective, material form to otherwise diffuse and inchoate sentiments of interpersonal anxiety and may become able to discharge their obligations to kith and kin in a relatively routinized fashion.

Thus, as she follows the model of the exemplary life of Kawai Mariko, each ascetic may enter into the sequence of intergenerational maturation evoked by the ritual cycle. She begins as a relative child, entirely dependent on the parental forces of the mountain, her teachers, the gods, and the ancestors. In time, she may come to be more and more closely identified with the mountain and other superior beings and take on a superior position relative to her own students and successive generations of younger worshipers. With time, she is expected gradually to move away from the strict dictates laid down by her teachers and to improvise, building up her own authoritative knowledge of the ways of the mountain. Recall that the priest Mr. Takeda, who had undertaken extensive shugyō, remained unconcerned that Fumiko, an experienced ascetic, had taken me up the Thirty-Three Kannonsama path in contravention of established rules.

This process of gaining spiritual autonomy, however, also parallels difficult aspects of maturation. Shugyō is held by its adherents to lead the ascetic worshiper toward a deepening awareness of her heavy "debt" to external forces, principally to the divinities and ancestors. The mediation of closely associated maternal figures—including the compassionate Bodhisattva Kannonsama, the sun goddess Amaterasu, the former demoness Onigamisama, the shrine's founder Kawai Mariko, and Akakura Mountain itself—makes possible such spiritual and psychological progress.

Fumiko's characterization of the mountain as her "mother's garden" thus evoked the regenerative and nurturing symbolism of the mountainscape, which in many respect functions as a maternal body through which dedicated worshipers are continuously nursed and reborn as pure servants of the divinities. In undertaking shugyō at varied maternally coded sites on this and adjacent mountains, women (and occasionally men) enter into enduring positive relations with maternal figures (their real and fictive mothers) and gradually constitute themselves as parental figures embedded in this sacred landscape.

At the same time, Fumiko's comment pointed to another, less obvious feature of the mountain. Gardens and sacred mountains are places of fecundity and new growth, which depend on human effort and attention. Like a garden (*niwa*), the Akakura mountainscape reflects progressive human labor, which helps to beautify it and to produce a place that one walks through. Gardens and sacred mountains are closely associated with aesthetic, embodied knowledge passed down through the generations. Just as the child gardens like parents and ancestors before her, so does the conduct of mountain shugyō express a commitment to follow (quite literally) the pathways of one's foremothers and forefathers, bringing refinement and knowledge learned from the parent to bear on a rough, unsocialized landscape.

The performance of a good shugyō is thus signaled by the ability to see the hidden bounty of the mountainscape. A dedicated ascetic may receive the gift of coming across a rare medicinal slug or herb. For example, during the July 1992 conversation, Mrs. Okuda recalled that at the conclusion of a recent stint of shugyō, a divinity possessed ("entered") her and gave her the ability to see the medicinal plant *mannensō* (*mannentake*, bracket fungus of the genus *Formes; Formes japonicus*) growing on the slope:

> I reached the fifth and last day of my gyō, and I gave thanks. It was the fifth day, you know. They entered. First the kamisama entered here [she gestured to her waist]. It's always like this. I thought, "During this time, the wind was a good thing." And the feeling, the spirit [of the kami] falls here and there. I was given *mannen* [the medicinal plant]. . . . The kami said, "There is mannensō," and I looked, and it had a grassy smell, so that I was granted mannensō, and I carried some back, and I thought, "Ahh."

The divine wind that enters her through her abdomen also brings to Okuda's awareness the faint fragrance of the sacred plant. Shugyō restores one's capacity to attune to a local landscape, to become aware, by smell and other senses, of the flora and fauna known to one's ancestors and antecedents. The greatest culmination of this process, veteran ascetics assert, is the ability to glimpse a secret garden hidden in the "heart" of the mountain.

Such imagery strikes particularly resonant chords in the contemporary quasi-agrarian households of Tsugaru. As noted above, although the postwar land reforms made modest land holdings possible for thousands of previously impoverished peasant families, the wider structure of the national economy has denied most local households the possibility of reproducing themselves through agrarian labor alone. My friends and informants often spoke of the ideal image of elders, adults, and grandchildren gathering wild mountain plants and productively toiling together in fields and gardens. Yet all acknowledged that given "high prices nowadays," such intergenerational solidarity was fleeting at best. Fumiko, like many members of the shrine association, frequently noted that the lure of wage labor, especially lucrative migrant labor (*dekasegi*) in the metropolitan core areas was tearing local families apart. Although a worker might pursue these forms of individuated labor out of obligation to provide financially for the older generation, such a person usually felt painfully aware of failing her more diffuse obligations to perform concerted, companionable labor with her elders. Many periodic migrants emphasized that although they dutifully sent back money and store-bought gifts to parents and relatives, these remissions seemed "empty," insufficient compensation for parents who had to "live and work alone." Nearly all migrants spoke wistfully of "missing the mountain" as they worked far away from Tsugaru.

Through the active labor of shugyō, worshipers represent, and to some extent resolve, the enormous burdens of dependence on, and obligation toward, parental figures, burdens all the greater under contemporary economic conditions. The varied work practices of shugyō help give objective form to one's endless obligations to human and divine progenitors, and make it possible to discharge these obligations through physical labor on an immense material landscape that comes to embody traces of one's remembered antecedents.

Gardening and shugyō are both domains of intense creativity, which demand sustained human bodily engagement in physical labor on a changing landscape. This process of giving objective and physical-phenomenal form to obligation proves both comforting and terrifying; although it at times allows for reassuring intimacy with benevolent and nurturing beings, it also demands continuous acts of separation. As we have seen, shugyō and related ritual practices at Akakura are often associated with themes of rejection, loss, expulsion, and frightening individuation. These themes are encompassed in the imagery of birth and weaning, and at times they recall motifs of violent, oral aggression associated with early childhood separation from the primal object of desire.

A long-term consequence of shugyō on Akakura, for women worshipers at least, would thus appear to be the production of tangible, embodied memories of their biological and spiritual mothers. Fumiko misses her late mother terribly. Yet climbing the mountain, she feels herself intimately in her presence, as it is still her "mother's garden." Every time Fumiko walks up and down the mountain, she encounters traces of her mother and of the charismatic women healers and ritual specialists who traversed this complex space before her.

Paradoxically, these intimate encounters with maternal forces are enabled by the worshiper's repeated detachment from prior objects of love and dependence. Each pilgrim undertaking shugyō separates herself from conventional linkages to family and friends for a period of time to become enmeshed in the complex small society of the shrine congregation, which its members often refer to as "my other family" or "my real family" (hontō no kazoku). In turn, the disciple must detach herself each morning from that small community as she ventures alone up the mountain paths. At selected sites along the mountain route, the worshiper becomes profoundly linked to the mountain divinities, at sacred rocks and watercourses, but she must quickly separate herself from these, too, in order to continue her ascent. Her disciplined attention and refusal to be diverted is dramatized by her repeated enunciation of the phrase, "Isshin!" (一心 One mind/one heart/in one moment). Fumiko often stressed that it was her own mother who had taught her this ritual phrase, which keeps the ascetic's attention from straying.

Through climbing the mountain, the experienced worshiper potentially realizes the promise first opened up to her as she began to learn how to make offerings to the divinities. Mountain asceticism is made possible by the intervention of a compassionate mother figure, but also through continuous separations from that mother figure and from her symbolic substitutes. In such a manner, the ascetic comes, over time, to internalize the capacity to act on others and to act as "mother" herself to successive generations of worshipers. Long in a state of profound dependence (amae) toward the mountain and its resident divinities, each successful ascetic gradually becomes the object of grateful dependence, tinged with fearful respect, for those who follow her footsteps through this beautiful, mountainous "garden."

6

i   a m   t h e   m i r r o r

The Political Dimensions of Representational Action

In the preceding chapters I have argued that the capacity to produce imitative representations of supernatural beings and elements helps the human worshiper establish productive conduits between worlds and propel herself into progressively more pure and elevated states. Through presenting offerings that resemble the gods and undergoing austerities modeled on their flowing perfection, the dedicated disciple may become more and more "like" the immortals and may in time earn the honored appellation *kamisama* (divine being). In this chapter I examine the relationship between visual representation and social progression more carefully, with particular attention to the subtle political dynamics of struggle and succession among kamisama spirit mediums.

I take as my point of departure a comment made during the July 1992 conversation in the Shinden. At one point, the aged kamisama Mrs. Narita declared "If you work honestly, and believe in the kami, then I am the mirror, am I not?" As noted in chapter 1, she delivered these words in the shrine's Inner Sanctuary below the sacred Shintō mirror, the instrument that recalls the cosmogenic mirror by which the sun goddess Amaterasu was tricked by fascination with her own image into leaving her cave hiding place to once more bless and give life to the universe. All animal and vegetative life depend on this initial quest for knowledge, on this primal journey to know the self through an image captured in a mirror. Not insignificantly, this cosmogenic moment has profound political significance: the imperial line claims direct descent from Amaterasu.

Mrs. Narita's assertion that she herself was "the mirror" of the divinities can be understood as the culmination of the broader logic of vision and representation in the Akakura system. At pivotal moments, a worshiper undertaking shugyō may come to apprehend aspects of her transforming selfhood through extraordinary revelatory visions. As she communicates these revealed images to others, the visionary ascetic may, like Mrs. Narita, become a "mirror" for a widening circle of worshipers. Reflecting back to the faithful their own aspirations for their future spiritual development, she becomes a vital conduit through which the life-giving blessings of the kami flow into the human world. At such moments, the profoundly personal transformations attained through shugyō become collective phenomena, with potential political implications. Given the tendency toward unroutinized charisma in kamisama-based religious institutions such as Akakura, a single reported vision may lead to a sizable following around a given ascetic or medium, reorganizing political lines of authority in the community and perhaps in time triggering a schism between groups of worshipers.

This chapter explores the political dimensions of imitative action at Akakura by examining in detail the events that followed the death in July 1991 of the great kamisama spirit medium Sugiyama Junko, Kawai Mariko's most charismatic disciple. We first examine closely the impact her death had on the already fraught relationship between the spirit mediums Mrs. Narita and Mrs. Okuda, two of the principal kamisama in the senior branch of the shrine, with particular attention to the July 1992 conversation in the Shinden sanctuary. I approach this three-hour interaction as a subtle rhetorical tournament of representational symbolism, in which the two charismatic figures each made claims to most perfectly embody imitative capacities and to be on the most intimate terms with the visible and invisible qualities of the kami.

We next consider the symbolic politics that unfolded in the junior branch of the shrine association following the death of Sugiyama Junko. Conscious of their enormous obligations to her living spirit, her daughter and adopted son-in-law faced a difficult set of challenges. How were they to carry on their mother's extraordinary spiritual status as mediator between this world and the other world? How were they to retain her extensive clientele and following? Like the spirit mediums Narita and Okuda, they sought to meet these challenges through a set of complex representational acts, publicly establishing their own intimate visual links to the universe's enduring, invisible forces.

The Narita-Okuda Relationship: Rivalry and Cooperation

As we have seen, Narita Emiko (b. 1912) was one of Kawai Mariko's first disciples and served for three decades as Kawai Mariko's representative (*dairi*) after the death of the founder. As the official "voice" of Kawai Mariko, Narita Emiko had to abstain from practicing spiritual healing. In contrast, Okuda Setsuko (b. 1931) never knew Kawai Mariko personally, although she claims to have heard Kawai Mariko's voice on numerous occasions while undertaking shugyō. Over the course of the 1980s, Okuda Setsuko emerged as the most charismatic medium associated with the honke branch of Akakura Mountain Shrine. Mrs. Okuda's charisma in the overall shrine community was exceeded only by Sugiyama Junko (1897–1991), the leader of the bunke or junior branch of the shrine, who for decades had presided over the climax of the Great Summer Festival, calling the kami into the kamado (cooking pot).

Sugiyama Junko's decline and death placed serious strains on the relationship between Narita Emiko and Okuda Setsuko. Now that Sugiyama Junko could no longer preside over the Cooking Pot rite at the Great Summer Festival, both women, I sensed, wished to take on this vital responsibility. At the 1991 summer festival, Mrs. Narita was assigned the primary leadership position for the rite, while Mrs. Okuda acted as her principal assistant. One month earlier, the two women had subtly jockeyed for a position during the Sword of Fudō rite. As Mrs. Okuda entered into possession, she explained in chant to the god Fudō that Mrs. Narita, who was waiting to be healed, needed his help.

As the chant progressed, Mrs. Okuda's voice took on an increasingly desperate, imploring tone, moving back and forth between her own voice and the posited "voice" of the supplicant Mrs. Narita: "She is appealing to you this time. Usually, when there are things she must do, she appeals to Akakura Daigongen and Shōkannonsama, and she asks for their protection because she is only a person, and with the proper feeling of gratitude [*arigatai*] she washes her hands. But today we are asking for your power today, Fudō, on the twenty-eighth day."

Although Mrs. Narita never publicly objected to this, Mrs. Okuda's statement was not, strictly speaking, accurate. Narita Emiko had prayed often to Fudō during her seven decades of service to the mountain kami, and had been instructed by messages written by Fudō in rice. She had at times "spoken" for Fudō during ritual performance and possession episodes. Nonetheless, Mrs. Narita listened patiently as Mrs. Okuda asserted that for the next three weeks (that is to say, up until one week before the Great Summer Festival) Mrs. Narita would have to change her ways and direct her prayers exclusively toward Fudō.

As it happened, Sugiyama Junko died on 30 June 1991, two days after this performance of the Fudō-ken. This particular performance of the Fudō-ken, widely discussed in the Akakura community, helped establish Mrs. Okuda as the shrine's principal intermediary with Fudō. One month later, on the morning of 29 July, Okuda Setsuko was to play a particularly prominent role at the Cooking Pot Ceremony, which Narita Emiko officially presided over. It was Mrs. Okuda who assembled the pot and performed the esoteric hand gestures of power over the boiling water. Mrs. Okuda, not Mrs. Narita, cried out "Gomen!" ("Forgive me!") repeatedly to the kami in the pot after the worshipers had deposited their offerings of rice and salt. Okuda Setsuko, not Narita Emiko, stayed behind to pick up virtually every grain of rice scattered on the Shinden sanctuary floor.

One year later, on the eve of the 1992 Great Summer Festival, the relationship between Mrs. Narita and Mrs. Okuda took another interesting turn. Sitting in the Shinden Inner Sanctuary of the shrine, the two mediums led a dozen lay women in an extraordinary three-hour conversation in which they discussed in remarkable detail their experiences of shugyō, emphasizing their revelatory visions of the mountain divinities. Why, on this particular night, were the kamisama mediums Mrs. Narita and Mrs. Okuda so willing to talk in detail about the mountain, usually treated with reverent obliqueness? Part of the explanation lies in the traumatic events of the previous year. In late September 1991 Typhoon Nineteen had devastated the Tsugaru apple crop on the eve of harvest. Many extended households had been torn apart as thousands of indebted men and women had left on extended circuits of migrant labor to Tokyo, Osaka, and Kobe. Although the national state eventually extended some financial assistance, farming families were rocked by heated, internal debates about the future of farming: was there any sense, many asked, in continuing in such a precarious occupation, given climatic irregularities and the looming threat of cheap North American apple imports? In her chanted performance just before the conversation, Mrs. Narita had taken heed of these concerns and had incorporated a detailed account of the typhoon and its ramifications in her ritual "report" to the divinities. Her singing had been painfully beautiful, and its spell lingered as she hobbled away from the drum at the front of the sanctuary. I sensed that she needed to talk as much as the women needed to hear her.

The unusual frankness of the conversation also resulted from the shifting relationship between Mrs. Narita and Mrs. Okuda. In a general sense, they had been structural rivals for two decades. Yet now, thirteen months after the death of Sugiyama Junko, the charismatic founder of the shrine's junior branch, the overall future of Akakura Mountain Shrine remained uncertain. Would Sugiyama's followers be reincorporated into the dominant honke branch, or would they split off to form an entirely different shrine? Now that Narita Emiko had taken over Sugiyama Junko's position as chief medium at the Cooking Pot rite, would Okuda Setsuko, a native of neighboring Akita prefecture who spoke with a distinct Akita-ben accent, be able to maintain her status among the Tsugaru majority of the congregation? Over the course of the 28 July conversation, the two mediums sought to shore up their reputations and to negotiate implicitly with one another over their respective areas of spiritual expertise. Significantly, they both devoted their considerable narrative skills primarily to emphasize their own capacity to emulate the divinities and function as tangible conduits of usually invisible forces and domains.

At the start of the conversation Narita Emiko explained that during her early ascetic exercises with Kawai Mariko seven decades earlier, she encountered the sun goddess Amaterasu. The passage, worth considering in some detail, begins with Mrs. Narita's description of her shugyō in the 1920s, as she began to climb the mountain before dawn. She returned to a place on the mountain where she had encountered a mysterious sound three days earlier:

> There, yes, where the temple/shrine is now, Akakura Shrine, was built, was built there, and then after three days [I] went again to that place, and then I lit candles, and prayed to Fudō-sama, and I prayed [Mrs. Narita claps to demonstrate how she prayed], and it became very bright, and I didn't have anything to do with it, and I thought, "Oh my!" and I saw a gold color appear . . . and it was beautiful, and I thought, "What is that coming out? Is it Amaterasu?"
>
> [The light] was coming directly into my eyes, and it was not a dream, you know, it was a deep blue sky and a streak of gold stretched across it, and suddenly, I thought, "What is that coming out? Amaterasu-sama?" Her hair was very beautifully coiffed and tied back, and she was wearing a splendid white twill kimono, and over it she wore an imperial kimono. I pressed my hands together in prayer, and I offered prayers, and I heard, then, little by little, the sound of her footsteps, and she showed me, Amaterasu that is, a round thing and entered, so then, I heard the sound of something breaking in half, and opening, and something came out. This was not a dream, it really happened. . . . So, because of that I climbed the mountain with a special purpose.

Soon afterwards, Narita Emiko explained, she discovered a magical "handkerchief of life" on the mountain and proceeded to wear it around her waist as a protective amulet. As in other such narratives at Akakura, an important being is envisioned and externalized from a quasi-animate landscape and then internalized into the dreamer's body or immediate environs in objective, material form.[1] Similarly, in her dream, Kawai Mariko saw Akakura Daigongen as a dragon "come out" of the left peak of the mountain. Later this same divinity gave her three sacred scrolls, condensed physical icons of the sacred three-peaked mountain.[2] Capable of flight between the mountain and the plain, the externalized dragon continues to link the descendants of Kawai Mariko to the mountain's powerful capacities.[3]

Like her teacher, Narita Emiko also saw something "come out" ("dete kita") of the rocky mountain face. She identified the being as Amaterasu. But in another sense, that which "came out" was a transformed image of Mrs. Narita herself. Recall that Amaterasu's mythic vision of another goddess was in fact a reflected image of Amaterasu herself, impelling her to be reborn into the world, resplendent and honored. Similarly, Mrs. Narita's vision gave her strength to be, in effect, reborn with a new identity and new powers. In the next extended episode of the narrative, Mrs. Narita went on to have her newfound miraculous gifts recognized by the kami, who renamed her "Koyoshi" or "Beautiful Voice."

Significantly both Kawai Mariko's and Narita Emiko's transformative visions featured beautiful women with strong maternal and reproductive associations. In Kawai Mariko's dream, the dragon transformed itself into a miniature woman who summoned the pregnant Kawai Mariko to a mountain shrine celebrated for aiding pregnant women. The aggressive dragon piercing Kawai Mariko's rooftop as she slept in a sense pierced her consciousness and presented her with a compressed image of herself as a powerful, assertive woman.[4] In Narita Emiko's vision, the golden orb of light opened to give birth to the exquisite sun goddess Amaterasu, the most important of all the kami venerated at the shrine. She thus recalled other well-known early visions at the shrine that highlighted virile masculine figures, especially the human male forms of Akakura Daigongen, as well as the paired male and female dragons, eagles, and trees through which the mountain divinity manifests itself.

We must in part understand Mrs. Narita's recounting of her vision of Amaterasu as a defensive speech act, establishing her special status. Not only had she known the founder Kawai Mariko, but she had beheld the heaven-sent apparition of Amaterasu that marked the precise spot where the shrine was later built. Her shugyō on the mountain received direct inspiration from Amaterasu herself and brought Narita Emiko further extraordinary visions. Later, in a reproduced dialogue with Kawai Mariko, Narita Emiko presented herself in the structural position of Kawai Mariko's daughter: "You know, it's the same when a mother asks her children, 'How was school today?' And this is the same as when Kawai Mariko always asked, 'How was your gyō today?' So I would say, 'Today this and that happened,' and Kawai Mariko would say, 'Oh, so that's the way it was,' and then [I'd say], 'That's what it was like.'"

From the start of the conversation, Mrs. Okuda was deeply respectful of her senior, Mrs. Narita, and initially said little. However, when she did begin to speak in earnest, about twenty minutes into the conversation, Mrs. Okuda quickly took on the most important voice of all, that of the long-dead kamisama Kawai Mariko, to emphasize her special spiritual connection to the "Great Mother":

> And when I descended [from the mountain], I went to [greet] Kannonsama, in her place [the statues of Kannonsama in the rear of the shrine]. . . . I heard Kawai Mariko's voice say, [Mrs. Okuda speaks in the voice of the late Kawai Mariko], "Oh, I followed behind you [on your way up to and back from Ubaishi]." That's what she said, so I replied, "Who is that?" And then, Kawai Mariko's [spirit] said, "I am the parent kami/head kami. I am the one that everyone calls Oyagami, Oyagami [Great Mother, Great Mother], and my name is Kawai Mariko. I am that one, and only you don't know about me."
>
> [Mrs. Okuda resumes her own voice]: I didn't know her, I didn't know. When my smallest daughter was born, Kawai Mariko was dead. Yes, that person, my daughter was born in April, and, that's when she was born, and Kawai Mariko died in February, so then, I didn't know anything [about Kawai Mariko] because my daughter was born, and after she was born, I came to Akakura, and [the person who inherited Kawai Mariko's place] said things about this person, Narita-san, Narita-san, even if they said that, I didn't know her name [at that time] I didn't know even that fact.

Mrs. Okuda then shifted into the voice of Kawai Mariko speaking to her at that time: "Chant 'Saigi, Saigi' while you are alone. Please, you should do this. And if you cannot, speak from your heart."

In this passage, Okuda Setsuko emphasized that in a conventional sense she knew neither Kawai Mariko nor her appointed representative Narita Emiko. Her connection with the "Great Mother" Kawai Mariko was direct and unmediated, emerging solely out of ascetic discipline on the mountain. Her claim, Mrs. Okuda seemed to imply, was superior to Mrs. Narita's. Although Mrs. Narita personally knew Kawai Mariko, Mrs. Okuda had leapfrogged into a senior structural position.

To establish further the legitimacy of this encounter with the spirit of Kawai Mariko, Mrs. Okuda at one moment even took on Mrs. Narita's voice, quoting Mrs. Narita addressing Mrs. Okuda many years ago: "The mother of the mountain, her power remains in you. You have that power because mother [Kawai Mariko] made you climb the mountain." Mrs. Okuda then reminded everyone that Mrs. Narita had been susceptible to a trick by one of the mountain's demons that had masqueraded as Mrs. Koike when Mrs. Narita returned one day from the mountain.

Although she did not directly respond to Okuda Setsuko, Narita Emiko did take the opportunity to remind everyone her prayers in the Reidō sustained the spirit of Kawai Mariko. At this point, Mrs. Narita stepped back a bit from her implied reproaches of Okuda Setsuko and turned her critical attention on another potential rival, Takeda Yuko.

MRS. NARITA: [Kawai Mariko] would climb the mountain every day, yes, every day, but on the contrary, the mother now [referring to Takeda Yuko] doesn't climb the mountain.

MRS. NAKAMURA: Yes, that's right.

MRS. NARITA: Yes, it's true. She doesn't climb the mountain. And that's no good at all. One should stand [in front of the kami], and if she accepts the role of an adept [*shugyōja*], then she [Takeda Yuko] should stand there in front of the kamisama and ask for their blessings—and if one is cured, it's very fortunate isn't it? And one should thank the kami. But she [Takeda Yuko] is not like that. And she mainly only stays in the shrine.

Toward the end of the conversation, the two mediums continued to agree with one another in this vein. In one fascinating exchange, they commiserated with one another over how terribly difficult it is to recognize the kami's presence and desires. The Great Mother had warned them how difficult it would be to determine the divine will, and as hard as they tried, sometimes they failed. Narita Emiko quotes her teacher Kawai Mariko, "'But both the good kami and the bad kami walk together. Because [one can mistakenly] receive power from the bad kami,' you know, those are the words of my teacher. Those are the words of Mariko-Sensei. The kami only walk in strange shapes, the kami only walk in strange shapes."

Mrs. Okuda agreed and offered as example her failure to recognize immediately that the spirit of Kawai Mariko had entered ("descended") into a rabbit on the mountain.

> MRS. OKUDA: Then, when I saw a rabbit come, this time when it turned up and around. It turned around and around. [That's when] it received—and the kami—who descended during this time, you know, mother [Kawai Mariko] entered here. It was the last time for the mother [the last sign Mrs. Okuda witnessed from Kawai Mariko]. It was the time the kami finished and left. When I went to the mother's place [the Mieidō shrine dedicated to Kawai Mariko] I said, "Mother?" And Kawai Mariko said, "Ah, yes, you are the person who just read and didn't give the answers" [meaning Mrs. Okuda just failed the examination]. So I was scolded by the kami [Kawai Mariko]. But why was I not able to answer the kamisama? I said, "Please forgive me." And [Kawai Mariko's spirit] said, "It's a good mountain for you to be attached to." And, you know, she knows everything about everyone.
>
> MRS. NARITA: She knows.
>
> MRS. OKUDA: Even at the gorge we offer/burn incense, and we receive blessings at the main shrine [goden] and at the place of Kannonsama. "It is very difficult with Kannonsama," that's what our mother said.
>
> MRS. NARITA: That's what she really said, even Mother said that.

In the end, then, the two women publicly asserted common cause, while maintaining a subtle oppositional stance: Deciphering the kami's signs is difficult, and we must all persevere despite our fear that we have failed our common Great Mother and the other divinities.[5] In so doing, however, each woman made claims to special intimate relations with the founding mother. Each presented herself as the exemplary charismatic mirror of Kawai Mariko and her fellow divinities. In some respects, Okuda Setsuko and Narita Emiko emerged out of the conversation with a deepened respect for one another's insights and spiritual fortitude in the face of the kami's unceasing demands. The old truce was more or less maintained, although the underlying tensions were not resolved. Narita Emiko remained the official "voice" of Kawai Mariko, Okuda Setsuko remained the preeminent healer.

However, my impression is that this conversation, although as deeply moving for Mrs. Okuda as it was for all who heard it, left her rather on edge, unsure as to how seriously the shrine community took her authority, and profoundly anxious about the great weight of obligation owed the divinities. Were Kawai Mariko's precise injunctions being remembered? Were the worshipers truly taking their responsibilities to the kami seriously?

The next morning, the most important of the ritual calendar, found Mrs. Okuda in a hard mood, even more exacting than usual in overseeing the ceremonial preparations. At one point, Mrs. Okuda directed her legendary anger at me, when she learned that I had the previous night slept in the Sugiyama's subshrine, not in the Akakura main shrine where I had stayed during shugyō: "You are confusing the kami," she told me bitterly. "I only know the kami here, I don't know what kami they are worshiping down there. You are confusing things terribly!"[6]

Matters did not improve at 11:00 A.M. when the kamado tipped over at the ceremony's climax, during the end of Mrs. Narita's chant. A great gasp of horror arose from the congregation. Although Mrs. Okuda and Mrs. Takeda quickly righted the pot, it never produced the hoped-for hum that would signal the blessing presence of the kami. Mrs. Okuda came to the fore, uttering piercing ritualized entreaties to the kami, pleading with them to manifest their presence. Takeda Seiji, the head priest, tried as well, praying in front of the altar. But the pot remained resolutely silent. The failure proved especially traumatic for Okuda Setsuko's close friend Takeda Yuko, who for the first time had helped officiate in the rite. Afterwards, her eyes slightly reddened with tears, Yuko quietly told my husband and me, "It is like this in any family. Here too, we have things that break the heart in two, so hard you can scarcely bear the pain." Her poignant words recalled the eighth line of the Akakura Prayer, "There are times when the heart becomes wretched."

Mr. Sugiyama Hideo, whose adoptive mother Sugiyama Junko had performed the kamado rite for decades, proved less than sympathetic. He was later heard to observe that the failure of the Cooking Pot indicated that the honke's current officials "did not know how to do things correctly." Feelings were bruised. One month later, on 28 August, Mrs. Okuda chose not to participate in the annual pilgrimage to Mount Hakkōda led by Hideo. The two avoided one another studiously at subsequent ritual gatherings.

In the months that followed Sugiyama Junko's death in June 1991, the Sugiyama circle had found itself caught up in a set of spiritual and practical challenges that recalled those faced by the shrine's senior branch after the loss of Kawai Mariko. Sugiyama Junko's death, which had reverberated throughout the entire Akakura community, posed thorny dilemmas for her descendants and for her immediate followers. Faced with the great burden of upholding her memory against substantial odds, they, too, endured pain that threatened to "break the heart in two." They, too, resorted to elaborate narrative and rhetorical measures to evoke the late medium's presence and to legitimate their spiritual links to her. As in the conversation between Mrs. Narita and Mrs. Okuda, the Sugiyama disciples deployed narratives of revelatory visions and imitative practices to build up their legitimacy and to give their followers a sense of the enduring presence of the Great Mother.

Let us now explore the varied representational strategies pursued in the Sugiyama network in the early 1990s as those who had directly experienced Sugiyama Junko's extraordinary power pondered what obligations they still owed her and how, if at all, her singular legacy might continue.

Sugiyama Junko's Extraordinary Career

Everyone in the extended Akakura Mountain Shrine community, as well as in her southeastern Tsugaru village, acknowledged that Sugiyama Junko (1897–1991) was "very different" from the other kamisama mediums of Tsugaru. In contrast to other leading ritual specialists, who might perform mountain shugyō hundreds of times in their life-long quest for spiritual authority, "Junko-san" had only undertaken shugyō once at Akakura. As her friends and family often told me, Sugiyama Junko's spiritual potency had been so extraordinary that this one session alone proved sufficient to transform her into a full-fledged kamisama spirit medium. Many considered her skill as a diviner and healer as unparalleled. "She could see so much," I often heard. Even at her advanced age, her ritual drumming and chanting were more rapid, "wilder" and louder than that of many of her peers. One of her followers compared her to a "brilliant flame." She had a deeply memorable personal charisma; she would hold the hands of her clients as she talked to them in a soothing voice, gently rocking back and forth and listening to them intently. Her tiny frame, I was often told, radiated waves of warmth and concern. (On a personal note, I, too, always found it deeply comforting simply to be in Sugiyama Junko's presence.)

Sugiyama Junko was also noteworthy for her longevity. Tsugaru residents often say that kamisama, who take on the pain and "impurities" of their clients, tend to suffer great anguish and die young. Sugiyama Junko, in contrast, never seem bowed by the daily line of worshipers who told her their most intimate concerns and tragedies; she always seemed to give each client her undivided attention and her prodigious energy seemed to grow as she aged. Until the age of eighty-eight, she continued to take long walking pilgrimages along the base of Mount Iwaki and up Mount Hakkōda, and she visited her worshipers in southern Hokkaido. Every year until her death, she continued to call down the kami at the Cooking Pot Ceremony during the Great Summer Festival at Akakura, the climax of the annual ritual cycle. Although she had established a subsidiary bunke branch of the shrine soon after the war, I sensed that she always managed to finesse relations with the dominant honke branch. She had been on good terms with Kawai Mariko's daughter and successor, Kimiko, and was especially warm toward Kimiko's daughter, Yuko and adopted son, Seiji, the chief priest at the shrine. Unlike many of her fellow kamisama, Sugiyama Junko had a markedly ecumenical attitude toward other popular religious traditions. She was on friendly terms with many itako mediums, and often took her clients to Osorezan, where the most important gathering of itako occurs each July.[7]

Sugiyama Junko had been a deeply loved member of her village, a largely agrarian community on the plain between Hirosaki and Aomori City. She was so well known in the village that, at school, teachers and schoolmates commonly referred to her grandchildren as "kamisama" instead of by their family name. Their house was simply known in the region as the "kamisama house."

As a prime example of Sugiyama Junko's generosity and breadth of spirit, many friends and relations pointed to the respectful under-

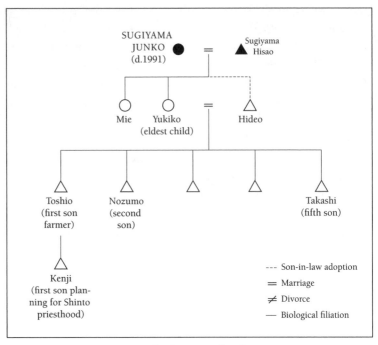

Within the figure:

SUGIYAMA JUNKO (d.1991) ● = ▲ Sugiyama Hisao

Mie ○ Yukiko ○ (eldest child) = △ Hideo

△ Toshio (first son farmer) △ Nozumo (second son) △ △ △ Takashi (fifth son)

△ Kenji (first son planning for Shinto priesthood)

--- Son-in-law adoption
= Marriage
≠ Divorce
— Biological filiation

33. The Sugiyama family

standing with which she had always treated her adopted son Hideo. Mukoyōshi, especially those from families as poor as Hideo's, are often treated as second-class citizens in rural Tsugaru, and they are usually required to sever all social and ritual relations with their natal kin. Yet Sugiyama Junko had always insisted that Hideo receive full respect within the Sugiyama family, that he be encouraged to keep up active relations with his natal family, and that he feel free to honor the ancestors of the family into which he had been born.

Although Sugiyama Junko's considerable income from her healing practice had paid for the orchard plot and continued to subsidize the family's agrarian enterprises, she had the tact never to mention this. She had always insisted, after her husband's early death, that Hideo was the real household head and that "his" orchard served as its financial foundation. She continued in this latter claim after primary responsibility for the orchard passed to Hideo's eldest son, Toshio.[8] She had encouraged Hideo's growing interest in spiritual matters, supervised his shugyō at Akakura, and assisted him as he studied for the Shintō priesthood.

Thanks to this long tutelage and to his considerable energy and drive, by the early 1990s Hideo had emerged a respected member of the local farming cooperative, one of the leading citizens of the village, and widely considered the neighborhood expert on religious matters. Each year at New Year's, he took the honored role of driving the village shrine's new shimenawa rice straw rope and demon mask through the village, expelling evil and allowing each household to partake in the rope's purity as he solicited donations for the local Shintō shrine. He assisted at Shintō ceremonials at the main branch of Akakura Mountain Shrine, and took the lead priestly role at rites within the junior branch.

Sugiyama Junko had also taken great interest in her grandchildren and great-grandchildren. Hideo and Yukiko had five sons, four of whom had families and children by the time Sugiyama Junko died. Sugiyama Junko had encouraged Hideo and Yukiko's second son, Nozumo, to pursue his dream of higher education and become an electrical engineer and, in time, a telecommunications executive in Tokyo. She took enormous pride in Nozumo, the only family member to achieve upper-middle-class professional status; it was considered widely appropriate that after her death, she chose to manifest her continuing presence to him before all others.

At age eighty-eight, Sugiyama Junko moved into semi-retirement. She ceased her lengthy walking pilgrimages and had herself photographed in front of her mountain altar in her favorite red kimono. Some of her followers expected that she would cease all healing in mediumship entirely, but in fact the next six years were to see her clientele and popularity grow steadily. The south wing of the family house became entirely dedicated to the practice. Often assisted by her daughter Yukiko, Sugiyama Junko would sit in front of her enormous, elaborate altar to the kami and pray for her many clients for hours on end.

In February 1991, Sugiyama Junko suddenly rose to even greater prominence. A local television station ran a documentary on Aomori spiritual healers. Sugiyama Junko was featured in the broadcast's title sequence and appeared in a three-minute segment within the show. Although she had always been popular, she and her family were unprepared for the deluge that followed. For the subsequent five months, requests for consultations and healing sessions swamped the household. Up until her death on the evening of 30 June 1991, clients began lining up outside the house by 5:00 A.M. each morning. Her extended family and large circle of friends agreed that exhaustion following the enormous upsurge in her clientele had caused her death. But all agreed she had died "at peace," a serene and successful matriarch of an extended family and a much-loved servant of the divinities.

Visions at the Funeral

On 3 July 1991, four days after Sugiyama Junko peacefully died at home in her sleep, four hundred mourners gathered in the village community hall for her funeral. All mourners paid their respects, lit incense from the candles beside her black-and-white memorial photograph, and rang the special funeral bell. A few hours before the formal Buddhist funeral service, several extraordinary things had been witnessed around these objects: Nozumo, Hideo's second son, observed that the two votive candles in front of Sugiyama Junko's memorial photograph had bent down toward one another as they melted. What is more, the left candle had melted into the shape of a dragon in flight. Nozumo hurriedly summoned his father, and the two men carefully photographed the candles three times. On examining the developed photographs, Hideo quickly concluded that the candle had transformed itself into a perfect representation of the dragon deity, Ryūjinsama, Sugiyama Junko's tutelary deity. As he gazed at the assemblage, he also saw the memorial photograph emit a miraculous glow, lighting up the candles from behind. The family would show and narrate these developed images to hundreds of friends over the coming months. Two images showed the miraculous left-hand (female) funeral candle, which had taken on the shape of the dragon. The third picture showed the male and female candles bending toward each other.

The carefully composed third photograph recalls the layout of many votive paintings at Akakura Mountain Shrine, which center on a left-hand (female) being facing a right-hand (male) one. In several paintings, a pair of dragons is shown facing one another, either within the upper reaches of Akakura Mountain or flying above it. Other paintings depict two sacred pine trees or birds leaning toward one another, or show Kawai Mariko on the left side of the mountain balanced against the male image of Akakura Daigongen or Kōbō Daishi on the right. As we have seen, ascetics annually reenact this motif at the 1 May Mountain Opening rite, when the great shimenawa rope is stretched over the Fudō Waterfall from a left-hand tree to a right-hand tree.

In turn, Hideo's photographed vision of the dragon candle backlit by Sugiyama Junko's miraculously glowing photograph recalls the shrine's most prominent votive painting (see frontispiece). The painting, depicting Kawai Mariko's miraculous nocturnal vision of the flying dragon, is hung over the front entrance of the Inner Sanctuary, precisely opposite the great altar and sacred mirror. In this striking black-and-white painting, the great dragon flies across the plain from the mountain, its huge head silhouetted against a large full moon. Scores of tiny people on the plain below point up to it in amazement. (Kawai Mariko's presence is indicated by a slightly larger figure, distinguished by a light halo around her head.)

In its basic structure, Mr. Sugiyama's vision recalls the revelatory visions of Kawai Mariko and Narita Emiko. In both these women's dreams, a flying element transmuted itself into a powerful maternal figure. Kawai Mariko saw a flying dragon become a miniature beautiful woman and Narita Emiko beheld "a streak of gold against a dark blue sky" transform itself into the sun goddess Amaterasu. Similarly, Hideo witnesses a miraculous dragon, which in turn leads him to see the illuminated photographic image of the Great Mother Junko-san.

It should be noted that, like many of their friends and neighbors, the Sugiyamas took it for granted that photographic images offered a privileged medium through which they could apprehend and venerate the dead. In metropolitan Japan, the practice of placing small photographs of former members of the family within the butsudan dates back to the late Meiji period (c.1890–1912). My impression is that wealthy Tsugaru families began this practice during the Taishō period. Memorial photographs were incorporated into the Sugiyama family altar soon after World War II. Some of my elderly informants could recall memorial photographs, such as the one at Sugiyama Junko's funeral, being used at local funeral services as early as the 1920s.

Television talk shows watched by the Sugiyama household often featured "mysterious" or paranormal photographs, within which are said to appear blurred images of troubled souls, such as murder victims and dead children, who continue to plague or afflict their living family. When I returned from a visit to Hiroshima, Sugiyama Yukiko remarked that negatives of the Genbaku (A-Bomb Dome) in central Hiroshima at times reveal shadowy figures standing at the windows, ghostly traces of those inside the building when the bomb exploded overhead on 6 August 1945.

For the Sugiyamas, as for many modern persons, photographs evocatively encapsulate some of the fundamental contradictions and conundrums of modernity. With increasing rationalization and with the loss of a sense of moral "authenticity" comes the deepening sense that conventional structures of meaning prove insufficient, that other truths must exist "out there." Yet paradoxically, these other truths are validated according to the reigning protocols of intelligibility, especially the quintessential authenticating device of modernity, the camera. In what Benjamin called "the age of mechanical reproduction," the real and the technologically visible have become increasingly synonymous (Benjamin 1974; Barthes 1981; Morris 1998). Under the intensely visual regime of knowledge associated with photography, a thing only "really" exists inasmuch as it is visible, or especially inasmuch as it may be captured on still or moving film. In many photographs of the odd, the blurred nature of the image becomes an index of its ambiguous interstitial state between the normal and the paranormal. From the standpoint of the Sugiyamas and their followers, the glowing photograph, and especially the blurrily developed photographs of the candles, thus gave tangible evidence that Sugiyama Junko's extraordinary spiritual influence continued to operate after her death.

Hideo's Dream: Amae Objectified

The night after witnessing the miraculous candle and glowing memorial photograph, Hideo fell asleep in front of the family butsudan, immediately adjacent to Sugiyama Junko's great saidan, where he had a powerful dream that he would reexperience several times. In the dream, he witnessed Sugiyama Junko sleeping in front of the family butsudan (or in some versions of the dream, he saw himself sleeping in front of the butsudan). Next he saw her atop a steep hill beckoning him to join her; in some versions she was standing in front of a beautiful old hilltop shrine, surrounded by trees. As he began to climb the steep flight of stone steps, he looked down and realized that the steps leading up to her were covered in human excrement. Confused and ashamed he stopped in his tracks, unable to reach his beloved mother/mother-in-law.

Hideo understood this dream, like the unusual behavior of the candles, as a clear message from the spirit of Sugiyama Junko, who was calling him and Yukiko to follow her in serving the kami. He surmised that he had to cleanse himself and his household of impurities before following her in her service to the divinities. He also concluded that he had a profound responsibility to share this dream with as many people as possible; over the subsequent year he was to tell many hundreds about it, which he considered the outstanding event of his life.

The dream's setting—facing up a hill from its base—has many referents. Many shrines and temples in the region are located at the top of forested hills, and worshipers reach them by stone staircases from the plain below. The dead are often thought to reside on hills and mountains, especially at Mount Osore (Mount Dread) on the Shimokita peninsula, where Sugiyama Junko often traveled with her clients. Thus no one considered it altogether surprising that her recently deceased spirit would beckon from a hilltop. The slope that Hideo tried to climb presumably has associations with Akakura, where ascetics often undertake shugyō as a form of memorialization for the recently deceased. Sugiyama Junko, one of Kawai Mariko's first disciples, had undertaken shugyō at Akakura in the 1920s. The path up Akakura Mountain begins with concrete steps. Hideo, who had undertaken shugyō in the 1950s under Sugiyama Junko's supervision, was intimately familiar with this sacred mountainscape.

As we have seen, images of Akakura Mountain encountered during shugyō or collective worship may produce mystically enhanced relations of kinship. Similarly, Hideo's dream of climbing the steps up a sacred hill allows him to enter fully into a line of ritual succession, moving him more closely into his adoptive household and toward the structural spiritual position of his late "mother." As in regular shugyō, these interactions with the symbolic mountain can prove psychologically fraught. A powerful condensation of relations of amae, the mountain can return the dependent climber or supplicant to the terrain of early childhood. Indeed, standing at the base of the hill, Hideo finds the steps up the slope covered in feces. Relative to the "great mother" Sugiyama Junko, he is a small, dependent child, reduced to infantile urges and uncontrolled bodily functions. Yet as he begins to climb the mountain, recapitulating the process of psychosocial maturation, he moves toward increasing self-consciousness. In the dream, after gazing up at his adoptive mother, he looks down and becomes acutely aware of his debased state. As is so often stressed by Akakura worshipers when they explain the ritual chant, "Saigi, Saigi," the first step in serving the gods and ancestors is to recognize one's own impure, sinful state. This aspect of the dream also recalls the Akakura Prayer's assertion that the "upper part of the body" (a pun on the term *kami*) must "become master" over the lower part of the body. Hideo must triumph over the dirty wastes from the lower half of the body in which his feet are mired and move up the mountainous stone steps toward the late Sugiyama Junko's elevated, spiritual position.[9]

In this regard, it seems striking that the dream's setting in part recalls the tableau of the Sugiyama family's domestic Buddhist altar, located next to Sugiyama Junko's great altar to the divinities. Hideo first had the dream while sleeping at the base of the butsudan; in subsequent versions he saw Sugiyama Junko sleeping before this altar. A miniature mountain, the vertically arranged butsudan serves as a dynamic, temporary abode for the dead, and it moves the deceased toward transmigration and rebirth. The butsudan constitutes the focal point of the Japanese extended household; inclusion within the butsudan epitomizes inclusion within the family line (Smith 1974). In part, the dream's image of climbing up the mountain toward a temple can be understood as equivalent to entering and ascending the family altar itself.

The Sugiyama butsudan represented a particularly fraught site for Hideo. As the adopted son of the house, he had been given primary responsibility for the altar's care and protection and for the veneration of the Sugiyama ancestors enshrined within it. Like a conventional bride, a mukoyōshi is viewed as a comparative outsider by the family into which he marries. He endures a long probationary period in which he must gradually convince his wife's family that he has truly severed himself from his natal family's ancestors and that he will capably lead his "new" family (Noguchi 1966). Even after six decades of marriage, and even after all of Sugiyama Junko's solicitude, Hideo remained acutely aware of his status as a relative outsider to the Sugiyama line. As he quietly mentioned to me several times, when he looked into the butsudan and gazed at the somber black-and-white

34. Memorial photograph of Sugiyama Junko on
altar of the junior (bunke) mountain shrine

photographs of the enshrined Sugiyama dead, he sometimes wondered
if he was worthy of fulfilling the great burden with which he had been
entrusted.

Significantly, Hideo first had his dream at the foot of the Sugiyama family butsudan, below these photographs of his late in-laws—
his classificatory mother and father. Just as the interior shelves of the
butsudan rise up to the central shelf housing the images, so in Hideo's
dream did he gaze up ancient stone steps leading up a hill to where
he could see the late kimono-clad Junko-san gesturing toward him.
In this sense, Hideo's dream recapitulated the structural predicament
he had faced throughout his adult life as a mukoyōshi: a comparative
outsider, he had continually attempted to rise in status, to enter fully
into the Sugiyama family line and into a higher generational plane—
in effect, to enter fully into the family's domestic altar. The dream's
central image of ancient stone steps leading up a hill to a shrine or
temple, seems to be a transformation of the terraced levels of the but-

sudan itself—a vision of movement into the family and ascent up to the next generational level.

As an adopted son-in-law, Hideo faced the disturbing possibility of becoming a muenbotoke, an unquiet soul memorialized neither in his natal or adopted families' altars. The dream evokes this terrifying sense of postmortem liminal separation and radical individuation. Hideo apprehends an image not only of the dead Sugiyama Junko but of himself after death, caught between worlds on the steps, even as the dream holds out the promise of eventual postmortem integration into the Sugiyama family butsudan. In the dream, as in his life thus far, this goal still eludes Hideo, for he finds himself mired in his insufficiencies.

In one sense, then, the lighted memorial photograph of Sugiyama Junko represents the elusive, interior centrality of the family line. Yet this magical glowing image also manifests the continuing power of Sugiyama Junko—Hideo and Yukiko's common "mother"—to bind husband and wife ever more closely together. Thus Hideo—by photographing the intertwined male and female candles and publicly narrating the wondrous glowing photograph of his "mother" Sugiyama Junko—sought to extend his intimate alliance with his wife, Sugiyama Junko's daughter. This union would follow the model of the *maeza-nakaza* (priest-shamaness) relationship in Japanese myth and cosmology, in which a charismatic shamaness and an interpreter-priest wield extraordinary religious power.[10]

The Family Orchard: Labor and Transcendence

The other major inspiration for the setting of Hideo's dream was also deeply imbued with his profound sense of obligation toward Sugiyama Junko and the Sugiyama family line. In many respects, the dream's steep hill recalled the Sugiyama's hillside apple orchard, the family's economic prize on which they had labored for half a century. Each morning Hideo would walk or drive through the (often muddy) flat fields that lay to the east of the village and then begin to climb up into the family orchard. This narrow one-acre plot stretched up a steep hill (forested to the right) that rose sharply from the lower plain toward thickly wooded hills above. Hideo had often mentioned that secreted within these high hills was a Shugendō (esoteric Buddhist) temple with which Junko-san had a special relationship. These hills gradually rose toward sacred Mount Hakkōda, fifteen miles further east. Every August for much of her long life Sugiyama Junko had journeyed as a pilgrim through these hills to the summit of Hakkōda; Hideo and Yukiko would continue to lead this pilgrimage each year after her death.

The narrow, hilly orchard was replete with further traces of Sugiyama Junko. She had purchased it during the MacArthur Land Redistribution, soon after the Asia-Pacific War. Sugiyama Junko had bought the plot with money earned from her many years as a labor migrant in Hokkaido fish canneries and her practice as a kamisama spirit medium. For Hideo, who had grown up in a bitterly poor seaside fishing village, the hillside orchard represented a priceless possession that epitomized the blessings that his adopted mother had brought into his life.

Sugiyama Junko herself had loved the orchard, widely admired in the community for its remarkably tasty apples, and spent much time working in it and praying each year for a successful harvest. At the hill's base was a tiny shrine to the field's protective deities; after Sugiyama Junko's death, the family became convinced that her spirit could be prayed to at this shrine as well. From the hill, one could gaze across the southern Tsugaru plain and see Akakura Mountain, the place where Sugiyama Junko had received her powers and where her formal shrine was located. (The mountain could not be seen from the Sugiyama's house in the village below.)

Even the excrement, in which Hideo found himself standing in the dream, may have been partly inspired by the family field. Mud often deeply covered the lower fields, but the hill did become drier the higher one climbed it. Hideo had often remarked to me that while the ground at the base of his field was messy and unkempt, the field's upper reaches were "clean" and well tended. He took great pride in the care with which he and his family pruned the apple trees, weeded the ground, removed dead branches and twigs, and delicately wrapped growing apples in tissue paper.

In the dream Hideo thus in part faced his adoptive mother from the familiar vantage point of his orchard, the place where he engaged each day in hard, concentrated work. This aspect of his dream recalls the emphasis on dedicated labor seen in the revelations experienced by the shrine's founding women. Narita Emiko was "seen by the kami" as she labored with grace and efficiency in the rice fields. Her vision of Amaterasu came to her at the place where she had carefully cooked the red fish. Kawai Mariko had seen the dragon emerging from the mountain that she looked on every day as she labored in the family fields. Hard, graceful work opens one up to transformative visions and to the blessings of the divinities, who are similarly graceful and productive.

Subsequent Journeys: Spreading the Vision

Hideo's dream became more widely disseminated after the extended Sugiyama family, including their children and grandchildren from Tokyo, took a day-long trip, forty-nine days after Sugiyama Junko's death, marking the traditional Buddhist transitional period when the soul of the deceased moves to the other world. At the Soto Zen temple of Entsu-ji, at Mount Osore on the Shimokita peninsula, they enshrined her *nodobotoke* (voice box, or larynx, lit. "throat Buddha"). In principle, the voice box could have been enshrined at a local Buddhist temple, but since Sugiyama Junko had often taken her clients to Osorezan, the most famous memorialization site in northern Japan, the family felt it only fitting that she take her next step toward Buddhahood there.

As we came into the open rocky field near the temple, everyone dismounted at the edge of the complex to walk over the red footbridge that marked the boundary between "this world" and the "other world." As Marilyn Ivy (1995) observes, Mount Osore's bleak, sulfur-drenched landscape marks one of Japan's most disturbing and "uncanny" zones. A Sainokawara (bank of the underworld river), it is believed to be inhabited by the pitiful unsettled souls of dead children who build up towers of stones, seeking to memorialize themselves and their family line, only to have their rocks overturned by demons. These beleaguered souls seek protection from the merciful Bodhisattva Jizō, whose statues stand throughout the area. Mount Osore is especially noted for the annual gathering of itako that takes place there each July, a few weeks before the annual Ōbon period of national ancestral veneration begins. Many thousands of worshipers gather to request prayers for the repose of their relatives and to consult itako, who speak enigmatically in the voice of the dead.

Now, no itako were present. The vast piles of flowers, pinwheels, and foodstuff left by worshipers for deceased relatives during the festival had all been cleaned up. Instead of thousands of visitors, only a few score roamed the desolate outcroppings. Hideo, always the conscientious teacher, carefully pointed out to me interesting sites, including a mound shaped like a ship, dedicated to those lost at sea. Looking up at the brooding shape of Osorezan, he also spoke at length about his dream of Sugiyama Junko on the hill. The usually effusive Yukiko seemed lost in her own thoughts.

The visit proved especially traumatic for Yukiko. After the whole family had boarded the bus, ready to depart, she stopped briefly into the first temple building, where we had left the remains of Sugiyama Junko's voice box. She emerged moments later and stood in front of the temple gate, crying inconsolably. Evidently unwilling to intrude on her sorrow, no one moved. Finally, I walked over to her and lightly put my arms around her; holding on to me, she slowly climbed on board the bus, continuing to cry. "Mother is really gone now," she whispered as the bus pulled out and we began the long drive home.

Riding the Dragon: Mr. Sugiyama's Speech

Immediately after returning from Osorezan, Hideo experienced an especially vivid version of his dream of Sugiyama Junko on the hilltop beckoning him to join her. He and Yukiko began to lay plans for a fall festival at Akakura, where Hideo would publicly announce his vision and dream to Sugiyama Junko's followers. These plans occasioned a good deal of spirited discussion and debate in the extended Akakura Mountain Shrine community. For many members of the senior branch, Sugiyama Junko's death presaged the long-awaited reunification of the two branches; they hoped that the Sugiyamas and their followers would consent to being subsumed under the direct mantle of Kawai Mariko's followers. The fall festival at the Takeda house in Hirosaki, in their eyes, should suffice for both branches. Others argued that so soon after the death of Sugiyama Junko, a fall festival was rather unseemly. Nonetheless, Hideo and Yukiko decided to proceed with the rite and invited Sugiyama Junko's followers to attend.

The service at the mountain shrine, on 1 September 1991, had a festive air. The apple harvest that year promised to be exceptionally good, and judging by their generous donations, many participants felt rather flush. With no inkling of the typhoon that a month later was to send local families into calamitous debts, Toshio (Hideo's eldest son) even told his boys just before the ceremony began that he was thinking of buying them a VCR.

Presided over by Mr. Takeda as senior priest, the ceremony followed the standard Shintō sequence, including the presentation of sakaki saplings by leading worshipers. Yukiko then sat before her mother's famous drum and drummed and chanted a prayer to the divinities. Her style recalled that of her mother, and was well received. Next, Hideo delivered a speech recounting his dreams and visions since his mother-in-law's death. As Hideo addressed the congregation, he stood in front of the large color photograph of Sugiyama Junko, taken when she was eighty-eight. The photograph showed her dressed in her ritual red kimono, posed in front of the great candelabrum in the shape of the mountain. The picture itself was placed directly on the altar just behind this same candelabrum. To the side was a sculpture of the dragon god Ryūjinsama, Sugiyama Junko's tutelary deity. In a quiet, steady voice, Hideo delivered the following words:

> In a flash I dreamt of her sleeping in front of the butsudan. Then I dreamt of very high stone steps, and Sugiyama Junko-san was standing at the top. Really dirty things were all over the steps.
>
> I was pulled up by my heart. . . . I had this dream four times. I woke up around 2:00, [thinking about] all the dirt. It shouldn't exist. If I clean it up, then I can go up [the steps]. . . . I felt this.
>
> The great mother. It can't be revealed in words. Then something made me stand in an anguished position. But I think I will never forget her. I was impatient, but nothing can be solved if—something made me impatient to do it. I myself am dirty. Many people support this building. [This] is the first step [without which we] could not hold this *matsuri* [festival]. [But we] received some bad telephone calls [from people who were jealous of our success]. But we wanted to hold the fall festival. And we suddenly decided that we had to hold to it.
>
> And we received money for Sugiyama Junko-san's funeral from a five-member family in Kanagawa. And when I told them about the wax in the shape of Ryūjinsama from the candle that burned at Sugiyama Junko-san's funeral, this woman said, "Oh! That's the

same thing I saw in my dream when Sugiyama Junko-san died! She allowed me to have that vision/dream!" And I said immediately, "Yes, that's right. Because she ended up herself riding the dragon."

Coming once more in front of grandmother [Junko-san], I suddenly saw the candle flow. When suddenly, from the core of the candle, with a snap it was like fireworks. And the candle began to melt out horizontally in the shape of a jointed piece of bamboo. One joint by one joint. It flowed like that out of the candle and then stood up like this [he gestures with his hand, wrist bent perpendicular to his arm]. And then the light shone out from behind her [Sugiyama Junko]. Thus things have been caused to be better.

Hideo' speech, considered by those who heard it as deeply elegant, moving, and sincere, is worth considering in some detail. After beginning with his dream and his startled awakening, he moves on to his anguish over his own insufficiencies and over negative feelings from unnamed others. He then mentions the support he has received for this fall festival, especially his delight at learning that another follower of Sugiyama Junko had had the same dream. He ends by returning in his mind's eye to the marvelous image of the left-hand dragonlike candle, the image he had carefully photographed and studied, and concludes with the glowing image of Sugiyama Junko's memorial photograph. In so doing, he rhetorically established a tangible tableau for his listeners of his own gradual transition from doubt and suffering to security and triumph. Many audience members subsequently told me that his speech made them feel "calmer" and gave them a profound sense that, through the blessings of the Sugiyamas, their own troubles might also ease.

From the start, Hideo's speech evoked the importance of photographic images in his postmortem encounters with Sugiyama Junko, whose butsudan photograph he stared at each morning and evening during prayers. The image of her sleeping at the butsudan's base came to him "in a flash." Next he sees her distant visage at the top of the steps, close yet unattainable, just like the black-and-white photograph within the butsudan's upper shelf. From this glimpse of the eternal, his attention shifts to his mortal, bodily insufficiency, to the excremental dirt in which he is mired. His wording, "I was pulled up by my heart," and his anticipation of climbing the ancient stone stairs to join

Sugiyama Junko recall the Akakura Prayer's fervent prayer: "There are times when the heart becomes wretched. . . . [May] the heart which is righteous, upright, and originary, become one with the beautiful heart of the great deity." Like any ascetic, he first confronts his internal mental and spiritual debasement, and only then prepares for personal reformation.

If facing the hill in the dream in part constitutes an exploration of Hideo's own psyche, then the mythic slope—like Akakura Mountain itself—evokes a sociocentric model of mind. The true value of the dream comes through opposition and alliance, as these are recreated in Hideo's spoken performances. He alludes to the shadowy enemies who have opposed his quest to continue Sugiyama Junko's mission and emphasizes that the dream of one of his distant supporters has corroborated his own dream. The dream is legitimate inasmuch as it is shared between individual consciousnesses. As in the many conversations among kamisama mediums, ascetics, and lay worshipers, knowledge gained by revelatory visions is here diffused through constantly circulating narratives. Hideo thus labors to create a vivid memory-picture of Sugiyama Junko among all worshipers, so that like him, they will "never forget her."

The woman's acknowledgment of their common dream leads Hideo to his epiphany: Sugiyama Junko is not simply dead; she remains an active force, moving effortlessly between worlds and among her followers. Like Kawai Mariko before her, she is unified with the divine being that moves between this world and the other world, between the plain and the mountain. She is, he realizes, "riding the dragon." Just as the dragon served as a messenger for Kawai Mariko's founding dream seventy years earlier, so now does the dragon spread Hideo's dream of Sugiyama Junko into the minds of the faithful.

The thought of the dragon inevitably returns Hideo to the deeply moving image of the animated funerary candle, which he reenacts with his outstretched arm. Through this physical performance, he himself becomes a tangible icon of the miraculous image, visibly embodying the presence of the usually invisible kami. Just as a possessed kamisama medium is thought to be filled with overpowering heat that bursts out into her surroundings, so does the candle burst out from its core, miraculously growing into the shape of the dragon lord. Like a living piece of bamboo, it rolls out "joint by joint." Its sudden awakening ("it stood up like that") signals the reawakening of Sugiyama Junko's spirit and the simultaneous reawakening of her followers, further signaled by Sugiyama Junko's glowing memorial photograph. Hideo, who takes on the physical qualities of the transforming candle, mimetically reperforms this reawakening, peformatively demonstrating, in his words, that "things have been caused to be better."

Typhoon Nineteen: Economic Disaster

The Sugiyamas' quest to succeed Sugiyama Junko received an unexpected impetus after Typhoon Nineteen swept through Aomori prefecture in late September 1991. The storm devastated the region's economic mainstay, its apple crops, on the eve of the harvest. As calamitous as the typhoon was for the local economy, it did seem to bring more of Sugiyama Junko's worshipers back into Hideo and Sugiyama Junko's orbit. As more and more members of local farming families had to travel to Kansai and Kanto as short-term migrant laborers, they or their parents came to ask Hideo and Junko to pray for their safety while away from home. Many recalled that Sugiyama Junko herself had first been blessed with healing powers when she worked as a labor migrant in Hokkaido, and that she had always provided protective prayers for migrants. Now, they asked Hideo and Junko to continue these prayers.

Hideo's dreams of Sugiyama Junko intensified during this period, and he and Yukiko began to visit many households, shrines, temples, and sacred sites that Sugiyama Junko had regularly visited during her long life, including Mount Hakkōda, Mount Taihei, Miyoshi Shrine in Akita, and Saruka Shrine. In so doing, Hideo and Yukiko repeatedly linked themselves to their common mother and helped constitute themselves as a sacral couple along the classic maeza-nakaza pattern. Rather like ascetics undergoing conventional mountain shugyō on the mountain slopes, they reaccessed microhistories embedded within charged landscape sites in order to locate themselves within a broader spiritual macrohistory.

Over the course of that winter, the Sugiyamas were blessed with a new client, Mr. Komatsu, a forty-year-old first son of a farmer family who remained unmarried and burdened with the responsibility of caring for his aging parents. Mr. Komatsu, in turn, introduced the Sugiyamas to a new set of families, who treated them with considerable respect. Buoyed by this experience, Yukiko and Hideo decided that spring to take a special trip through southern Hokkaido, visiting many of Sugiyama Junko's former clients and followers, who welcomed them warmly as a respected priest-medium couple.

Carrying the Photograph: The May 1992 Mountain Opening Ceremony

Two weeks after the Hokkaido trip, on 1 May 1992, I joined Hideo and Yukiko at the annual Mountain Opening Ceremony at Akakura. As we began the ascent, Yukiko bewildered me by patting her knapsack and excitedly whispering to me, "Obāchan ga koko ni itte" (I have grandmother here with me). Up at the waterfall, as Hideo and the other men hung the great shimenawa rope, I learned what Yukiko meant. Within her backpack she had carried the color photograph of Sugiyama Junko-san dressed in her kimono, the same photograph in front of which Hideo had delivered his September 1991 speech. Carefully extracting it, she posed with Hideo and the photograph, insisting that I take pictures, then carefully erected the photograph in the snow, lit candles, and laid out offerings before it. She recited prayers softly as Mr. Takeda led the entire congregation in collective chanting to the mountain kami.

Since Sugiyama Junko's death, the color photograph had stayed in Sugiyama Junko-san's altar in the Sugiyamas' mountain subshrine. But the evening after the Mountain Opening climb, Yukiko brought the photograph back to her home in the village, and set it within the great altar to the divinities, where it would stay permanently. That night, she told me, she slept better than she had since her mother's death. She later remarked to me, "It was a beautiful day on the mountain, wasn't it?" Hideo also remarked how good it had felt to pray to the photograph on the mountain. From this day on, Hideo or Yukiko ceased expressing doubts as to their ability to succeed Sugiyama Junko or to uphold their obligations to her. Renewed with purpose, they enthusiastically continued their healing practice and service to the kami. The leading figures of the senior branch soon afterward abandoned their campaign to absorb the junior branch and began to assign increasingly important ritual tasks to Hideo and Yukiko at major collective ceremonies.

35. Sugiyama Junko's photograph carried by her
daughter and son-in-law up Akakura Mountain during
the 1992 Mountain Opening Ceremony

Why did the Sugiyamas carry Junko's photograph? Why did this
particular ritual episode help put their lingering doubts to rest? And
why did it help solidify their emerging high status in the shrine association? To begin with, their act must be understood in relation to
Hideo's dream. In the dream, Hideo tried to travel up a slope toward
his mother, only to find himself stopped in his tracks by his polluted,
debased state. Now, in contrast, Hideo and Yukiko traveled together up
the sacred mountain with an incarnation of Sugiyama Junko, during a
rite of collective purification. After Sugiyama Junko's death, her senior
children and principal heirs had been overcome with anxiety that they
could not live up to her extraordinary legacy. How could they begin to
follow in her footsteps? How could they begin to memorialize so vast
a spirit? The sacral photograph, which quite literally dominated their
field of vision, provided a kind of solution: here was a tangible icon of
Sugiyama Junko's powerful and enduring presence that they could suc-

cessfully care for. In contrast to the diffuse, infinite obligations to the soul of Sugiyama Junko-san, the photograph offered visual immediacy and tactile limitations; it could be held, put in a backpack, carried up the mountain, and set out before them. In caring for the photograph, Yukiko and Hideo could do something for Sugiyama Junko, respectfully elevating her stature as they, in turn, raised their own status.

In a cultural context that places such emphasis on memorial photography and postmortem photographic encounters with the dead, photographs can carry compressed tangible traces both of remembered living human personalities and of dead spirits. This is largely possible because a photographic print simultaneously evokes presence and absence. It constitutes on the one hand a compact and proximate object, yet it manifestly depicts something separated from the viewer in space and time. The photographic image seems to present an image like that available through ordinary vision, yet it hints at greater knowledge, at a truth beyond general apprehension. Under the correct conditions, the photograph, like the Shintō mirror, functions as a virtually perfect instance of mitate, in Yamaguchi's sense of the term.

These dynamics call to mind Lévi-Strauss's argument that the aesthetic power and intelligibility of miniaturized artworks depends on the radical suppression of some dimensions of the thing represented. This reduction of size, scale, or weight makes the aesthetic element more "grasp-able," more understandable by the viewer, who is enabled to apprehend the thing as a whole before perceiving its constituent parts (Lévi-Strauss 1966).[11] Similarly, for Hideo and Yukiko, the immediacy of these material objects subsumed other dynamics and made it possible for them to redeploy these elements creatively in a ritual context.

The Mountain Opening rite offered a particularly appropriate arena for this symbolic redeployment. As discussed in chapter 3, the dramatic hoisting of the shimenawa allows the assembled congregation, whose labor and vision the rope collectively embodies, to experience vicariously a miraculous flight up the sacred mountain. In this ritual of concentrated visual attention, worshipers gaze at the breathtaking upper reaches of the mountain. They are oriented toward a soaring, dragonlike rope, in which the visions and aspirations of the community have been tangibly invested. All attention is directed toward the invisible gods, who at this moment seem just beyond the threshold of immediate apprehension.

Situated in this ritual context, Sugiyama Junko's photograph appears to have taken on a similarly overwhelming immediacy, filling the actors' horizon of concern and blotting out other dynamics and anxieties. The photograph co-participated, in effect, in this soaring animation of the great rope, an instrument closely associated with the dragon lord Ryūjinsama, Junko's tutelary deity. The color picture even showed Sugiyama Junko in her auspicious red kimono, the same color as the red Rising Sun of Amaterasu directly overhead, in the Japanese national flag hanging from the rope.

Carrying Sugiyama Junko's photograph up the mountain during the Yamabiraki thus constituted a powerful realization of Hideo's dream. He and Yukiko responded to Sugiyama Junko's invitation to join her in an elevated space, overlooking the plain below. Their mother's face was no longer at a distant, elevated remove, but was instead transported into a familiar realm, where it could be intimately caressed and talked to as it became merged with Amaterasu and the other mountain divinities.

Like the shimenawa rope and the ritual elements that we have explored in the preceding chapters, the photograph of Sugiyama Junko provided a tangible link between mother and child even as it helped establish a beneficial degree of separation between two subjects. I remember the intense joy in Yukiko's face as she carried her mother's color photograph up Akakura. As we retraced the snow-covered route that mother and daughter had climbed together so many times before, Yukiko stressed that Sugiyama Junko was "right here with me!" This was a poignant claim, for when we reached the sacred waterfall on the high mountain slopes, the vital threshold between the human and divine domains, mother and daughter did not kneel beside each other, as they had always done before. Instead, Yukiko placed the photograph in the snow in front of her and prayed to the picture, while Hideo and the rest of the congregation prayed to the mountain gods. Through such acts, Sugiyama Junko was moved more toward the status of a full-fledged kami. Hideo and Yukiko, in turn, returned to the plain below better prepared to succeed Sugiyama Junko as living intermediaries between worlds.

Hideo and Yukiko apprehend in the image of their mother's face a reflected image of their own hopes and possibilities. At the funeral, as Hideo wonders if he has within himself the capacity to serve as a vessel of the kami, he looks up to see the photographic image of his adoptive mother's face radiating an accepting light, illuminating the wax image of her dragon familiar. In his dream, he gazes up to see her face smiling down at him, signaling her belief that he has the capacity to become like her. As he retold this story and repeatedly contemplated the mysterious candle photographs, he reexperienced this validating vision of his classificatory mother's face. In his speech of 1 September 1991, Hideo mimetically enacted all of these maternal roles: he stood with his arms outstretched to demonstrate Sugiyama Junko's accepting posture at the top of the stone steps, and his arm became the magically extended dragon candle which Junko "rode."

Finally, at the May 1992 Mountain Opening Ceremony, he and Yukiko creatively engaged with the powerful reflective qualities of their mother's face; they carried her image (a close-up of her face and upper body) up the mountain, experienced with the congregation the annual rite of cosmological marriage, and brought her image back from the mountain into their home. No longer at a structural distance from the mother's face, they internalized her face's positive reflected image of themselves. Freed of self-doubts, they became more capable of following in her footsteps with creative improvisation, developing novel representational rites. In gazing on their mother's image at the great gorge, the Sugiyama couple were able to move beyond a long-term structural childhood and come more into their own as mature actors, confidently defending their interests and their following against other leading figures in the association.

Becoming "the Mirror": Attaining Mastery

In the *Kojiki*, Amaterasu's initial response to having committed incest with her brother (and having witnessed his acts of defilement that reiterated the incestuous violation) is to retreat into the uterine cave, to break off all contact with the world. She is enticed out only by the mirror, which tricks her into thinking she sees a rival goddess. This "mistake" of the self for the other and in the other constitutes a necessary misrecognition, perhaps one of the foundations of culture. It compels one to enter into the social world, to interact with others, and eventually to pursue an alternate solution to the problem of incest—to marry a person from outside one's immediate group.

A worshiper at Akakura invests her inmost hopes and conditions within the mountain and its symbolic substitutes, which represent macrocosmic and microcosmic transformations of the maternal body. She may later access and reinternalize these transformed qualities and energies from the maternal mountain, which teaches her about aspects of herself that she had never recognized or understood. Significantly, this new knowledge and reinvigoration often comes about by beholding visions of a woman's beautiful face or by disciplinary operations on the surface of Akakura, colloquially referred to as the *ura no kao* (reverse face) of the mountain. These reflected visions of the self are often conflated with visions of the empowering, phallic dragon deity. Kawai Mariko first learned of her spiritual calling by seeing the flying dragon detach itself from the mountain and become a beautiful woman standing beside her pillow. Narita Emiko was transformed by her vision of the beautiful face of Amaterasu, soon after a dragon god renamed her "Beautiful Voice." Sakurai Fumiko in time came to apprehend the healing mountainscape, in which she encountered visions of its resident green dragon, as her "mother's garden." For all these women, important transformations took place as they looked into the carved, compassionate faces of the Kannonsama stupas along the great ridge. As we have seen, especially important transitions took place at the eighteenth "Rock Door" Kannon, within Ubaishi. Inside the narrow birth tunnel of this complex reflective space, ascetics talk aloud to the divinities and hear back deep truths about themselves.

Each day, a kamisama medium strives to become more and more like the kami she venerates, a visible reflection of the perfect beauty of the gods. Through shugyō, meditation, ritual performance, and prayer, the medium's body increasingly takes on the irresistible, shimmering, graceful, and flowing qualities of light itself, which she—as a human mirror—refracts back to her human worshipers. At the same time, as a mediating mirror, she also reflects back to her worshipers that which they have invested in their relationship with her, and through her, with the divinities. It is perhaps for this reason that even though my informants nearly always reported fear at being so "transparent" and "exposed" to the medium's unwavering eyes during consultations, they usually recalled a deep sense of tranquility and serenity once the conversation was completed. For better or worse, a worshiper sees in the kamisama's visage a fundamental aspect of herself.

These publicly dramatized positive enhancements of the self may have social and political consequences in the larger shrine community. Revelatory visions function as a kind of communication currency in the Akakura network, establishing some actors as particularly charismatic, others as less so. Those mediums who must effectively transmit to worshipers the reflected light of the divinities, and who best mirror the worshipers' emerging sense of selfhood, are most likely to develop sizable followings and to be called on to perform important divination and healing rites. As the story of Hideo's revelatory dream vision of his mother's face circulated through various Tsugaru social networks, the Sugiyama couple became increasingly in demand as a priest-medium pair for local rites and blessings. They were able to resist the senior branch's attempt to absorb the Sugiyama-led junior branch of the shrine, and they enhanced Sugiyama Junko's status as an important deity of the entire shrine.

These interpersonal struggles, waged in a deeply familial idiom, rarely rise to the level of explicit confrontation. As in conventional families, these initiatives entail complex, shifting alliances and are frequently punctuated by explicit assertions of solidarity between interlocutors. They are often pursued through subtle rhetorical means and indirect retellings of the quasi-genealogical lines through which the leading worshipers are connected representationally to the shrine founder. Important mediums and prominent worshipers vie to establish their particular memories as definitive and as speaking for the Akakura family as a whole as they seek to encompass others' personal accounts within their own broader imitative narratives of the ever changing mountain. As living "mirrors," they condense other persons and trajectories within fixed representational frames, functioning as authoritative intermediaries between supplicant mortals and the undying divinities. Through bodily enactments and rhetorical performances, these politically and spiritually powerful ascetics dramatize and reconfigure the sorrows and pain of this world; they ritually articulate unarticulated aspirations and give tangible form to hitherto invisible forces. In so doing, they establish compelling representations of the full range of human experience, from mundane labor to spiritual transcendence. They make real their followers' most deeply held immortal wishes.

c o n c l u s i o n

Immortal Wishes — Dependence and Interdependence

This book draws its title, *Immortal Wishes,* from Freud's classic meditation on the nature of unconscious desire. Writing of the Western bourgeois subject, Freud assumed the immortal wishes to be childish, libidinal urges that must be repressed in order for an independent, masterful ego to emerge triumphant. Yet in the particular Japanese context that we have explored, what are the salient "immortal wishes"? To what extent are they repressed or sublimated within this particular sacred mountain and the minds of its dedicated worshipers?

At least in this particular Japanese context, the ultimate temptation or unconscious desire would seem to be the fantasy of infinite amae, of complete maternal dependence. Possessed by a demon, Kawai Mariko urged all her disciples to join her in an *onsen,* a hot springs bath, associated with indulgent, childlike pleasure. All novice ascetics learn of worshipers who have been tricked by demons calling their names in their mothers' voices, leading them to disappear forever within the maternal mountain. In this respect, the famous early scene in the *Kojiki* of the sun goddess Amaterasu hiding in the cave would seem to depict the most fundamental immortal wish: she retreats back into a womb, out of all contact with others, returning to primal unity with the mother.

At one level, such utter inward retreat proves deeply dangerous: were Amaterasu to stay in her cave forever, all light and life would fade from the universe. Were the Dragon Princess to have stayed forever in her muddy pool, she never would have conjoined with the male god; agriculture and history would never have come to Tsugaru. Yet at another level, this sort of turning inward proves vital for the ultimate reproduction of life. In a perceptive discussion of the metaphysical dimensions of uchi/soto relations, Rosenberger (1994) argues that Shintō cosmology is founded on an implicit contrast between externally oriented relations of fixed, authoritative hierarchy and internally directed sources of compressed energy. She characterizes these two orientations through the metaphor of a tree going through its annual cycle. The tree in winter folds in on itself, "consolidating its energy in its roots and returning to its inner essence for generativity." In contrast, the tree in spring and summer grows outward, manifesting its authority through properly ordered differentiated parts (Rosenberger 1994, 100). Adapting Bradd Shore's discussion of the two potentialities of *mana* (creative or generative power) in Polynesia, Rosenberger argues that in Japan the generative energy and spontaneity of the interior domain of uchi serves as a necessary complement to the more restrictive, disciplined hierarchies associated with the external public domains of soto, the principles that ultimately govern social relations with others. In Japan, Rosenberger notes, "Sources of generative power, such as nature and women, are literally roped into human use: the rope around the unique rock on the coast, the *obi* binding the kimono-clad woman, the knot on envelopes containing money" (Ibid, 100–101).

At Akakura, the extraordinary discipline of shugyō on the mountain helps to intensify the ascetics' interior reservoirs of generative energy. Appropriately, this inner intensification often occurs within highly interior (uchi) spaces, while crawling repeatedly under the tunnel of Ubaishi, meditating under the cold waterfall of Fudō within the narrow gorge, boiling sacred water in the compressed cooking pot. As they anticipate and conform to the wishes of the gods, even the outer rock face of the mountain becomes a comforting interior space, as intimately familiar as one's "mother's garden." As befits an uchi zone, the mountain becomes the staging ground for spontaneous acts of aesthetic representation; recall the flowing grace with which Sakurai Fumiko and other ascetics leap across boulders or fashion offerings that are always said to emulate the divinities' beauty yet turn out different each time. Each performance of "Saigi, Saigi" or the Sword of Fudō rite by an important kamisama medium constitutes a unique event, as she deftly incorporates unexpected references to recent events, to persons present and absent, and to the worshipers' deepest fears and aspirations. Such spontaneous eruptions would appear shocking and unseemly if performed by a male priest during a formal Shintō service governed by the hierarchical, ordered principles of the exterior (soto) domain. Yet they are considered miraculous blessings of the life-giving kami when performed by a female kamisama medium in interior contexts. Witnessing and hearing these unruly performances by the "mothers of the shrine" stimulates the growth of plants and persons, causing the "hearts and minds" of worshipers to more properly resemble the spontaneous divinities.

In other words, excessive maternal dependence is dangerous, yet maternal dependence also serves as the necessary foundation of all positive development. As we have seen, the ascetic on the mountain gradually learns to accept total dependence on the all-powerful maternal mountain, and in time she learns to project this sense of dependence onto other persons, beings, and forces. The two kinds of dependence are so close that they may prove difficult to distinguish. Yet by repeatedly traversing the sacred mountain, with a heart fully open to indulgence by the divinities, one may come to know oneself more fully in relation to these good and bad others. Filled with love for the life-giving divinities, the worshiper ideally enters into expanding relations of exchange with a host of others—ancestors, remembered Great Mothers, and the invisible divinities. As these sacred beings reciprocate her dedicated labor and grant her revelatory visions, she may in time become a "mirror" for herself and others, attaining a form of transcendent selfhood and achieving recognition as an honored "mother" of her dependent children. In so doing, she necessarily comes to stand in competitive opposition to other maternal figures, including demonesses and fellow kamisama spirit mediums, who, she may suggest, pose considerable dangers for their mortal worshipers.

The worshiper can easily misconstrue an image of her emerging self-hood in the maternal mountain's shifting, multifaceted features. Significantly, demons tempt a worshiper by calling out her name; if the climber turns for an instant, she will be possessed and return to an infantile state, eager only to return to the mother's embrace, forgetting all adult obligations and responsibilities. In Freud's terms, the repressed "immortal wishes" of the Titans continue to rumble beneath the psychic apparatus cast down by the Father of the Gods.

On this point, Mrs. Narita and Mrs. Okuda do not seem far removed from Freud. They ruefully agreed during the July 1992 conversation that it is terribly easy to be led astray on the mountain since it is hard to recognize the divinities when they enigmatically manifest themselves. For all her pride in her many years of service, even Mrs. Narita, ultimately, comes to a tragic conclusion: "The good kami and the bad kami walk together. . . . The kami only walk in strange shapes, the kami only walk in strange shapes."

The maternal mountain, after all, makes for a profoundly fearful place. The opening lines of the Akakura Prayer refer to the "fear and reverence" with which worshipers face and climb the mountain. The mountain, as nearly all my informants told me, is a severe (*kibishii*) and fear-inducing (*osoroshii*) mistress. "Fear"—of divinities, demons, ancestral beings, biophysical illness, and economic catastrophe—manifestly motivates disciplinary service on the mountain slopes and in the shrine precincts. Kawai Mariko carried out her initial shugyō at Ōishi Shrine and its subsidiary subshrine Ubaishi, sites dedicated to protection against difficulties and death in childbirth. To this day, Akakura Mountain Shrine's ritual practices are organized with reference to the disturbing symbolism of human childbirth and the regenerative cosmological "womb" of the life-giving mountain. In repeated ascetic exercises modeled on human procreative and gestational processes, Akakura worshipers traverse the "fearful" mountain landscape. They also present exquisitely crafted offerings of food, rice wine, and water to divinities and ancestors, and they may in turn receive revelatory visions of the divinities' "pure beauty." In so doing, worshipers gradually transpose qualities of their own "fear," insufficiency, and devoted labor into material media, the mountain, and transcendent qualities of light. "Beautiful" offering trays, shrine buildings, and physical sites on the mountain body thus function as microcosmic and macrocosmic reconstructions of tenuous, hoped-for exchange relations between persons, ancestors, and gods.

Worshipers are continually made aware that these positive relations with the nurturing divinities may be suddenly and violently severed. Even an experienced ascetic such as Mrs. Okuda may forfeit whatever credit she has earned with the divinities through momentary inattention. A ritual may fail, leaving one's heart "torn in two." Like human childbirth, these processes of biocosmological gestation and bodily reconstruction may culminate in death, not life. Like the shimenawa rope that slowly frays over the gorge each year, the umbilical cord binding mortal worshipers to the sacred divinities may easily snap. The mirror face of the maternal mountain, which promises the enhancement of the self, may lead to its annihilation.

Gender and Power

Fraught relations with other women motivate many women to pursue asceticism at Akakura, and ritual action on the mountain is often organized around the symbolism of ambivalent female roles or tense female-female interaction. Kawai Mariko was first drawn to ascesis out of deep anxieties over her failures as a mother, triggered by her daughter's skin affliction and hair loss. She responded to Akakura Daigongen's call when pregnant with her second son and faced with renewed worries over her fitness as a mother. Mrs. Narita also experienced her early visions as she confronted the early challenges of marriage and motherhood and was consumed by worries that she might fail in the obligations to her husband's household. The medium Mrs. Okuda, in turn, underwent transformative visions as she performed memorialization for her grandmother on the mountain slopes. A flying dragon from the Akakura summit also summoned Kawai Mariko's daughter Kimiko to the mountain to follow in her mother's vocation as a kamisama spirit medium. In turn, at the point during her mountain austerities when she began to think of Akakura as her "mother's garden," Sakurai Fumiko, anxious that she had failed to provide grandchildren for her mother-in-law, beheld a great green dragon coiled up at the Fudō Waterfall.

These women's revelatory visions (which oral narratives in the shrine community continually recall) may be understood as complex encounters with refracted images of their own selves and of their relations with their own mothers, grandmothers, sisters, and daughters. As they become increasingly oriented toward the mountain, the sacred landscape reforges them and their closest kin bonds, constituting each woman as a spiritual "Great Mother" of the community of worshipers—in alliance and competition with the other maternal forces of the mountain.

How are we to understand the marked emphasis at Akakura on positive and negative maternal figures and feminine capacities? To some extent, this ambivalence reflects broader structures of patriarchy in Japan. Social and spiritual ties within the (overwhelmingly female) Akakura Mountain Shrine congregation often exhibit the tensions and crises between mothers and daughters—as well as mothers-in-law and daughters-in-law—that characterize conventional modern Japanese households. Applying Melanie Klein's concept of projective identification to Japanese family organization, Anne Allison argues that in contemporary Japanese culture, symbolic mother figures are often feared and raged against precisely because of the extraordinarily deep, enduring bonds promoted, and then partially ruptured, between mother and child. To be sure, distance from the primary maternal object of affection can trigger anger in any historical moment or cultural context. However, this potential has enormously intensified in Japan since the Meiji period. The dominant state-sponsored ideology of "Good wife, wise mother" widely inculcated an image of an omniscient mother who would anticipate and meet all of her child's needs, yet willingly sacrificed the child to the service of the nation and society in arenas of education, marriage, military service, or employment. As a result, Allison demonstrates, a "split" image of the mother developed in mass and popular culture, oscillating between an intensely loved, asexual, "pure" being, and an eroticized, sadistic, demonic creature (Allison 1996).

In a comparable sense, as dependent worshipers follow the footsteps of their Great Mother Kawai Mariko on the maternal mountain of Akakura, they repeatedly encounter, and are possessed by, "good" and "bad" divinities, usually conceived of as female, who alternately seek to nurture and consume them. Inasmuch as the dominant deity,

Akakura Daigongen, is (in Melanie Klein's terms) "a combined parental figure," fusing the male alien conqueror and the indigenous female demoness, it is difficult to disentangle a worshiper's varied affective relations to the object of veneration. Yet the greatest anxiety expressed by worshipers usually does seem directed toward female demonesses and female-coded landscape sites.

The shrine unquestionably reproduces conventional gender hierarchies. As in nearly all Japanese institutions, males occupy virtually every formal leadership position in the shrine association. As we have seen, women ascetics work considerably harder than their male counterparts, especially at cleaning and food preparation. As in many other Japanese institutions which places women in close association with one another, including households and community organizations, friction among them, especially between older and younger women, probably has the net effect of deflecting attention away from taken-for-granted structures of patriarchy. Many women report that worship at the shrine helps them to become "better adjusted" to their roles as women, better able to help their fathers, husbands, brothers, and sons and to be "less gloomy" about the challenges of everyday life.

Yet, clearly, it would be far too simplistic to ascribe misogyny, or even exclusively "traditionalist" gender conceptions, to the women of Akakura Shrine. All stress that dedicated service on the mountain has made them proud of their accomplishments as women, and they point with delight to their successes in wage labor as well as home life. Many older women take enormous pride in their professional daughters or granddaughters, and they pray for their success in university examinations and corporate career tracks (as well as in finding suitable husbands and bearing children). Although the shrine community unquestionably occupies the lower orders of the postindustrial Japanese economy, it is certainly difficult to conceive of the shrine women as passive victims of circumstance in any obvious sense. A decade of intermittently living and working in the shrine has only deepened my admiration for the fortitude, solidarity, passion, and hilarity that pervades this close-knit community of women.

So far as I can tell, most women experience shugyō as deeply liberatory. All stress that time at the shrine differs distinctly from conventional domestic or labor contexts. Sites such as the shrine kitchen constitute valued zones of female creativity and autonomy beyond any direct form of male supervision or control. Ascetics usually have female spiritual teachers and, once on the mountain, are nearly always on their own, guided only by their memories and their emerging sense of the gods' looming presence. High on the mountain paths, women worshipers accomplish extraordinary feats of physical prowess, confidently confronting cliffs, crevices, and wild animals. The spirits of the male fire god or of aggressive male conquerors may possess them, and the women may, in ritual action, wield swords and gohei wands in a manifestly "masculine" fashion.

Asceticism, in short, affords women extraordinary possibilities for autonomy and self-fashioning. Exercises of mountain shugyō, the fabrication of offerings, and participation in collective ritual action on the mountain allow practitioners the opportunity to attain deeply fulfilling modes of personhood, creatively integrating themselves into expanding networks of interdependence.

The Joys of Exchange: Differentiating and Binding Self and Other

As I have argued, the processes of positively expanding the person become especially evident in the practices through which worshipers, singularly and collectively, fabricate simulated images (mitate) of other beings with which they pursue productive exchange relations. As they master the art of creative imitation, the faithful are increasingly able to project or transpose themselves into potent landscape sites and become more and more "like" the mysterious divinities that reside within the sacred mountain.

In a provocative recent essay, Judith Feher Gurewich (1999) proposes that Lacan's concept of the "*jouissance* of the Other" makes it possible to bridge Freud and Lévi-Strauss's perspectives on incest, marriage, exchange, and the origins of culture, approaches usually seen as diametrically opposed to one another. In Lacan's usage of the term, "jouissance" refers to the formal rights to use or abuse a thing and not, significantly, to desire that thing. Unlike the desiring gaze of the other, which the gazed-on person can often anticipate or negotiate, the imputed gaze of jouissance is profoundly enigmatic, mysterious, and terrifying, for it cannot on its own terms be fulfilled. The child's emerging recognition that the mother does not solely exist for her or him is in a sense beyond comprehension and is read as fundamental "lack" (which for Lacan is the lack of the "phallus," the capacity for assertive self-definition). The mirror stage, in which the child attempts initially to constitute her or his own selfhood through readings of the mother's face, thus exposes the developing child to a terrifying blankness, an absence that for Lacan is beyond signification (Lacan 1977, 1–7). Under conditions of successful analysis, a patient and analyst can participate in productive exchanges of language and imagery that obviate and transcend the terror imputed to this blank other imagined in early childhood. In Feher Gurewich's terms, "The process of psychoanalysis consists in coming to realize that the Other whose *jouissance* we both fear and envy is in fact within us, yet not as all-powerful and malevolent, but simply as traces, as legacy of the marks of psychic separation from the primordial others of our childhood" (Feher Gurewich 1999, 15).

In a similar sense, Feher Gurewich implies, the impulse toward exchange, and especially toward the culturally foundational meta-exchange of marriage, might be understood as a universal effort to defuse and transcend the imputed unknowability of the primal other. In this respect, Lévi-Strauss's well-known statement (Lévi-Strauss 1992, 47–48) that the goal of marriage is not so much to gain a wife as to gain a brother-in-law (or, as he also put it, "to convert enemies into friends"), could be read as having fundamental psychological — as well as political — origins and ramifications. The basic exchange transaction of marriage, like the other exchange circuits it enables and signifies, helps establish its participants as social, sentient beings. As Mauss (1954) tells us, material exchange media invariably carry projected aspects of the personhood of the giver and simultaneously demand reciprocal counterprestations that, in turn, bring aspects of the donor's personhood back into the orbit of the original giver, who may tangibly grasp, control, and comprehend them. Through exchange — of shells, food, words, or siblings and affines — we come to know others, and thus, ultimately, to know ourselves. Hence Mauss characterizes the gift as a "total social fact," which produces the social field in which persons, who are irreducibly relational beings, interact.

Might the Akakura Mountain Shrine system be understood as a comparable psychosocial field of constitutive action? Seeking spiritual rebirth and struggling to relearn fundamental modes of orientation toward the universe and the object world, worshipers in time encounter that which lies beyond the general capacity to represent or signify, an alternate space that one may variously associate with the glimpsed face of the mother long ago or the long-forgotten face of indigenous antecedents. Such blankness is especially disturbing since it calls into question the worshipers' capacity to know themselves and to function as autonomous beings. In a manner that partly recalls psychoanalysis and other interactive therapies, this anxiety drives a vast range of exchange transactions: aesthetically pleasing offerings and prayers are presented to the divinities, elaborate rites are directed to the gods, ascetic discipline takes one up to the kami's precincts to interact tangibly with their traces on rock and wind.

Mythologically, life in Tsugaru began with an exchange, as the Dragon Princess arose from her muddy pool and presented a gift to the strange male conqueror, who reciprocated by enshrining her at the mountain base. In turn, Akakura Mountain Shrine began with an exchange, with a dream given to Kawai Mariko by the dragon flying out of the mountain. Kawai Mariko spent the rest of her lifetime trying to reciprocate, through austerities and offerings dedicated to the god, who in turn gave her further dream visions and concretized icons of the mountain for her to distribute among her human followers. As we have seen, the ritual calendar Kawai Mariko instituted is oriented around the most fundamental kind of exchange, a cosmic marriage on the mountain, through which worshipers seek to reconcile profoundly different orders of being—the heavens with the plain, the mother with the father, the parent with the child, the indigenous with the conqueror, the old with the new. All rites on the mountain entail the creative fabrication of simulated images of the graceful divinities, reflecting back to the gods the beauty that they have given to their mortal children. Spontaneously produced by dedicated worshipers, these offerings constitute extensions both of the donor's selfhood and of the media through which exchange with the distant gods is possible: each offering represents, in the most positive sense, the externalized other within the self. Significantly, all such ritual encounters culminate in the joyous consumption and exchange of the offered familiar substances—as rice, rice wine, fruits, and commonplace manufactured crackers and sweets. Joking, laughing, and chatting, worshipers trade off these well-known, purified foods as they disseminate the divinities' counterprestations. At many levels, then, exchange renders the strange familiar.

Might it be that exchange at Akakura is not so much a means to an end as it is an end in and of itself? In laboring to exchange with gods, ancestors, and other mortals to constitute a cosmological marriage between immortal forces, do worshipers solely seek to overcome their own physical mortality? Or do they strive as well to transcend the initial fear of the unknown other that is the very precondition of mortal existence and of human consciousness?

Reproductive Symbolism and Landscape:
Ritual Creativity in an Industrialized Periphery

If there is a fundamental drive for exchange at Akakura, the broader historical sweep of Japanese capitalism has conditioned its expression. Reproductive mountain imagery may well have existed for millennia in Japan, but the particular forms these schemas have taken at Akakura reflect the layered post-Meiji history of northern Honshu. The system's foundations were laid during the economic turmoil of the late nineteenth and early twentieth centuries, when the remembered mountain-oriented iconography of the Yonaoshi world renewal movements took on renewed salience. In Tōhoku, impoverished women, moving back and forth between farming households and factory labor, sought the power of mountain divinities to heal breaches in their bodies and in local social networks. Modern female mountain asceticism in Tsugaru is also, to some degree, an artifact of the systematic state repression of unorthodox female ritual specialists during periods of growing surveillance by the militarist state. Kawai Mariko and Sugiyama Junko experienced their founding revelatory visions at a time when many other female popular religious and healing figures suffered routine harassment, and each of the two spent time in prison. As many of my oldest informants recall of the 1920s and 1930s, the only "safe places" were on the high mountain slopes.[1]

At the same time, in many respects Akakura Mountain Shrine is one of "MacArthur's children." Only the Freedom of Religion Clause of the postwar constitution made its establishment possible, and the shrine's principal constituency of smallholder farmers emerged out of postwar land reforms. Most of these families had long worked the land, but they only gained title to plots around mid-century. Formal ownership quickly bound them to new forms of dependence on state-organized cooperatives and enmeshed most families in cyclical patterns of seasonal labor migration to urban, industrial centers (Kelly 1986, 1991; McCormack 1996). At precisely the moment that the dream of agrarian autonomy seemed realized, farming families found themselves unable to reproduce themselves solely through working the land.

Under these circumstances, the rambling, farmhouse-style shrine at Akakura offered profound compensations. Its extended fictive family constituted a tangible replacement for the idealized image of the stable, multigenerational agrarian household held together by the coordinated labor of many women. Its busy, efficient kitchen, filled with dozens of hardworking women at festival times, provides a deeply moving tableau of social solidarity and moral harmony. The lubricating water of the gods flowing through the kitchen, a gift of the Dragon Princess, helps keep this all-female space "clean" and "pure." The agrarian household, women's labor, and female reproductive capacities are further celebrated in the triannual ritual of the kamado (a synonym for *cooking pot* and *household*), when the Dragon Princess's water boils in a womblike miniature house of the gods.

Furthermore, in the context of high rates of cyclical migration to core urban zones and disappearing family farms, the mountain provided a stable image of centrality, a fulcrum firmly set in the local land. Although many worshipers no longer directly farm, and very few actually farm the supreme crop of rice, the shrine allows them all to co-participate in the symbolic rice economy, long oriented toward the mountain divinities. Every spring during the Mountain Opening, each and every worshiper takes hold of the great rice straw rope, produced out of the rice fields of one of the shrine members, as the congregation gives thanks to the mountain divinities for watering the plain below. Although they may have moved far from the villages, houses, and graves of their forefathers, all can return to the mountain, "our real home," to perform kuyō for the ancestors.

In this sense, the Akakura system functions as a compensatory home, a symbolic bulwark against the vast social and economic pressures breaking up extended multigenerational agrarian houses. To this day, my informants strongly feel that farming, land, and locality matter, and that ancestral veneration must continue in some form, even if the idealized extended households no longer exist. In the great "storehouse/granary" of Akakura, they find a tangible image of agrarian surplus, moral containment, and ancestral propriety.

Nonetheless, it would be misleading to characterize these quests for cosmological regeneration as simply reactive, nostalgic, or archaic. Although Akakura offers its worshipers many compensations, its ritual processes do not merely make up for the alienation of capitalist modernity. The great kamisama Mrs. Narita took enormous pride in the money she earned as a hardworking farm laborer. Mrs. Okuda equally boasted of her income as an Amway distributor, work she regarded as part of her divinely mandated healing practice. All worshipers maintained that dedicated service to the kami was likely to increase one's income and lead to better employment. Some claimed gyō made them better apple farmers; others believed it made them more efficient workers in resort hotels or automobile factories. Economic disasters and the failure to earn money, in turn, were widely interpreted as signs of divine disfavor, of the worshipers' lack of spiritual discipline and dedication to the divinities and ancestors who safeguarded the welfare of their families. In a manner that recalls Weber's characterization of the "Protestant work ethic" in the West, worldly material success functions as a signifier of spiritual election, and vice versa.[2]

Thus the forms of deep anxiety that we have explored do not simply derive from ahistorical familial psychodynamics "traditionally" evoked by the ancient mountain, but from the manner in which the contemporary political economy pressures and constrains northern Japanese families. Consider, for example, the enormous consternation in the Akakura Shrine congregation on the morning that the Cooking Pot rite failed and the blessing sound of the gods did not resonate through the Inner Sanctuary. Again and again that afternoon, worshipers quietly voiced their fears that the coming year was full of potential economic dangers and that the loan defaults and related financial pressures brought on by Typhoon Nineteen might worsen. As a number of friends and informants told me, the rite's failure showed that no guarantees of anything existed in this life. Even on the mountain, sad things could happen, things that, in Takeda Yuko's words, "break the heart in two." Even the most dedicated and disciplined labor may not gain rewards, no matter how worshipers struggle and persevere.

And yet the prevailing mood of that afternoon at Akakura was not one of gloom or foreboding. Immediately after the priests had concluded their formal Shintō rites, two visiting priests clothed in a grand *shishimai* (masked lion dance) lion mask costume unexpectedly burst into the Inner Sanctuary. Its wooden mouth chomping loudly, the lion wildly grabbed at the coins and bills offered it, and then (amidst much raucous laughter) dragged a dozen startled worshipers (one anthropologist among them) up to the altar to be blessed by the gods.

Since my friend Sakurai Fumiko had helped prepare the kamado that morning and had served as one of the attending women during the Cooking Pot Ceremony, I had expected her to feel chastened for having inadvertently contributed to the failure of the rite. However, she expressed delight at finally having presided at the most important rite of the year: "Please tell your husband to make a copy of the videotape as soon as possible, so I can take it home to my husband and show him what it is like here!" Like the others, she agreed that the coming year would present special difficulties: perhaps her hotel's debts would become too great, perhaps she would not be able to balance her obligations to perform ascetic discipline and manage the hotel. Yet months later, Sakurai Fumiko would still proudly recall that day of extraordinary beauty in which men and women gracefully served the mountain divinities.

This complex mixture of joy and sorrow, confidence and trepidation, pervades Akakura and the related institutions of Tsugaru kamisama spirit mediumship. The worshipers and ritual specialists of Akakura Mountain Shrine offer no totalizing panaceas. While they strive to conjoin work and worship, they are often painfully aware of their mortal failings in honoring their obligations to the gods, ancestors, and their kith and kin. Setbacks should occasion not despair, but renewed efforts tinged with sober reflection. Even during hard times, one's obligation to serve the divinities demands joyous consumption of all their gifts. Ritual action at the shrine always concluded with carnivalesque revels of commodity distribution and consumption, and the Great Summer Festival of 1992 was no exception. Vast quantities of store-bought, wrapped foodstuffs, purified by the divinities during ritual events, were quickly taken down off the altar and, amidst much hilarity and repartee, exchanged with those of friends and neighbors.

In these conflations of work and worship, actors have not sought to "retreat" from modernity into the disengaged comforts of ahistorical nostalgia. They have creatively evoked, recombined, and mobilized the disciplinary circuits through which their foremothers and -fathers have sought for generations to coordinate and navigate material and symbolic worlds. In so doing, they have been repeatedly drawn, like Kawai Mariko before them, to fleeting images of the mountain—where invisible and visible forces tentatively meet, conjoin, and disengage. In pursuing these visions of a knowledge that lies just beyond conventional human understanding, these worshipers and workers have, in part, come to better understand the underlying conditions of production, exchange, and consumption within their own social environs, at their own moments in history. In "finding their own path up the mountain" and in gazing on the mountain's symbolic extensions, they have partially confronted the basic processes, in the here and now, through which they produce and reproduce themselves as social beings.

It is worth recalling, in this light, that during the important July 1992 conversation, Mrs. Narita did not romanticize the early phase of her life as noncommodified or premonetary. She remained intensely proud of the money she earned, a sign of her particularly favored status in the eyes of the gods. She and Mrs. Okuda repeatedly stressed that their working lives had exemplified the positive interpenetration of gods and humans in the context of a money economy, within which financial wealth served as the preeminent visible sign of the invisible gods' blessings, and in which money earned by the production of rice is especially blessed.

As I have argued, the worshipers' emphasis on the great importance of women's therapeutic and ritual capacities and their labor must be understood in terms of the changing political economy of the Tsugaru region. Although postwar land reforms made modest land holdings possible for thousands of previously impoverished peasant families, the wider structure of the national economy has denied most local households in northern Japan the possibility of reproducing themselves through agrarian labor alone (Kelly 1986, 1991, 1992; McCormack 1996). Under these conditions, women's mundane and reproductive labor activities have come under profound revaluation at Akakura. Cooking, food presentation, childbearing, nursing, agrarian piecework, and labor migration have come to dominate the community's religious imagination. Through practical and symbolic elaborations of these labor processes in ritual contexts, members of the overwhelmingly female congregation seek to make themselves more and more like the divinities that they serve. In so doing, they strengthen their households and honor their obligations to their living kin and their ancestors.

Indigenous Traces: The Return of the Repressed?

In borrowing Freud's Olympian metaphor for the title of this book, I have sought to evoke the simultaneous capacity of landscape forms to reveal and conceal, to make manifest and to repress. I have argued that as a dynamic model of the human mind and body, the Akakura mountainscape at times recapitulates the psychic terrain of early childhood for those who traverse it, reevoking the hopes and fears of infancy as it moves the climber toward spiritual and social maturity. In order to attain purity and spiritual mastery, the worshiper must engage in a rigorous journey of self-discovery, uncovering long-forgotten or denied aspects of the self. Like Hideo in the dream, immersed in his own bodily wastes, the dedicated ascetic must first come to terms with her or his own baser instincts before ascending the heights. For this very reason, shugyō opens one up to the temptations of infantile libido, associated with the demons who urge one to give into the most fundamental narcissistic desire, the desire to monopolize the mother. The volcanic mountain, abode of the parentlike gods, is riven with fissures and vents through which repressed childlike wants may unexpectedly erupt. Immortal wishes, in this sense, are never very far from the surface.

I have argued that a deep, mythic history embedded in the mountainscape has largely conditioned these enduring psychodynamics. Kawai Mariko and her associates developed a brilliant, synthetic solution to the long-term tensions between "foreigner" and "native" in Tsugaru cosmology. A "compromise formation," fused of the "male" conquering Yamato culture hero and the indigenous female demoness, Akakura Daigongen functions as a "combined parental figure," linked to worshipers in multiple ways—as parent, as lover, and as adoptive classificatory sibling/spouse. As such, this complex being simultaneously evokes love and jealousy, filial piety and infantile rage, sibling affection and sexual attraction. The reemergence of familial dynamics in ritual arenas, in other words, constitutes a legacy of the long-term repression of indigenous ritual capacity and its formal encompassment within the dominant Shintō-Buddhist synthesis. The earliest form of the mother, the ancient Demon Queen, is not directly accessible to worshipers; encounters with her, as we have seen, are mediated through cultural acts of marriage and adoption that enmesh her and all worshipers within a complex cosmological kinship system.

Yet, ultimately, how successful has this repression of the indigenous proven? Does modern veneration of the mountain inadvertently trigger mytho-historical "slippage," bringing to light glimpses of long-forgotten or denied cultural histories? A northern Tōhoku legend has it that the head of Aterui, an Ainu leader executed by the Yamato state in Kyoto in the early eighth century, flew back to Tōhoku and still haunts the region.[3] Rather like the Titans in Freud's myth, are these lords of an earlier epoch unexpectedly emerging from the rock face? At the dawn of the new millennium, can we speak of the "return of the repressed" at Akakura?

These questions have seemed especially salient in recent years, as a small movement of Tsugaru and Hokkaido intellectuals has proposed a hybrid, métis identity, an interstitial status between "Yamato" and "Ainu" affiliations (Tanaka 1997, 1998a). Admittedly, this discourse of postmodern hybridity has not, as of this writing, held any appeal for my informants. Although they remain deeply proud of their Tsugaru heritage, they insist that Akakura Mountain Shrine is thoroughly "Japanese," and that these same kinds of rites and ceremonies can be found at any regular Shintō establishment throughout the nation. They note that the principal deity worshiped at the shrine is clearly identified as Amaterasu in the first line of the Akakura Prayer and that ascetics have beheld her in numerous visions for seven decades. As a national divinity from whom the imperial line claims descent, Amaterasu is immortalized in the *Hinomaru*, the Rising Sun national flag, which is hung each year from the great shimenawa rope strung across the waterfall of Fudō. A preeminent maternal figure at Akakura, Amaterasu binds the worshipers into the larger collectivity of the Japanese nation. So, too, do the shrine's statues of Kōbō Daishi, the founder of Japanese esoteric Buddhism, who is popularly believed to have sailed to Tsugaru in the ninth century to found nearby Kōbōji Temple, and the statue of Sakanoue Tamuramaro, Yamato conqueror of Tsugaru and its Demon Queen. Onigamisama, no longer a hostile demoness, is in principle fully domesticated within the Shintō pantheon and closely linked to Amaterasu herself.

Yet I have long been struck by the fact that from the mountain, worshipers gaze down into a section of the Tsugaru plain rich in archaeological excavations. These neolithic Jōmon and pre-Jōmon sites, many of which long preceded Yamato conquest and settlement of northern Honshu and the expulsion of indigenous communities, fascinate most members of the congregation. Alleged ancient rituals of the prehistoric inhabitants were lovingly reproduced at the 1992 Un Doko extravaganza at Morita village, excitedly attended by the Sugiyamas. At the annual Nebuta and Neputa festivals, the greatest aesthetic creativity and enthusiasm seems reserved for painting extravagant images of bearded aboriginal warriors and the ancient demons allied to the Ezo and Ainu. Although ostensibly long-banished or exterminated, the region's original inhabitants continue to exercise a deep hold on the Tsugaru moral imagination.

Ainu long ago hunted bears and performed sacrifices on Akakura; the earliest inhabitants of Tsugaru are said to have lived and worshiped inside caves. Might an enduring sense that the powers of the earth have not yet been fully placated or encompassed partly motivate contemporary rituals at Akakura, oriented toward the mountain's tunnels and rocky formations? Consider the Mountain Opening Ceremony, which so strikingly contrasts with the three female-controlled Cooking Pot Ceremonies spaced out through the rest of the annual cycle: a large phallic rope, carried by men, penetrates into the depths of the vaginal gorge. As I have argued, this rite may be understood as a relatively foreign, masculinized attempt to inseminate and dominate a relatively autochthonous, female-coded landscape site. Yet does the large Rising Sun flag hanging from the shimenawa over the waterfall represent simply an unambiguous sign of victory and incorporation within a national frame? Or might it, inadvertently, signal the farthest limit of "Japanese" influence: beyond this line, in the mysterious upper reaches of the mountain, lies something else, something strange, something other.

Recall that the spirit medium Mrs. Okuda, known for her markedly "male" persona, was guided on the mountain by the ninth-century protonationalist figure of Sakanoue Tamuramaro, who ethnically cleansed the indigenous Ezo and Ainu and established Yamato state control in far northern Honshu. Mrs. Okuda insists that Sakanoue himself performed shugyō on Akakura, which he first climbed when looking for timber to rebuild his naval fleet and link Tsugaru to the Japanese heartland. In Tsugaru, as elsewhere in Japan, early mountain ascetic discipline had a colonizing edge to it, taking hold of local landscapes as it projected a synthetic Shintō Buddhist schema and reorganized proximate sites in terms of a cosmological ecumene (see Grapard 1989).[4] Mrs. Okuda, who herself came north into Tsugaru from the prefecture of Akita, appears as heir to this tradition, protected on the dangerous landscape by the vanguard of Japanese national expansion.

More than eleven hundred years after Sakanoue Tamuramaro's conquest, is this mytho-historical process of ritual encompassment entirely complete? Mrs. Okuda herself was ever mindful of the mountain's hairy demons, whom she emphasized were very, very old. They could enter your body in an instant and force you to speak in a language entirely unlike Japanese. The gods themselves, as we have seen, speak traces of an unintelligible language. The line of thirty-three Kannon stupas, stretching up the ridge past the "Sumo Ring of the Demons," "The Garden of the Demons," and the "Guidepost of the Demons," represents, in many respects, transmuted, domesticated local demons. Yet these animated statues at times behave in an unlicensed, irregular fashion, making strange noises, twirling themselves around, and walking up and down the mountain on their own accord.

When Mrs. Narita enigmatically noted that "the gods only walk in strange shapes, the gods only walk in strange shapes," did some of these shapes recall the mountain's aboriginal inhabitants? Votive paintings depict Akakura Daigongen as a remarkably hairy male, an image that recalls the stereotypical image of the Ainu as much more hirsute than the "ethnic Japanese." (To be sure, yamabushi itinerant mountain priests typically had long hair and went unshaven, but some worshipers elaborated that Akakura Daigongen was "hairy all over" and was a "great hunter.")[5] Each February in the Dragon Princess Rite, worshipers capture the first, pure trickle of the feminine gods' own water, in order to inseminate it with a silver staff that recalls the initial mythic gift of the demoness to the Japanese conqueror. Yet in digging down through the deep snow cover to the buried river, are worshipers returning to a source that, in a sense, lies beyond their own remembered history, to a time before the demoness surrendered to the conqueror? My informants' nightmares of dragons, demons, and subterranean caverns would seem to suggest some persistent anxiety, an enduring sense that the fusion of "Japanese" and "indigenous" histories is less than seamless.

Finally, what of Sugiyama Hideo's dream? Might his vision of climbing up ancient stone steps toward his dead adoptive mother evoke a hoped-for movement back toward an earlier, forgotten historical epoch, back toward a pre-Yamato mythic moment, back into the land itself? After all, he and Yukiko carried Junko's photograph back up the sacred upper gorge to the very frontier of ritually purified space. In Kawai Mariko's founding vision, the dragon burst out of the mountain's peak and turned into a beautiful woman, a transformed version of the local demoness. A lifetime later, as Sugiyama Junko is seen "riding the dragon," is she flying back into the mountain, returning to a fundamentally mysterious, indigenous space? Is the aged grandmother, back once more on the summit, rejoining the ancient Demon Queen?

Edification by Puzzlement

It strikes me as entirely appropriate that our discussion of Akakura should end on this avowedly speculative note, confronting the most enigmatic features of the sacred mountain. From the moment of Kawai Mariko's first dream, Akakura has generated not so much definitive answers as enduring questions. As James Fernandez (1982) observes of another synthetic religious movement, attaining deep knowledge at Akakura Mountain Shrine depends not so much on dogma as on "edification by puzzlement"(563–73). Indeed, the various aspects of the modern Akakura synthesis explored by this book can be restated as a series of linked conundrums: If a violent dragon, a manifestation of a wild, masculine deity, can appear as a beautiful woman, what then does it mean to be a woman or to be a man? If a mortal woman can become a kamisama, a synonym for divinity, what then does it mean to be a deity or to be a mortal? Must one always strive to learn new strategies of imitation and representation, or does there come moment when one is truly a "mirror," perfectly embodying the gods' reflective capacities? If the divinities can speak to housewives by silently writing on their morning rice, what function, if any, does an elaborate bureaucracy of official Buddhist and Shintō priests serve? If the "good" gods and the "bad" gods walk together, how does one manage to live a righteous life? Is each person's destiny fixed from childhood, or can one "find one's own path on the mountain"? Does the power given by the mountain pass automatically through blood from mother to child, or must it be gained anew by each generation, through individual and varied discipline on the sacred mountainscape? Do we ever truly know our parents as we grow up, or do we only really encounter them, and those that come before them, as we labor in adulthood at demanding tasks? Are "we" and our most distant predecessors one people, or are we fundamentally distinct? Are we the heirs of a metropolitan civilization that conquered alien aboriginals, or are we still those barbarians? Or are we, somehow, both? Are our most fundamental, immortal wishes to be fulfilled by returning home, to our childhood, to the mother, to an earlier time beyond memory? Or can the route to transcendence incorporate cherished memories of maternal love while using that primary emotional orientation to produce a viable future, joyously recognizing the other within the self?[6]

Once more, I find myself recalling Sakurai Fumiko's enigmatic words of guidance, "The mountain will teach you through your body." For her and her fellow worshipers at Akakura, the deep commitment to embodied pedagogy does not mean that they accept uncritically whatever they hear or experience on the high slopes. Each time Sakurai Fumiko came down from the mountain, she always eagerly wished to talk to her teachers and friends in the shrine, to tell them stories, to listen, to argue, to ask them for explanations of what the day had brought. Each act of dedicated labor on the mountain brings awe and puzzlement. Each climb generates its own forms of wonder—and inspires new and different questions.

a p p e n d i x

Guide to Persons Mentioned in Text

Note: All names are pseudonyms. Family names are followed by given names.

Abo Yoshi. Male kamisama spirit medium. Teacher of Sakurai Fumiko.

Hirata Eiko. Novice female ascetic at Akakura. Psychologist.

Kawai Hisao. Brother of the shrine's founder, Kawai Mariko. Carved Shōkannonsama statue at Akakura summit. Father of Kenji.

Kawai Kenji. Secretary of Akakura Mountain Shrine. Son of Kawai Hisao, nephew of Kawai Mariko.

Kawai Mariko. Founder of Akakura Mountain Shrine. Farmwife.

Koike Fumiko. Informal caretaker at Akakura Mountain Shrine.

Kinoshita Hideo. Ascetic and informal handyman at Akakura Mountain Shrine.

Komatsu Yoshitake. Farmer from Morita village. Client of Sugiyama Yukiko and Hideo

Nakamura Yuko. Female ascetic. Talkative listener in the July 1992 conversation.

Narita Emiko. Senior kamisama spirit medium at Akakura Mountain

Shrine. From a fishing community on Tsugaru's west coast. Offical "voice" of the late Kawai Mariko. Participant in the 28 July 1992 Shinden conversation.

Okuda Setsuko. Important kamisama medium at Akakura Mountain Shrine. From Akita prefecture. Participant in the 28 July 1992 Shinden conversation.

Sakurai Fumiko. Ascetic at Akakura Mountain Shrine. Underwent a ten-year shugyō (1986–96).

Sugiyama Hideo. Adopted son-in-law of Sugiyama Junko, husband of Yukiko.

Sugiyama Junko. Prominent kamisama medium. Founder of junior (bunke) branch of Akakura Mountain Shrine.

Sugiyama Miyako. Married to Toshio. Daugher-in-law of Hideo and Yukiko.

Sugiyama Nozumo. Second son of Hideo and Yukiko. Telecommunications executive in Tokyo. First witnessed the miraculous candles at his grandmother Junko's June 1991 funeral.

Sugiyama Takashi. Fifth son of Hideo and Yukiko. Municipal government employee.

Sugiyama Toshio. First son of Hideo and Yukiko. Apple farmer and occasional labor migrant.

Sugiyama Yukiko. Eldest daughter of Junko, wife of Hideo. (Also known by the technonym *Toshio no Kāsan* ("mother of Toshio," after her first son).

Takeda Kimiko. Kamisama medium and healer. Daughter and heir of Kawai Mariko. Mother of Takeda Yuko.

Takeda Seiji. Priest of Akakura Mountain Shrine. Adopted son-in-law of Takeda Kimiko. Married to Takeda Yuko.

Takeda Yuko. Daughter of Takeda Kimiko, granddaughter of Kawai Mariko. Nurse and schoolteacher. Married to Takeda Seiji.

Yamamoto Emiko. Important disciple of Kawai Mariko. Female kamisama spirit medium associated with Akakura Mountain Shrine.

n o t e s

Introduction

1   In *Medusa's Hair: An Essay on Personal Symbols and Religious Experience,*
    Gananath Obeyesekere also finds in Freud's reading of a classical Greek
    myth inspiration for an ethnographic analysis of a non-Western social in-
    stitution, although he does not accept all of Freud's interpretations of the
    myth in question. Similarly, I do not find Freud's reading of the Tartarus
    legend, which he largely adapts from Rank, entirely convincing. However,
    like Obeyesekere in *Medusa's Hair,* I have found that Freud's allegorical sen-
    sitivity to classical motifs has led me to reinterpret a popular religious move-
    ment with attention to the dynamic reciprocal links between psychological
    and social dimensions of symbolic action.

2   Freud makes two further references in *The Interpretation of Dreams* to Zeus's
    attack on the Titans described in Hesiod's *Theogony* (1993, chap. 716), with
    emphasis on Zeus's emasculation of his father Kronos (Freud 1983, 290, 657;
    see also Freud 1914). In the 1914 (fourth) edition of the *Interpretation,* Freud
    refers approvingly to Otto Rank's (1909) analysis of this myth, which em-
    phasizes the violent attributes of the hero. Obeyesekere, criticizing Rank,
    notes that heroic figures are not necessarily parricides and that they tend to
    achieve legitimization not simply through violent usurpation, but through
    separation from their royal origins and intimate nurturance at the hands of
    the populace (Obeyesekere 1981, 47–50). In any event, these passages in the

Interpretation anticipate Freud's exploration of the mythic theme of parricide in *Totem and Taboo* (Freud 1961), *Moses and Monotheism* (1939), and *Civilization and its Discontents* (1949). Freud's analyses in these "cultural books" are critiqued, and built on, by Robert Paul (1992, 1996).

3   Freud appears to have been deeply interested in the enduring power of autochthonous cults in the face of conquering states and world religions. (See, for instance, the opening of *Civilization and its Discontents*.) Freud's contemporaries, including Nietzsche, Spengler, and Momsen, read such mythic narratives as evidence of "Aryan" invasions and the subjugation of autochthonous Mediterranean peoples, a view later developed and popularized by Graves (1997).

4   Classical scholarship since Freud's time has enormously complicated our understanding of ancient Greek mythology and political history. The so-called Aryan hypothesis has been criticized as overly literalist by structuralists such as Vernant (1980) and as Eurocentric by Afrocentrists (e.g., Bernal 1987). Comparative treatments of myths of conquering "stranger gods," building on and revising Frazer (1894), include Dumézil (1973) and Sahlins (1985).

5   No regular term was used consistently in the shrine community for a person undergoing shugyō, in part because all worshipers were referred to by their family name, not their role, in this very small community. Occasionally, the terms *gyōja* (行者 ascetic), *shinja* (信者 believer), or *deshi* (弟子 apprentice) were employed. I refer to those undertaking shugyō as *ascetics* or *worshipers*. Since the vast majority of ascetics were female, I use the feminine pronoun when referring to the worshipers and concentrate on women's experiences of shugyō.

6   In recent years, many Japanese farmers have sought to marry foreign brides, in part because of the unwillingness of young women to take on the extraordinary physical and emotional demands of the farm wife role. Kenji's father strongly opposed bringing a foreign woman into the family.

1. Predicaments of History

1   My abbreviated account of Tsugaru history draws heavily on Ravina (1991 and 1999), Ikegami (1987 and 1992), and the unpublished historical research of Tazawa Tadashi, a Hirosaki intellectual. See also Kodate (1980 and 1986) and Sako (1992).

2   A recent movement of local intellectuals and activists celebrates this hybrid heritage, asserting a métis identity impossible to reduce either to purely "Yamato" or "Ainu" histories (Tanaka 1997 and 1998a).

3   I follow the convention of listing pre-Meiji dates by year and lunar month.

4   Pesticides are sprayed on apple trees about fourteen to sixteen times during the growing season.

5   The Rokkasho Plutonium Reprocessing Plant became the principal campaign issue of a bitterly contested prefectural gubernatorial race in 1990. Protesters, allied with Tokyo-based environmental organizers, held a series of public demonstrations against the plant. One such rally centered on Shimokita itako spirit mediums and Native North American ritual specialists who drummed and prayed in protest against the plant. The "pro-plutonium" candidate, a member of the ruling Liberal Democratic Party, won the election handily, amidst widespread allegations of fraud and voter intimidation. This same governor was the featured guest speaker at the 1991 Great Summer Festival at Akakura Mountain Shrine, at which he made no mention of Rokkasho, but instead spoke only of his plans to bring the Shinkansen bullet train line to Aomori prefecture.

6   The historical relationship between Ezo, Ainu, and Jōmon-era settlements in northern Honshu (such as the recently excavated Sannai-Maruyama in Aomori City) is contested. Aomori prefectural officials and most local scholars maintain (or imply) that the Ainu arrived on Honshu after the fall of Jōmon civilization. In contrast, Tanaka (1997) argues for a more or less unbroken line of continuity between northern Jōmon, Ezo, and Ainu societies.

7   Prominent Sainokawara sites in Aomori prefecture include Osorezan ("Mount Dread") on the northern Shimokita peninsula and Kawakura Sainokawara in Kanagi-Nakasato in the north central Tsugaru plain.

8   Tanaka reports, "A temple in Kiraichi [in central Tsugaru] preserves a gruesome reminder of the great famines at the beginning of the nineteenth century: a carving of a woman in the last stages of starvation, with huge black holes for eyes and her ribs jutting from her skin" (1998b, 5).

9   Scholarly treatments of itako include Sakurai (1970); Takamatsu (1983); Blacker (1975); Ivy (1995); and Kodate (1986).

10 The principal scholarly study of contemporary kamisama mediumship in northern Honshu is Ikegami (1987). See also Ikegami (1992, 1999) and Kodate (1980, 1986).

11 As Naoe (1983) notes, some of what he calls western Tsugaru female gomiso are associated with Takayama Inari Shrine in Shariki village. See also Smyers (1999, 40). In my experience, kamisama mediums from elsewhere in the region view these women with suspicion and argue that they were "just trying to become itako." I worked closely with one woman who, through close affiliation with Inari Takayama, did move from kamisama to itako status over the course of the 1970s and 1980s (Schattschneider 2001).

12 For example, the great kamisama medium Sugiyama Junko (discussed in chapter 6) routinely brought her clients to Sōtō Zen temple of Entsū-ji, at Osorezan, for many decades. After her death, her family enshrined her *nodobotoke* (voice box or "throat Buddha") at this temple.

13 The relevant passages of the *Tsugaru ittoshi*, the official history of the Tsugaru house, are given in Sako (1992). See also Liscutin (2000).

14 Ikegami's argument is summarized in Liscutin (2000).

15 The name *Hyaku-zawa* may be related to the Tendai esoteric Buddhist concept of *hyakkai,* the one hundred realms of existence in the universe (Inagaki 1988, 115).

16 Literary representations of Mount Iwaki continue to emphasize its seductive, feminine qualities. Promotional campaigns and official presentations throughout modern Aomori prefecture often quote novelist Osamu Dazai's first vision of the mountain on returning home to Tsugaru after many years in Tokyo: "The mountain really did seem to be floating, unencumbered by weight. A lush deep green, it hovered silently in the blue sky, more feminine than Mount Fuji, its lower slopes like a gingko leaf standing on its wavy edge or like an ancient court dress folded open slightly, the symmetry of the folds exactly preserved. The mountain resembles a woman of an almost translucent grace and beauty" (Dazai 1987, 121). As Robertson (1991) has noted, in such twentieth-century nostalgic discourses, "The generic mountainous landscape now associated with *furasato* [old home place] appears to be at once a gateway and the land inside."

17 Masculinity in the southern Tsugaru region is still strongly tied to Iwaki's front side. Young men still take great pride in their participation in the Ōyamasankei. After my husband Mark climbed the front side of mountain with a male friend a few weeks after our arrival in Hirosaki, many people told me, "Now, he looks like a real man!" A local Tsugaru artisan and merchant, an active promoter of the revival of Tsugaru-ben, told me that on his return from studying in Europe in the 1960s, he immediately climbed Mount Iwaki, "So that I would really be back in Tsugaru." Not realizing that a "skyway" and tram lift had been built during his absence, he was shocked to encounter young women at the summit, a place he had always considered an exclusively male space.

18 My account of Kawai Mariko's life draws heavily on Ikegami (1987 and 1992) as well as on my interviews with Kawai Mariko's descendants and many other members of the Akakura Shrine community.

19 Strictly speaking *gongen* means "temporary manifestation" or "avatar." My impression, however, is that most members of the Akakura Mountain Shrine congregation employed *Dai-gongen* (Great gongen) simply as an honorific term for kami (divinity). The term *gongen* is strongly associated with *yama-bushi* (indigenous mountain-oriented esoteric priests) who were later assimilated into esoteric Buddhist Shugendō practice. The avatar Sannō Gongen (Mountain King) serves as a central figure of Tendai Buddhism.

20 The ties between these two families were strengthened several years later when the widow of Takeda Yuko's brother married Mr. Takeda Seiji's natal brother.

2. Between Worlds

1 Akakura mountain is venerated by many different Shintō associations, Buddhist temples, spirit mediums, and new religions. Although these various institutions are often in close proximity to one another, and although their adherents often encounter each other on mountain paths, they tend to ignore each other. I discuss only the system of shugyō practiced by worshipers at Akakura Mountain Shrine (Akakura Yama Jinja).

2 Like other novices, I always felt out of joint arriving for my first afternoon and evening on the eve of starting a stint of shugyō. It always seemed to me that one was fundamentally disconnected from the rhythms of the community until one had slept at and awakened at the shrine.

3 Even my middle-class Hirosaki friends, who generally expressed skepticism over shamanism and folk religious practice, often acknowledged the curative powers of the mountain. A high school teacher remarked that she was glad she knew me, because if terrible misfortune were to befall her or her family, she would have a connection to Akakura.

4 The image of dragon-king pairs facing one another and playing with a cosmic sphere constitutes a common Chinese-derived convention in East Asia. I discuss dragon symbolism more extensively in chapter 3.

5 Although villagers near the mountain make frequent reference to Onigami-sama, and venerate her at nearby Oni Jinja, her precise status is a rather murky and sensitive issue at Akakura Mountain Shrine. I return to the question of the demoness's ultimate fate in the conclusion.

6 Until recently, bears were also hunted on the mountain for their medicinal organs.

7 As discussed in chapter 3, the Akakura Mountain Shrine kō (association) now holds thirteen collective ceremonies during the year. During these rites, the temporary population of the shrine may swell to several hundred, as worshipers sleep on futon mats throughout the living areas of the complex.

8 Once, when my husband Mark attempted to dry dishes after a large lunch, he was emphatically shooed out by the senior spirit medium Mrs. Okuda, who appeared visibly upset and not in the least amused. "He is a man. This place is for women only!" she declared.

9 See the introduction and chapter 6 for discussions of Fumiko's background and the peculiarities of her shugyō.

10 Note that the image of the hot water pot seems to have been especially apposite to Fumiko's sense of feeling intense internal pressure.

11 This shrine takes its name from the presence of the founder's statue; a Mieidō is a hall where a portrait or image of the founding priest is enshrined (Inagaki 1988, 206).

3. Labor and Rebirth

1   For the full title of each calendrical rite in English, transliterated Japanese, and kanji, please see the glossary. Unless otherwise noted, I describe the ceremonies as I observed and participated in them in 1991, 1992, 1997, and 1999. The sequence of ceremonies has been constant since the late 1950s.

2   Stein (1990, 235–38) argues that the image of hearths or stoves as sacred mountains is an ancient and widespread East Asian architectural motif. He cites 1500-year-old Chinese examples of hearth mountains.

3   One of the most prominent such rites is the Fuji-no Yamabiraki (Fuji Mountain Opening) held each 1 July at the start of the climbing season on Mount Fuji.

4   Once the new rope is hung, the gorge takes on the visual appearance of an enormous shrine (or conversely, the shrine below might be understood as a condensed model of the gorge and mountain). Enclosed on both sides by the walls of the canyon, the worshipers gaze up toward the craggy, convoluted volcanic formations above them, and toward the obscured summit beyond. The space immediately below the sacred rope becomes a kind of altar, on which believers place offerings. Indeed, the shimenawa rope arching across the sky bears some resemblance to the beautifully prepared offering of a fish on the altar, which is tied from tail to head with string in order to emulate its leaping in the air above the sea's waves. As noted in chapter 4, such offerings of the products of human labor please the divinities, who themselves are beautiful, radiant, and soaring.

5   The progression of the embryo toward birth is a prominent motif in many Shugendō rituals (Blacker 1975; Earhart 1970; Hardacre 1983). In 1992, the priest's wife insisted that all of the worshipers carry the rope nearly all of the way up the mountain. Most members of the congregation considered this irregular and noted that it was ordinarily men's responsibility to carry the rope up most of the way, before men and women together bring the rope into the gorge's entrance.

6   Thirty-Three Kannonsama pilgrimage routes are found throughout Japan. Miniature Thirty-Three Kannonsama circuits, along the lines of the one at Akakura, are often found on the grounds of Shintō and Buddhist establishments.

7   I do not know of any other Shintō or Buddhist institution with an ofuro inside a sanctified space. Note that unlike regular ofuro, this "bathtub" only provided the source of sacred water for offerings and medicinal consumption; no human body entered into it. Cold-water austerities at Akakura are performed in the regular bathtub in the living quarters, not in the Mieidō bathtub. The only explanation I ever heard for the presence of a bathtub in the Mieidō came from Kawai Mariko's granddaughter Takeda Yuko: "Grandmother always loved taking baths, so her shrine has an ofuro." The Mieidō bathtub is evidently an aspect of the intimate, "homey" qualities of Aka-

kura Mountain Shrine. The spirit of Mariko continues to live in this small building, and her followers, as her living family, seek to make their common "mother" as comfortable as possible.

8   The length of 275 days is important in yamabushi (山伏) observances elsewhere. For example, the Akamine ritual performed by a Shugendō sect at Mount Haguro in Yamagata prefecture traditionally lasted for seventy-five days, representing the "275 days during which the embryo was believed to gestate in the mother's womb" (Blacker 1975, 218 quoting Shimazu 1937; Earhart 1970).

9   Human-made composite images of dragons are often deployed in Japanese communities for ritual purposes. For example, northern Tōhoku villagers sometimes construct dragons out of rice straw in order to call rain or expel pollution from a community (Bownas 1963). I once observed such a rice straw dragon at a small shrine in Kanagi. One family in North Tsugaru venerates a dragon rock shrine, chiseled out of a nearby mountain (Tanaka 1999). At Nagasaki's leading Shintō establishment, Suwa Shrine, an annual festival culminates in a dragon dance, in which eight dancers guide a great dragon costume as it pursues a golden globe (presumably signifying the universal orb, or tama). Nelson (1996, 149–51) speculates that this Chinese-derived Nagasaki dragon dance constitutes a rainmaking rite, and he notes that it dates back to the sixteenth century, when the dragon was constructed out of straw baskets used in unloading foreign ships. Prominent dragon dances are also performed at Oyamato-Jinja and Nāngu-Jinja (Herbert 1967, 177).

10 At the annual Autumn Festival of Tsugaru Akakura Jinja, Akakura Mountain Shrine's "brother" shrine in the central Tsugaru peninsula, worshipers bring the metal dragon statues that ordinarily live on the *kamidana* (神棚 Shintō divinities' household altar shelf) in their homes to be blessed for the year.

11 Terence Turner (1980) notes that the most profoundly cultural, constitutive acts are often produced through the recombination of the most fundamental natural elements. In this regard, it is striking that the ritual dragon images are produced out of water and rice, the most basic elements of the surrounding environment.

12 Architectural evocations of spiraling dragons are found in many East Asian contexts. For example, a seventh-century Korean tomb features a deep circle "formed by a . . . dragon whose tail curls down in a spiral" (Stein 1990, 321 n. 40). In China, the twelfth-century pagoda of Pai-t'a features a double spiraling staircase, called the "staircase of the pair of dragons" (*shuang-lung t'i*), on which "people climbing up do not meet until they reach the top" (Ibid, 241). In the Beijing Well of Heaven (1444), eight dragons wind themselves around ceiling columns, constituting a ritual "window to Heaven" (Ibid, 153–54).

4. Miniature Mountains

1 As many commentators have noted, rice is the archetypal medium of consumption and exchange in Japan, at both mundane and sacred levels. See, for example, Yanagita (1982); Harootunian (1988); Heine (1991); Robertson (1991); and Ohnuki-Tierney (1993). Its cultivation, transactions, and transformations into food and alcohol elegantly condense human labor and divine intervention. These interrelated processes have been at the heart of the various "moral" and "market" economies of precapitalist and capitalist Japan.

2 As Karen Smyers (1999) documents, Inari veneration is widespread throughout Japan, and it holds deep attraction for many spirit mediums. In my experience, most Tsugaru kamisama mediums expressed deep suspicion of Inari.

3 Mrs. Narita's narrative of the miraculous rice bag also bears some resemblance to Blacker's description of the initiation of a blind itako spirit medium, who undergoes her first possession by her tutelary deity while surrounded by three bags of rice (Blacker 1975, 146).

4 The divinities are sometimes said to "drink tea" during the evening services.

5 During the times I performed shugyō in 1991 and 1992, I was initially responsible for the morning circuits of water and, later, for the rice presentations. I was never given permission to prepare the full meal offerings.

6 I was never able to obtain an explanation as to why Kawai Mariko's spirit received no food, only water and incense. Mrs. Narita, the kamisama medium considered closest to the founder, simply said that Mariko only needed the "breath" of her worshipers.

7 These special days are determined by the priest through calendrical calculations. Special meals for the kami in the Shinden, Ryūjinsama, or Godaimyōō Shrines might include pickles, rice, fish, miso soup, sake, squash, or other vegetables.

8 As we have seen, eight female angels (tennin)—presumably the eight Puja-bodhisattvas whose offerings are compared to celestial clouds by Kūkai (1972, 160–61) in his *Precious Key to the Secret Treasury*—are represented in the Five Lords Shrine. The Akakura Prayer refers to "Eight Heavenly Clouds" (line 40), perhaps associated with these eight celestial maidens. If the Shinden's five pairs of bowls in the right (male) tray evoke the Five Fierce Lords, perhaps the nine pairs of bowls in the left (female) tray honor the eight divinities plus the superordinate female spirit of Amaterasu or Onigami-sama.

   In this sense, the left Shinden tray may recall the Inner Sanctuary of the Imperial Palace in Tokyo, which honors eight named *musubi-kami* (divinities of birth and becoming) arranged in a three by three grid of nine squares that recalls the vertical and horizontal layout of the Akakura trays. Priests speculate that the unidentified central square of the imperial Shinden is occupied by Ame-no-minaka-nushi (Herbert 1967, 395). This would bring the total of kami honored to nine, the same number as in the Akakura Shinden left tray.

9 Mr. Kawai stressed to me that three days before this event he had experienced a prophetic dream, in which he beheld large hands reaching into this same water offering jar.

10 This basic principle is not limited to Akakura Mountain Shrine. Little children in Japan are often admonished to eat all of their rice, since "there are seven kami in every grain of rice." This attention to the realm of the miniature stresses the extraordinary condensation of value in such blessed media.

5. My Mother's Garden

1 Fumiko was by no means the only ascetic who felt guided by her mother when performing shugyō. At the July 1992 shrine conversation, the ascetic Mrs. Nakano recalled that she had tried to follow her mother's routes of shugyō: "Since my mother was really deceived by other people all the time, I used to come here [to Akakura] every month and wouldn't say a word. . . . I wouldn't tell any secrets, I would just go and pray once, twice. That's how my mother did it, and she said, 'You should go at least as far as The Eighty-Eight Place [about three-quarters up the mountain] and that will be good, that will be good.'"

2 One woman who arrived for a week-long shugyō was an extremely nervous chain-smoker, but by the end of the week she was down to three cigarettes per day, and much more relaxed. Everyone said that also was not uncommon; as one lived in proximity to the kami, and climbed the mountain, eventually the body would "heal" itself. According to Inagaki (1988, 247–48), the six roots of perception are *gen* (eyes), *ni* (ears), *bi* (nose), *zetsu* (tongue), *shin* (tactile body), and *i* (mind).

3 *Banzai* is a phrase of exultation, literally meaning "ten thousand years." It is usually addressed to the emperor, but sometimes is expressive of a great accomplishment by oneself or others.

4 For comparable cases, see Parmentier (1987) and Obeyesekere (1981).

5 Hardacre analyzes the contrasting gendered experience of men and women undergoing a Shugendō esoteric Buddhist rite within a cave at Mount Ōmine in central Honshu. Practitioners explicitly describe the cave as a womb, specifically the Womb World Mandala, occupied by Dainichi. Hardacre reports that entrance to this cave requires claustrophobic passage through a narrow shaft, as the pilgrims shout out the proclamation of repentance, "Rokkon shōjō!" or, "Purify our six roots of perception!" (Hardacre 1983, 153). See also Stein (1990, 54–58, 345) for a provocative discussion of the symbolism of narrow cave entrances in East Asian religious, especially in reference to initiation and mystical transport.

6 Although novices are told to be silent as they crawl through Ubaishi, some veteran ascetics, such as Mrs. Okuda, state that they pray and talk to the

kami as they move forward and that they hear the divinities' voices within the tunnel.

7 The Kannon statues at the Demons' Sumo Ring might be regarded as domesticated local "demons," encompassed within a familiar esoteric Buddhist framework. The propensity of the Kannon statues to behave in unexpected and irregular ways, such as noisily shaking and spinning themselves around in place, would suggest that the encompassment and taming of indigenous or "demonic" capacity is not complete.

8 Oshirasama are said to "enjoy traveling" and are considered to have a special fondness for Akakura. Owners of oshirasama in the congregation normally bring them to the Great Summer Festival and on the summer Tsugaru Thirty-Three Kannon, Mount Taihei, and Mount Hakkōda pilgrimages.

6. I Am the Mirror

1 This dynamic of landscape externalization and bodily objectification bears some resemblance to aboriginal Australian narratives of dreamtime, in which ancestral forms embedded in the terrain "come out" of the land and enter into the bodies of the dreamer and his or her descendants (see Munn 1970; Myers 1986; Povinelli 1993).

2 The motif of a dragon emerging from a mountain bearing spiritual gifts has precedents in Japan. A passage of the *Rokugō Kaizan Nimmon Daibosatsu Hongi*, a nineteenth-century text associated with Shugendō and Hachiman mountain veneration on Kyūshū's Kunisaki peninsula, describes an ascetic's search for the jewel that symbolizes the quest for awakening: "Before thirty years elapsed, a divine dragon emerged from the rock, clutching the pearl in its claws, and presented it to Hōren." Grapard suggests this passage is based on the Dragon Princess episode in the twelfth chapter of the Lotus Sutra (Grapard 1989, 178).

3 This pattern of a revelatory vision leading to an objective physical icon of a sacred mountain is not unusual in Tsugaru. Consider the history of the Kasai family of Kiraichi village (about sixty miles north of Akakura), which for several generations has venerated a Ryūjinsama rock found in a nearby mountain. Cultural historian Sherry Tanaka offers the following description of how her great-grandfather, Kasai Manzoku, a local hunter, gatherer, and mountain charcoal-maker, obtained this rock: "Dreams brought our family a treasure we would not trade for anything. During World War II, my father spent some time in the village of Kiraichi with my grandmother's family. My great-grandfather went to the mountain with his peers to work and one night, he had a dream. In his dream, he encountered a powerful dragon spirit, which told him that he must find it in the mountain and bring it home. Next day he told his companions about the dream and so they began searching. They found the "dragon," and my great-grandfather carried it down from the mountain to his home on his back, as my father witnessed in

a state of awe. It was a large ammonite fossil in a cube of rock nearly a foot square and deep! He brought home this huge spiral gift from aeons of years ago, and the cosmic dragon is still at its home in Kiraichi today" (Tanaka 1999, 8; see also Tanaka 1998b). Rather as Kawai Mariko dreamed of the flying dragon and brought home the sacred scrolls, Kasai Manzoku dreamed of Ryūjinsama on the mountain and then brought home the dragon fossil encased in ammonite to serve as the family shrine.

4   Blacker (1975) and Smyers (1999) note that dragons and snakes figure prominently in the esoteric visions of their Japanese women informants. Following Obeyesekere (1981), Smyers suggests that serpentine symbolism is particularly attractive to female mystics as it evokes or encapsulates their "masculine" spiritual capabilities (Smyers 1999, 237). In addition to seeking visions of dragons and snakes, Akakura worshipers also try to consume small, elongated slugs, referred to as tiny snakes, while undertaking ascetic discipline.

5   It may be significant that the most eventful and traumatic shugyō undertaken by Mrs. Okuda was done so as memorialization for her grandmother, whom she dearly loved yet with whom she often fought. Klein (1975b) argues that mourning for a loved one, which often recalls early childhood fears of abandonment and fantasies of revenge, may occasion internally and externally directed rage and anxiety (see also Stephen 1998).

6   At the time, I was devastated by Mrs. Okuda's criticism. In retrospect, no lasting harm appears to have been done to our relationship.

7   On at least one occasion, however, Sugiyama Junko urged her clients not to consult itako.

8   When I first visited the Sugiyamas in 1987 to meet Junko, Toshio insisted that I accompany him to the orchard to see the fruits of Junko's labor; as we stood in the orchard, he emphasized the family's fears that cheap North American apple imports would undercut Japanese apple production.

9   Ritual contrasts between the polluting nature of excrement and dramatic acts of purification are common in the region. In traditional Tōhoku rainmaking, a Jizō statue is either submerged in water or it is daubed overall with manure. Only cleansing rainfall will efface this pollution (Bownas 1963, 127).

10 Some commentators consider the Japanese emperor system to be based on this ancient maeza-nakaza relationship (Blacker 1975).

11 I am grateful to Bradd Shore for bringing this aspect of Lévi-Strauss's argument to my attention.

Conclusion

1   Tamanoi (1998) explores political consciousness and popular expression among agrarian Japanese women under conditions of prewar militarist nationalism.

2　These apparent parallels between Western and Japanese systems of economic discipline call for careful historical investigation along the lines of
Weber's (1958) exploration of the rise of the "spirit" of European capitalism into processes of appropriation and reconfiguration. Practices of ascetic discipline rather similar to the ones I have documented may well have
played a role in the early modern emergence of the "spirit" of Japanese capitalism and in the mass dissemination of industrial labor discipline. But just
as early ideologues of Western industrial capitalism appropriated the external forms of Calvinism's worldly asceticism without necessarily internal-
izing its doctrinal content, so have modern Japanese technicians of labor
discipline drastically altered the "interior" content of mountain veneration
and shugyō (see Harootunian 1988). For instance, the discipline of compulsory corporate retreats (explored in Kondo 1990) may borrow extensively
from the symbolic repertoire of popular synthetic Shintō Buddhist ascesis,
but it rarely seeks to locate those performing austerities in a regenerative,
life-giving economy of the sort posited at Akakura.

3　Tanaka (1998a) reports that Aterui is commemorated by a 1988 memorial
stone at a shrine in Atori, Iwate prefecture. The marker is inscribed, "Hero
of the Northeast in Ancient Times. Commemorative Tablet of the Festival
Marking the Twelve Hundredth Year of King Aterui."

4　Grapard argues that early forms of mountain-oriented asceticism in Japan
reflected and supported the emerging state's politico-religious view of the
"sociocosm," and as such may be regarded as forerunners of later national-
istic ideologies (Grapard 1989, 187).

5　This is not to imply that there are, or were, "objective" racial or biological
distinctions between the various peoples of northern Japan. I am referring
simply to the way in which the cultural categories of "Yamato," "Ezo," "Ainu,"
and "Japanese" may be mobilized or confounded on the mountain.

6　These fundamental questions are also raised (often obliquely) in ritual, performance, and literary genres elsewhere in Japan. For example, Schnell
(1995) discusses how Shintō ritual performances have been used to in-
terrogate the status quo in agrarian communities. In metropolitan contexts,
Jennifer Robertson (1998) demonstrates that unresolved problems of gender
ambiguity are centrally engaged in many modern Japanese social and cultural contradictions; performance genres such as the all-female *Takarazuka*
theatrical review dramatize these contradictions within carefully controlled
frames. In her exploration of contemporary Japanese moral imaginations
and structures of historical amnesia, Norma Field (1991) argues that within
the fissures opened up by the death of the Emperor Shōwa, many "ordinary" people used the genres of personal letters as well as quasi-public ritual
events to question seemingly taken-for-granted assumptions about account-
ability, remembrance, and affluence. Gluck (1997) detects within the public
arena an increasing willingness to raise thorny questions about "the Other

within" in reference to foreign workers and long-term minority communities. Molasky (1999) argues that such contemporary debates were largely anticipated and framed by literary and poetic meditations on national, gender, and racial distinctions during the occupation era.

glossary

Akakura Daigongen: 赤倉大権現 the Great Avatar or Manifestation of Akakura

Akakura Norito: 赤倉祝詞 Akakura Prayer

Akakura-san Jinja Kaki Taisai: 赤倉山神社夏季大際 Akakura Shrine's Great Summer Festival

Akakura Yama Jinja: 赤倉山神社 Akakura Mountain Shrine

Akakura Yama Jinja-kō: 赤倉神社講 Akakura Mountain Shrine Association

Akita Taiheizan Mairi: 秋田大平山参り pilgrimage to Mount Taihei of Akita prefecture

amae: 甘え dependence, indulgence

Amaterasu: 天照 sun goddess; one of the principal divinities venerated at Akakura Mountain Shrine

Aomori-ken: 青森県 Aomori prefecture

Fudō Myōō: 不動 Sanskrit: Acalanātha or Acala (lit., the immovable, or the unshakable); the god of fire

Ganki: 巌鬼山 "left-hand" peak of Mount Iwaki; the summit of Akakura Mountain (lit., Stone Demon Mountain)

giri: 義理 obligation

Godai Myōō: 五大明王 the Five Great Lords

gofu: 護府 purified food tasted by the kami; protective amulet, charm, or talisman

gohei: 御幣 purification wand (a wooden stick or staff with sacred white paper strips attached) *goshiki:* 五色 the five sacred Buddhist colors corresponding to the five directions (north: black, purple; east: blue, green; south: red; west: white; center: yellow)

Hakkōda-san Mairi: 八甲田山参り pilgrimage to Hakkōda Mountain in central Aomori prefecture

Hannya Shingyō: 般若心經 Heart Sutra

Hoke-kyō: 法華經 Lotus Sutra

Honden: 本殿 sanctuary of the divinities; at Akakura Mountain Shrine, the Honden is located directly behind the Shinden, linked by a bridge, and is only opened during the Great Summer Festival

hōnō: 奉納 offerings

hotoke-sama: 仏様 ancestor

isshin: 一心 one heart-mind

itako: イタコ northern Japanese spirit mediums; often blind women

kamado: 竈 cooking pot, synonym for house; Ceremony performed three times a year at Akakura Mountain Shrine

kamado no kami: 竈の神 divinity of the kitchen

kami: 神 divinities (or kamisama, 神様 divine beings)

kamidana: 神棚 household altar shelf honoring the divinities

kamisama: 神さま northern Japanese spirit mediums (sometimes derisively termed *gomiso* ゴミソ)

kami no mizu: 神の水 the water of the gods

Jizō: 地蔵 (Sanskrit: Ksitigarbha, lit., earthy repository) Bodhisattva in the Matrix-store Realm Mandala, especially noted for aiding the souls of dead children

Kannonsama: 観音様 (Sanskrit: Avalokitesvara, lit., One who observes the sound of the universe) Bodhisattva of mercy in the Matrix-store Realm Mandala; in China and Japan, worshiped as a female figure

kō: 講 association

kura: 倉 storehouse, granary, or treasury.

kusuri: 薬 medicine

kuyō: 供養 ancestral memorialization

mannengusa: 万年草 also pronounced "mannensō" (lit., ten-thousand-year/eternity plant); a medicinal mountain plant, a variety of moss, gathered by ascetics on mountain slopes

Mieidō: 御影堂 hall in which the portrait or image of a founding priest or religious figure is enshrined; at Akakura, the Mieidō is the rear left building containing a seated statue of Kawai Mariko

Miyoshi Jinja: 三由神社 Miyoshi Shrine (Akita prefecture)

Miyoshi no ōkami: 三由の御神 Miyoshi divinity

mukoyōshi: 嫁養子 adopted bridegroom (or son-in-law)

nodobotoke: 喉仏 voice box or Adam's apple (lit., throat Buddha)

Ōishi Jinja: 大石神社 Great Stone Shrine, located a mile downhill from Akakura

Mountain Shrine; dedicated to Batō Kannon. Base of Kawai Mariko's original shugyō

okāsan: お母さん Great Mother; term of respect for important women at Akakura Mountain Shrine, especially the founder Kawai Mariko

omiki: お神酒 divinely purified rice wine

oni: 鬼 demon

Oni Jinja: 鬼神社 Demon Shrine located in the plain about four miles from Akakura

Onigamisama: 鬼神様 ancient demoness of Mount Iwaki; the term through which villagers still refer to the dominant divinity of Iwaki, enshrined at Iwaki-san Jinja

onna no koto: 女の事 the womanly/feminine aspect; opening in the Akakura gorge

Oya Gami Yaku Jō Yama Tatsu Hime no Mikoto Sai: 親神薬乗山龍姫乃命際 Rite for the Powerful Mountain Dragon-Princess's Great Deities' Medicine

Reidō: 霊堂 Ancestor Hall; at Akakura, the hall next to the Shinden Inner Sanctuary

rokudō: 六道 (Sanskrit: *samsara*) the six realms of existence

Ryūjinsama: 竜神様 dragon divinity

saidan: 祭壇 altar

sange: 懺悔 (Sanskrit: *ksama;* Tsugaru-ben: *saigi*) repentance or purification

San-jū-san Kannon: 三十三観音 the Thirty-Three Kannon

senzo kuyō: 先祖供養 ancestral memorialization ritual

shimenawa: 注連縄 sacred rice straw rope

Shinden: 神殿 Inner Sanctuary

shishimai: 獅子舞 lion dance

Shōgatsu Yama Sai: 正月山際 New Year's ritual on the mountain

Shōkannonsama: 聖観音様 common incarnation of Kannonsama

Shugendō: 修験道 school of Buddhism emphasizing ascetic practices on mountains to attain mystical powers

shugyō: 修行 ascetic discipline, religious austerities

Shūki Taisai: 秋季大際 Great Autumn Festival

Taiheizan: 大平山 Mount Taihei (Akita prefecture)

sakaki: 榊 evergreen sapling presented in Shintō rites

soto: 外 outside; exterior

tama: 玉 universal jewel

tamagushi: 玉串 sakaki branch offering

tane: 種 seed

Tsugaru: 津軽 western section of Aomori prefecture

Tsugaru-ben: 津軽弁 dialect (or dialects) of the Tsugaru region

Tsugaru Akakura Jinja: 津軽赤倉神社 Tsugaru Akakura Shrine, along the Iwaki River in the central Tsugaru plain

Tsugaru 33 Kannon Mairi: 津軽33観音参り pilgrimage to the Tsugaru Thirty-Three Kannonsama

uchi: 内 inside; interior

yama: 山 mountain

yamabiraki sai: 山開き際 Mountain Opening Ceremony

yamabushi: 山伏 mountain ascetic practitioners (lit., those who sleep in the mountains)

yanagi: 柳 willow

b i b l i o g r a p h y

Allison, Anne. 1994. *Nightwork: Sexuality, Pleasure, and Corporate Masculinity in a Tokyo Hostess Club.* Chicago: University of Chicago Press.

——. 1996. *Permitted and Prohibited Desires: Mothers, Comics, and Censorship in Japan.* Boulder, Colo.: Westview.

Asano-Tamanoi, Mariko. 1988. "Farmers, Industries, and the State: The Culture of Contract Farming in Spain and Japan." *Comparative Studies in Society and History* 30 (3): 432–52.

Bachnik, Jane M. 1994. "Indexing Self and Society in Japanese Family Organization." In *Situated Meaning: Inside and Outside in Japanese Self, Society, and Language,* ed. Bachnik and Charles J. Quinn Jr., 143–66. Princeton, N.J.: Princeton University Press.

Bargen, Doris G. 1988. "Spirit Possession in the Context of Dramatic Expressions of Gender Conflict: The Aoi Episode of the Genji Monogatari." *Harvard Journal of Asiatic Studies* 48 (1): 95–130.

Barthes, Roland. 1981. *Camera Lucida: Reflections on Photography.* Trans. Richard Howard. New York: Hill and Wang.

Ben-Ari, Eyal. 1996. "From Mother to Othering: Organization, Culture, and Nap Time in a Japanese Day-Care Center." *Ethos* 24 (1): 136–64.

Benedict, Ruth. 1947. *The Chrysanthemum and the Sword: Patterns of Japanese Culture.* London: Secker and Warburg.

Benjamin, Walter. 1974. "The Work of Art in the Age of Mechanical Reproduction." In *Illuminations.* Trans. Harry Zohn. London: Fontana.

Berger, Peter L., and Thomas Luckmann. 1966. *The Social Construction of Reality: A Treatise in the Sociology of Knowledge.* Garden City, N.Y.: Doubleday.

Bernal, Martin. 1987. *Black Athena: The Afroasiatic Roots of Classical Civilization.* New Brunswick, N.J.: Rutgers University Press.

Bernstein, Gail Lee. 1983. *Haruko's World: A Japanese Farm Woman and Her Community.* Stanford, Calif.: Stanford University Press.

Bix, Herbert P. 1986. *Peasant Protest in Japan, 1590–1884.* New Haven, Conn.: Yale University Press.

Blacker, Carmen. 1975. *The Catalpa Bow: A Study of Shamanistic Practices in Japan.* London: Allen and Unwin.

———. 2000. "Initiation in the Shugendō: The Passage through the Ten States of Existence." In *Collected Writings of Carmen Blacker,* 186–98. Tokyo: Edition Synapse.

Bocking, Brian. 1997. *A Popular Dictionary of Shinto.* Lincolnwood, Ill.: NTC Publishing Group.

Boddy, Janice. 1989. *Wombs and Alien Spirits: Women, Men, and the Zar Cult in Northern Sudan.* Madison: University of Wisconsin Press.

Born, G. 1998. "Anthropology, Kleinian Psychoanalysis, and the Subject in Culture." *American Anthropologist* 100: 373–86.

Bourdieu, Pierre. 1977. *Outline of a Theory of Practice.* Trans. Richard Nice. Cambridge: Cambridge University Press.

Bownas, Geoffrey. 1963. *Japanese Rainmaking and Other Folk Practices.* London: Allen and Unwin.

Brandon, Reiko Mochinaga, and Barbara B. Stephan. 1994. *Spirit and Symbol: The Japanese New Year.* Honolulu: Honolulu Academy of Arts.

Brumbaugh, Thoburn Taylor. 1934. *Religious Values in Japanese Culture.* Tokyo: Kyo bun kwan.

Bunn, David. 1994. "Our Wattled Cot: Mercantile and Domestic Space in Thomas Pringle's African Landscapes." In Mitchell, 127–73.

Caudill, William A., and Tsung-yi Lin, eds. 1969. *Mental Health Research in Asia and the Pacific.* Honolulu: East-West Center Press.

Comaroff, Jean. 1985. *Body of Power, Spirit of Resistance: The Culture and History of a South African People.* Chicago: University of Chicago Press.

Comaroff, Jean, and John L. Comaroff. 1992. *Ethnography and the Historical Imagination.* Boulder, Colo.: Westview.

———. 1993. Introduction to *Modernity and Its Malcontents: Ritual and Power in Postcolonial Africa,* xi–xxxvii. Chicago: University of Chicago Press.

———. 1995. *Of Revelation and Revolution: The Dialectics of Modernity on a South African Frontier.* Chicago: University of Chicago Press.

Crump, John. 1983. *The Origins of Socialist Thought in Japan.* New York: St. Martin's.

Dazai, Osamu. 1987. *Return to Tsugaru: Travels of a Purple Tramp.* Trans. James Westerhoven. 1944. Tokyo: Kodansha.

Dobbins, James C. 1989. *Jōdo Shinshū: Shin Buddhism in Medieval Japan.* Bloomington: Indiana University Press.

Doi, Takeo. 1973. *The Anatomy of Dependence.* Trans. John Bester. Tokyo: Kodansha.

Dumézil, Georges. 1973. *The Destiny of a King.* Trans. Alf Hiltebeitel. Chicago: University of Chicago Press.

Earhart, H. Byron. 1970. *A Religious Study of the Mount Haguro Sect of Shugendō: An Example of Japanese Mountain Religion.* Tokyo: Sophia University.

Erikson, Erik H. 1987. *A Way of Looking at Things: Selected Papers from 1930 to 1980.* Ed. Stephen P. Schlein. New York: Norton.

Feeley-Harnik, Gillian. 1991. *A Green Estate: Restoring Independence in Madagascar.* Washington, D.C.: Smithsonian Institution Press.

Fernandez, James W. 1982. *Bwiti: An Ethnography of the Religious Imagination in Africa.* Princeton, N.J.: Princeton University Press.

Field, Norma. 1991. *In the Realm of a Dying Emperor.* New York: Pantheon.

Frazer, James George. 1894. *The Golden Bough: A Study in Comparative Religion.* New York: Macmillan.

Freud, Sigmund. 1914. *Psychopathology of Everyday Life.* Trans. A. A. Brill. London: Unwin.

———. 1939. *Moses and Monotheism.* Trans. Katherine Jones. New York: Knopf.

———. 1949. *Civilization and Its Discontents.* Trans. Joan Riviere. London: Hogarth.

———. 1959. "The Unconsicous." 1915. In *The Collected Papers,* 4:98–136. Trans. Joan Riviere. New York: Basic Books.

———. 1961. *Totem and Taboo: Some Points of Agreement between the Mental Lives of Savages and Neurotic.* 1913. Trans. James Strachey. London: Routledge and Kegan Paul.

———. 1983. *The Interpretation of Dreams.* 1900. Trans. James Strachey. New York: Avon.

Gennep, Arnold van. 1960. *The Rites of Passage.* Trans. Monika B. Vizedom and Gabrielle L. Coffee. London: Routledge and Paul.

Giddens, Anthony. 1979. *Central Problems in Social Theory: Action, Structure, and Contradiction in Social Analysis.* Berkeley: University of California Press.

Gluck, Carol. 1997. "The 'End' of the Postwar: Japan at the Turn of the Millennium." *Public Culture* 10 (1):1–23.

Grapard, Allan G. 1982. "Flying Mountains and Walkers of Emptiness: Toward a Definition of Sacred Space in Japanese Religions." *History of Religions* 21 (2): 195–221.

———. 1984. "Japan's Ignored Cultural Revolution: The Separation of Shintō and Buddhist Divinities in Meiji (Shinbutsu Bunri) and a Case Study: Tonomine." *History of Religions* 23 (3): 240–65.

———. 1989. "The Textualized Mountain—Enmountained Text: The Lotus Sutra in Kunisaki." In Tanabe and Tanabe, 159–90.

————. 1992. *The Protocol of the Gods: A Study of the Kasuga Cult in Japanese History.* Berkeley: University of California Press.

Graves, Robert. 1997. *The White Goddess: A Historical Grammar of Poetic Myth.* Ed. Grevel Lindop. Manchester: Carcanet.

Groner, Paul. 1989. "The Lotus Sutra and Saichō's Interpretation of the Realization of Buddhahood with This Very Body." In Tanabe and Tanabe, 57–74.

Gurewich, Judith Feher. 1999. "A Plea for a Measure of Universality, or, The Return of Lévi-Strauss." Presented at the conference "The Repressed and Its Comeback: Anthropology in the Shadows of Modernity," Amsterdam.

Hanks, William F. 1990. *Referential Practice: Language and Lived Space among the Maya.* Chicago: University of Chicago Press.

Hardacre, Helen. 1982. "The Transformation of Healing in the Japanese New Religions." *History of Religions* 21 (4): 305–20.

————. 1983. "The Cave and the Womb World." *Japanese Journal of Religious Studies* 10 (2–3): 149–76.

————. 1984. *Lay Buddhism in Contemporary Japan: Reiyukai Kyodan.* Princeton, N.J.: Princeton University Press.

————. 1986. *Kurozumikyō and the New Religions of Japan.* Princeton, N.J.: Princeton University Press.

————. 1989a. "The Lotus Sutra in Modern Japan." In Tanabe and Tanabe, 209–24.

————. 1989b. *Shintō and the State, 1868–1988.* Princeton, N.J.: Princeton University Press.

Harootunian, H. D. 1988. *Things Seen and Unseen: Discourse and Ideology in Tokugawa Nativism.* Chicago: University of Chicago Press.

————. 1991. "Cultural Politics in Tokugawa Japan." In *Undercurrents in the Floating World: Censorship and Japanese Prints,* by Sarah E. Thompson and Harootunian, 7–28. New York: Asia Society Galleries.

Hashimoto, Mitsuru. 1982. "The Social Background of Peasant Uprising in Tokugawa Japan." In *Conflict in Modern Japanese History: The Neglected Tradition,* ed. Tetsuo Najita and J. Victor Koschmann, 145–63. Princeton, N.J.: Princeton University Press.

Heine, Steven. 1991. "From Rice Cultivation to Mind Contemplation: The Meaning of Impermanence in Japanese Religion." *History of Religions* 30 (4): 373–403.

Herbert, Jean. 1967. *Shintō: At the Fountain Head of Japan.* New York: Stein and Day.

Hesiod. 1993. *Works and Days and Theogony.* Trans. Stanley Lombardo. Indianapolis: Hackett.

Higuchi, Tadahiko. 1983. *The Visual and Spatial Structure of Landscapes.* Trans. Charles S. Terry. Cambridge, Mass.: MIT Press.

Hori, Ichiro. 1968. *The Folk Religion in Japan: Continuity and Change.* Ed. Joseph M. Kitagawa and Alan L. Miller. Chicago: University of Chicago Press.

Ikegami Yoshimasa. 1984. "Iwaki-san shinkō no kinseiteki engen—shūkyōgaku-teki shiten kara no I chikōsatsu." In *Tsugaru-han no kisoteki kenkyū,* ed. Hasegawa Seiichi, 577–615. Tokyo: Kokusho Kankōkai.

———. 1987. *Tsugaru no kamisama: Sukui no kōzō o tazunete.* Tokyo: Dōbutsusha.

———. 1992. *Minzoku shūkyō to sukui: Tsugaru, Okinawa no minkan fusha.* Kyoto: Tankōsha.

———. 1999. *Minkan fusha shinkō no kenkyū: Shūkyōgaku no shiten kara.* Tokyo: Miraisha.

Inagaki, Hisao. 1988. *A Dictionary of Japanese Buddhist Terms: Based on References in Japanese Literature.* Union City, Calif.: Heian International.

Inoue Nobutaka. 1994. *Shintō jiten.* Tokyo: Kōbundō.

Ivy, Marilyn. 1995. *Discourses of the Vanishing: Modernity, Phantasm, Japan.* Chicago: University of Chicago Press.

Jackson, Michael. 1989. *Paths Toward a Clearing: Radical Empiricism and Ethnographic Inquiry.* Bloomington: Indiana University Press.

Jackson, Michael, and Ivan Karp. 1990. Introduction to *Personhood and Agency: The Experience of Self and Other in African Cultures,* 15–30. Uppsala: Academiae Upsaliensis.

Karp, Ivan. 1978. *Fields of Change among the Iteso of Kenya.* London: Routledge and Kegan Paul.

———. 1980. "Beer Drinking and Social Experience in an African Society: An Essay in Formal Sociology." In *Explorations in African Systems of Thought,* ed. Karp and Charles S. Bird, 83–119. Bloomington: Indiana University Press.

———. 1990. "Power and Capacity in Iteso Rituals of Possession." In *Personhood and Agency: The Experience of Self and Other in African Cultures,* 79–93. Uppsala: Academiae Upsaliensis.

Karp, Ivan, and Kent A. Maynard. 1983. "Reading the Nuer." *Current Anthropology* 24 (4): 481–503.

Katō, Bunno, Yoshirō Tamura, and Kōjirō, trans., with revisions by W. E. Soothill, Wilhelm Schiffer, and Pier P. Del Campana. 1975. *The Threefold Lotus Sutra.* New York: Weatherhill.

Katō, Genchi. 1973. *A Historical Study of the Religious Development of Shintō.* Trans. Shōyū Hanayama. Tokyo: Japan Society for the Promotion of Science.

Kelly, William W. 1985. *Deference and Defiance in Nineteenth-Century Japan.* Princeton, N.J.: Princeton University Press.

———. 1986. "Rationalization and Nostalgia: Cultural Dynamics of New Middle-Class Japan." *American Ethnologist* 13 (4): 603–18.

———. 1991. "Directions in the Anthropology of Contemporary Japan." *Annual Review of Anthropology* 20: 395–431.

———. 1992. "Tractors, Television, and Telephones: Reach out and Touch Someone in Rural Japan." In *Re-made in Japan: Everyday Life and Consumer Taste in a Changing Society,* ed. Joseph J. Tobin, 77–88. New Haven, Conn.: Yale University Press.

Kendall, Laurel. 1996a. *Getting Married in Korea: Of Gender, Morality, and Modernity.* Berkeley: University of California Press.

———. 1996b. "Initiating Performance: The Story of Chini, A Korean Shaman." In *The Performance of Healing*, ed. Carol Laderman and Marina Roseman, 17–58. New York: Routledge.

Kishimoto, Hideo. 1960. "The Role of Mountains in the Religious Life of the Japanese People." In *Proceedings of the Ninth International Congress for the History of Religions*, 545–49. Tokyo: Maruzen.

Kitagawa, Joseph Mitsuo. 1966. *Religion in Japanese History.* New York: Columbia University Press.

Klein, Melanie. 1975a. *Love, Guilt, and Reparation, and Other Works, 1921–1945.* London: Hogarth.

———. 1975b. *The Psychoanalysis of Children.* Trans. Alix Strachey. London: Hogarth.

Kodate Chūzō. 1980. *Iwakisan shinkōoshi.* Hirosaki: Hoppō Shinsha.

———. 1986. *Aomori-ken no minkan shinkō.* Hirosaki: Hoppō Shinsha.

Komatsu Kazuhiko. 1978. *Kamigami no seishinshi.* Tokyo: Hatsubai gendai janarizumu.

Kondo, Dorinne K. 1990. *Crafting Selves: Power, Gender, and Discourses of Identity in a Japanese Workplace.* Chicago: University of Chicago Press.

Kūkai. 1972. *Major Works.* Trans. Yoshito S. Hakeda. New York: Columbia University Press.

Lacan, Jacques. 1977. *Écrits: A Selection.* Trans. Alain Sheridan. New York: Norton.

LaFleur, William. 1983. *The Karma of Words: Buddhism and the Literary Arts in Medieval Japan.* Berkeley: University of California Press.

Lambek, Michael. 1981. *Human Spirits: A Cultural Account of Trance in Mayotte.* Cambridge: Cambridge University Press.

———. 1993. *Knowledge and Practice in Mayotte: Local Discourses of Islam, Sorcery, and Spirit Possession.* Toronto: University of Toronto Press.

Lebra, Takie Sugiyama. 1984. *Japanese Women: Constraint and Fulfillment.* Honolulu: University of Hawai'i Press.

Lévi-Strauss, Claude. 1966. *The Savage Mind.* Chicago: University of Chicago Press.

———. 1992. *The View from Afar.* Trans. Joachim Neugroschel and Phoebe Hoss. Chicago: University of Chicago Press.

Lewis, I. M. 1971. *Ecstatic Religion: A Study of Shamanism and Spirit Possession.* Harmondsworth, U.K.: Penguin.

Liscutin, Nicola. 2000. "Mapping the Sacred Body: Shinto versus Popular Beliefs at Mt. Iwaki in Tsugaru." In *Shinto in History: Ways of the Kami*, ed. John Breen and Mark Teeuwen, 186–204. Honolulu: University of Hawai'i Press.

Lock, Margaret M. 1980. *East Asian Medicine in Urban Japan: Varieties of Medical Experience.* Berkeley: University of California Press.

———. 1981. "Japanese Psychotherapeutic Systems: On Acceptance and Responsibility." *Culture, Medicine, and Psychiatry* 5(3): 303–12.

———. 1987. "Protests of Good Wife and Wise Mother: The Medicalization of Distress in Japan." In *Health, Illness, and Medical Care in Japan: Cultural and Social Dimensions*, ed. Edward Norbeck and Lock, 139–217. Honolulu: University of Hawai'i Press.

———. 1988. "New Japanese Mythologies: Faltering Discipline and the Ailing Housewife." *American Ethnologist* 15(1): 43–60.

———. 1996. "Centering the Household: The Remaking of Female Maturity in Japan." In *Re-imagining Japanese Women*, ed. Anne E. Imamura, 73–103. Berkeley: University of California Press.

Long, Susan. 1996. "Nurturing and Femininity: The Ideal of Caregiving in Post-war Japan." In *Re-imagining Japanese Women*, ed. Anne E. Imamura, 156–76. Berkeley: University of California Press.

MacGaffey, Wyatt. 1993. "The Eyes of Understanding." In *Astonishment and Power*, 30–89. Washington, D.C.: National Museum of African Art, Smithsonian Institution Press.

Marx, Karl. 1967. *Capital: A Critique of Political Economy*. Ed. Frederick Engels. Vol. 1. New York: International Publishers.

Matisoff, Susan. 1992. "Holy Horrors: The Sermon-Ballads of Medieval and Early Modern Japan." In *Flowing Traces: Buddhism in the Literary and Visual Arts of Japan*, ed. James H. Sanford, William R. LaFleur, and Masatoshi Nagatomi, 234–61. Princeton, N.J.: Princeton University Press.

Matsunaga, Alicia. 1969. *The Buddhist Philosophy of Assimilation: The Historical Development of the Honji Suijaku Theort*. Tokyo: Sophia University.

Matsunaga, Daigan, and Alicia Matsunaga. 1974. *Foundation of Japanese Buddhism*. Los Angeles: Buddhist Books International.

Mauss, Marcel. 1954. *The Gift: The Form and Functions of Exchange in Archaic Societies*. Trans. Ian Cunnison. Glencoe, Ill.: Free Press.

———. 1973. "Techniques of the Body." *Economy and Society* 2: 70–88.

McCormack, Gavan. 1996. *The Emptiness of Japanese Affluence*. Armonk, N.Y.: Sharpe.

Meech-Pekarik, Julia. 1986. *The World of the Meiji Print: Impressions of a New Civilization*. New York: Weatherhill.

Merleau-Ponty, M. 1962. *The Phenomenology of Perception*. Trans. Colin Smith. London: Routledge and Kegan Paul.

Mitchell, W. J. T., ed. 1994. *Landscape and Power*. Chicago: University of Chicago Press.

Molasky, Michael S. 1999. *The American Occupation of Japan and Okinawa: Literature and Memory*. London: Routledge.

Molasky, Michael S., and Steve Rabson, eds. 2000. *Southern Exposure: Modern Japanese Literature from Okinawa*. Honolulu: University of Hawai'i Press.

Morris, Rosalind C. 1998. "Surviving Pleasure at the Periphery: Chiang Mai and the Photographies of Political Trauma in Thailand, 1976–1992." *Public Culture* 10 (2): 341–70.

Munn, Nancy D. 1970. "The Transformation of Subjects into Objects in Walbiri and Pigantjatjara Myth." In *Australian Aboriginal Anthropology: Modern Studies in the Social Anthropology of the Australian Aborigines,* ed. Ronald Berndt, 141–63. Nedlands: Australian Institute of Aboriginal Studies.

———. 1986. *The Fame of Gawa: A Symbolic Study of Value Transformation in a Massim (Papua New Guinea) Society.* Cambridge: Cambridge University Press.

———. 1994. "Creating a Heterotopia: Spacetime in Olmstead and Vaux's Central Park." Presented at Northwestern University, February 2.

Myers, Fred R. 1986. *Pintupi Country, Pintupi Self: Sentiment, Place, and Politics among Western Desert Aborigines.* Washington, D.C.: Smithsonian Institution Press.

Naoe Hiroji. 1983 "Inari Shinko fukyu no minzokuteki kiban." In *Inari Shinko,* ed Naoe, 113–33. Tokyo: Yuzankaku Shuppan.

Nelson, John K. 1996. *A Year in the Life of a Shinto Shrine.* Seattle: University of Washington Press.

Nitzschke, Gunter. 1995. "Building the Sacred Mountain: Tsukuriyama in Shinto Tradition." In *The Sacred Mountains of Asia,* ed. John Einarsen, 110–18. Boston: Shambala.

Noguchi, Takenori. 1966. "Mortuary Customs and the Family-Kinship System in Japan and Ryūkyū." In *Folk Cultures of Japan and East Asia,* ed Toichi Mabuchi, 16–36. Tokyo: Sophia University Press.

Nuckolls, Charles. 1996. "Spiro and Lutz on Ifaluk: Towards a Synthesis of Cultural Cognition and Depth Psychology." *Ethos* 24: 695–717.

Obeyesekere, Gananath. 1981. *Medusa's Hair: An Essay on Personal Symbols and Religious Experience.* Chicago: University of Chicago Press.

———. 1990. *The Work of Culture: Symbolic Transformation in Psychoanalysis and Anthropology.* Chicago: University of Chicago Press.

Ohnuki-Tierney, Emiko. 1984. *Illness and Culture in Contemporary Japan: An Anthropological View.* Cambridge: Cambridge University Press.

———. 1993. *Rice as Self: Japanese Identities through Time.* Princeton, N.J.: Princeton University Press.

Ono, Sokyo. 1962. *Shinto: The Kami Way.* Rutland, Vt.: Tuttle.

Ortner, Sherry. 1984. "Theory in Anthropology since the Sixties." *Comparative Studies in Society and History* 26 (1): 126–66.

Parmentier, Richard J. 1987. *The Sacred Remains: Myth, History, and Polity in Belau.* Chicago: University of Chicago Press.

Paul, Robert A. 1976. "The Sherpa Temple as a Model of the Psyche." *American Ethnologist* 3 (1): 131–46.

———. 1989. "Psychoanalytic Anthropology." *Annual Review of Anthropology* 18: 177–202.

———. 1992. "Freud's Anthropology: A Reading of the Cultural Books." In *Understanding Freud: The Man and His Ideas,* ed. Emanuel E. Garcia, 10–30. New York: New York University Press.

————. 1996. *Moses and Civilization: The Meaning behind Freud's Myth.* New Haven, Conn.: Yale University Press.

Philippi, Donald L. 1968. *Kojiki.* Tokyo: University of Tokyo Press.

Povinelli, Elizabeth A. 1993. *Labor's Lot: The Power, History, and Culture of Aboriginal Action.* Chicago: University of Chicago Press.

Pye, Michael. 1977. "The Heart Sutra in Its Japanese Context." In *Prajñāpāramitā and Related Systems: Essays in Honor of Edward Conze,* ed. Lewis Lancaster and Luis O. Gómez, 123–34. Berkeley: University of California Press.

Rank, Otto. 1957. *The Myth of the Birth of the Hero: A Psychological Interpretation of Mythology.* Trans. F. Robbins and Smith Ely Jelliffe. 1909. New York: Brunner.

Ravina, Mark. 1991. "Political Economy and Statecraft in Early Modern Japan." Ph.D. diss., Stanford University.

————. 1999. *Land and Lordship in Early Modern Japan.* Stanford, Calif.: Stanford University Press.

Reader, Ian. 1991. *Religion in Contemporary Japan.* Honolulu: University of Hawai'i Press.

Reader, Ian, and George J. Tanabe Jr. 1998. *Practically Religious: Worldly Benefits and the Common Religion in Japan.* Honolulu: University of Hawai'i Press.

Robertson, Jennifer. 1984. "Sexy Rice: Plant Gender, Farm Manuals, and Grass-Roots Nativism." *Monumenta Nipponica* 39 (3): 233–60.

————. 1991. *Native and Newcomer: Making and Remaking a Japanese City.* Berkeley: University of California Press.

————. 1998. *Takarazuka: Sexual Politics and Popular Culture in Modern Japan.* Berkeley: University of California Press.

Rosenberger, Nancy R. 1994. "Indexing Hierarchy through Japanese Gender Relations." In *Situated Meaning: Inside and Outside in Japanese Self, Society, and Language,* ed. Jane M. Bachnik and Charles J. Quinn Jr., 88–112. Princeton, N.J.: Princeton University Press.

Sahlins, Marshall David. 1985. *Islands of History.* Chicago: University of Chicago Press.

Saitō Akitoshi. 1984. "Kōbō Daishi densetsu." In *Kobo daishi shinkō,* ed. Hinonishi Shinjō. Tokyo: Yūsankaku.

Sakō Nobuyuki. 1992. *Sanshō dayū densetsu no kenkyū: Anju Zushiō denshō kara sekkyōbushi Mori Ōgai made.* Tokyo: Meicho Shuppan.

Sakurai Tokutarō. 1970. "Tsugaru itako no fūzoku." In *Tsugaru no Minzoku,* ed. Wakamori Tarō, 297–346. Tokyo: Yoshikawa Kōbunkan.

————. 1976. "Minkan shinkō to sangaku shūkyō." In *Sangaku shūkyō to minkan shinkō no kenkyū,* ed. Sakurai, 13–32. Tokyo: Meicho Shuppan.

————. 1988. *Nihon shamanizumu no kenkyū.* 2 vols. Tokyo: Yoshikawa Kōbunkan.

Sato, Kanzan. 1983. *The Japanese Sword.* Trans. Joe Earle. Tokyo: Kodansha.

Saunders, E. Dale. 1960. *Mudrā: A Study of Symbolic Gestures in Japanese Buddhist Sculpture.* New York: Pantheon.

Schattschneider, Ellen. 1996a. "Circuits of Discipline: Production, Reproduction, and the Work of the Gods in Tsugaru, Northern Japan." Ph.D. diss., University of Chicago.

———. 1996b. "The Labor of Mountains." *positions* 4: 1–30.

———. 1999. "Our House Will Be Shattered: Murder and Money's Promise in Northern Japan." Presented at "Pathologies of Consumption" conference, Vernacular Modernities Program, Emory University, March 16.

———. 2000. "My Mother's Garden: Transitional Phenomena on a Japanese Sacred Mountain." *Ethos* 28 (2): 147–73.

———. 2001. "Buy Me a Bride: Death and Exchange in Northern Japanese Bride Doll Marriage." *American Ethnologist* 28 (4): 854–80.

Schnell, Scott. 1995. "Ritual as an Instrument of Political Resistance in Rural Japan." *Journal of Anthropological Research* 51(4): 301–28.

———. 1999. *The Rousing Drum: Ritual Practice in a Japanese Community.* Honolulu: University of Hawai'i Press.

Schutz, Alfred. 1967. *The Phenomenology of the Social World.* Trans. George Walsh and Frederick Lehnert. Evanston, Ill.: Northwestern University Press.

Segal, Hanna. 1979. *Melanie Klein.* New York: Viking.

Sered, Susan. 1999. *Women of the Sacred Groves: Divine Priestesses of Okinawa.* New York: Oxford University Press.

Shinamura Izuru. 1969. *Kōjien.* Tokyo: Iwanami Shoten.

Shore, Bradd. 1996. *Culture in Mind: Cognition, Culture, and the Problem of Meaning.* New York: Oxford University Press.

Silverberg, Miriam. 1990. *Changing Song: The Marxist Manifestos of Nakano Shigeharu.* Princeton, N.J.: Princeton University Press.

Smith, Henry D., II. 1988. *Kiyochika: Artist of Meiji Japan.* Santa Barbara: Santa Barbara Museum of Art.

Smith, Robert J. 1974. *Ancestor Worship in Contemporary Japan.* Stanford, Calif.: Stanford University Press.

Smyers, Karen A. 1999. *The Fox and the Jewel: Shared and Private Meanings in Contemporary Japanese Inari Worship.* Honolulu: University of Hawai'i Press.

Stefánsson, Finn. 1993. "Shingon Buddhist Mandalas." In *Japanese Religions: Past and Present,* by Ian Reader, Esben Andreason, and Stefánsson, 183–85. Honolulu: University of Hawai'i Press.

Stein, Rolf A. 1990. *The World in Miniature: Container Gardens and Dwellings in Far Eastern Religious Thought.* Trans. Phyllis Brooks. Stanford, Calif.: Stanford University Press.

Stephen, Michele. 1998. "Consuming the Dead: A Kleinian Perspective on Death Rituals Cross-culturally." *International Journal of Psycho-Analysis* 79: 1173–94.

Stevens, John. 1988. *The Marathon Monks of Mount Hiei.* London: Rider.

Swanson, Paul. 1981. "Shugendō and the Yosino-Kumano Pilgrimage: An Example of Mountain Pilgrimage." *Monumenta Nipponica* 36 (1): 55–79.

Takamatsu Keikichi. 1983. *Shimokita hanto no minkan shinkō: Fuzoku to takaikan ni kansuru minzokugakuteki kenkyū.* Tokyo: Dento to Gendai sha.

Tamanoi, Mariko Asano. 1990. "Women's Voices: Their Critique of the Anthropology of Japan." *Annual Review of Anthropology* 19: 17–37.

———. 1991. "Songs as Weapons: The Culture and History of *Komori* (Nursemaids) in Modern Japan." *Journal of Asian Studies* 50 (4): 793–817.

———. 1998. *Under the Shadow of Nationalism: Politics and Poetics of Rural Japanese Women.* Honolulu: University of Hawai'i Press.

Tamura Eitaro. 1960. *Yonaoshi.* Tokyo: Yuzankaku.

Tanabe, George J., Jr., and Willa Jane Tanabe, eds. 1989. *The Lotus Sutra in Japanese Culture.* Honolulu: University of Hawai'i Press.

Tanaka, Sakurako. 1997. "Death by a Thousand Cuts: The Un-making of Ainumoshiri." Unpublished manuscript.

———. 1998a. "The Head of Aterui: Aboriginal History and the Conquest of Japan." Unpublished manuscript.

———. 1998b "Forbidden-to-Come-Place." Presented at the Eighth Conference of Hunter-Gatherer Societies, October 1998, Aomori, Japan. Unpublished manuscript.

———. 1999. "Bringing Home a Dragon: A Spiritual Cartography from Northern Tsugaru." Unpublished manuscript.

Tsing, Anna Lowenhaupt. 1993. *In the Realm of the Diamond Queen: Marginality in an Out-of-the-Way Place.* Princeton, N.J.: Princeton University Press.

Turner, Terence. 1980. "The Social Skin." In *Not Work Alone: A Cross Cultural View of Activities Superfluous to Survival,* ed. Jeremy Cherfas Roger Lewin, 112–40. Beverly Hills, Calif.: Sage.

Turner, Victor W. 1967. *The Forest of Symbols: Aspects of Ndembu Ritual.* Ithaca, N.Y.: Cornell University Press.

———. 1969. *The Ritual Process: Structure and Anti-Structure.* Chicago: Aldine.

Uryū Naka and Shibuya Nobihiro. 1999. *Nihon Shintō No Subete.* Tokyo: Nihon Bungeisha.

van Bremen, Jan. 1995. "Introduction: The Myth of the Secularization of Industrialized Societies." In *Ceremony and Ritual in Japan: Religious Practices in an Industrialized Society,* ed. van Bremen and D. P. Martinez, 1–22. London: Routledge.

Vernant, Jean Pierre. 1980. *Myth and Society in Ancient Greece.* Trans. Janet Lloyd. Atlantic Highlands, N.J.: Humanities Press.

Walthall, Anne. 1986. *Social Protest and Popular Culture in Eighteenth-Century Japan.* Tucson: Association for Asian Studies.

Weber, Max. 1958. *The Protestant Ethic and the Spirit of Capitalism.* Trans. Talcott Parsons. New York: Scribner's.

Winnicott, D. W. 1971. *Playing and Reality.* London: Tavistock.

Yamaguchi, Masao. 1991. "The Poetics of Exhibition in Japanese Culture." In *Exhibiting Cultures: The Poetics and Politics of Museum Display,* ed. Ivan Karp and Steven D. Lavine, 57–67. Washington, D.C.: Smithsonian Institution Press.

Yanagita Kunio. 1982. "Koe no chikara." In *Yanagita Kunio-shū,* 36 vols., 14:240–58. Tokyo: Tsukuma Shobō.

i n d e x

Ellen Schattschneider is Assistant Professor
of Anthropology at Brandeis University.

Library of Congress Cataloging-in-Publication Data
Schattschneider, Ellen.
Immortal wishes : labor and transcendence on a Japanese
sacred mountain / Ellen Schattschneider.
p. cm.   Includes bibliographical references and index.
ISBN 0-8223-3075-X (cloth : alk. paper)
ISBN 0-8223-3062-8 (pbk. : alk. paper)
1. Akakura Yama Jinja (Iwaki-machi, Japan) 2. Kawai,
Mariko. 3. Mountain worship—Japan—Iwaki-machi.
4. Iwaki-machi (Japan)—Religious life and customs.
5. Mountain worship—Japan—Tsugaru Region. 6. Tsugaru
Region (Japan)—Religious life and customs.   I. Title.
BL2225.I832 A337 2003   299'.561'095211—dc21   2002151231